REMEMBERING THE KANJI 1

BY THE SAME AUTHOR

Remembering the Kana: A Guide to Reading and Writing the Japanese Syllabaries in 3 Hours Each. Honolulu: University of Hawai'i Press, 2007 (1987)

Remembering the Kanji 2: A Systematic Guide to Reading Japanese Characters. Honolulu: University of Hawai'i Press, 2008 (1987)

Remembering the Kanji 3: Writing and Reading Japanese Characters for Upper-Level Proficiency (with Tanya Sienko). Honolulu: University of Hawai'i Press, 2008 (1994)

Kanji para recordar I: Curso mnemotécnico para el aprendizaje de la escritura y el significado de los caracteres japoneses (with Marc Bernabé and Verònica Calafell). Barcelona: Herder Editorial, 2005 (2001)

Kanji para recordar II: Guía sistemática para la lectura de los caracteres japoneses (with Marc Bernabé and Verònica Calafell). Barcelona: Herder Editorial, 2004

Kana para recordar: Curso mnemotécnico para el aprendizaje de los silabarios japoneses (with Marc Bernabé and Verònica Calafell). Barcelona: Herder Editorial, 2005 (2003)

Die Kanji lernen und behalten 1. Bedeutung und Schreibweise der japanischen Schriftzeichen (with Robert Rauther). Frankfurt am Main: Vittorio Klostermann Verlag, 2006 (2005)

Die Kanji lernen und behalten 2. Systematische Anleitung zu den Lesungen der japanischen Schriftzeichen (with Robert Rauther). Frankfurt am Main: Vittorio Klostermann Verlag, 2006

Die Kana lernen und behalten. Die japanische Silbenschrift lesen und schreiben in je drei Stunden (with Klaus Gresbrand). Frankfurt am Main: Vittorio Klostermann Verlag, 2006

Kana. Snel Japans leren lezen en schrijven (with Sarah Van Camp). Antwerpen: Garant, 2009

Kanji. Snel Japans leren schrijven en onthouden door de kracht van verbeelding (with Sarah Van Camp). Antwerpen: Garant, 2010

REMEMBERING THE KANJI

VOL. 1

*A Complete Course on How Not to Forget
the Meaning and Writing
of Japanese Characters*

James W. Heisig

SIXTH EDITION

University of Hawai'i Press
HONOLULU

Copyright © 1977, 1985, 1986, 2001, 2007 by James W. Heisig
All rights reserved, including the right to reproduce this book or portions
thereof in any form without the written permission of the publisher.
Printed in the United States of America

Fifth edition: 24ᵗʰ printing, 2008
Sixth edition: 1ˢᵗ printing, 2011

16 15 14 13 12 11   6 5 4 3 2 1

Library of Congress Cataloging-in-Publication Data

Heisig, James W., 1944-
    Remembering the kanji : a complete course on how not to forget the meaning
    and writing of Japanese characters / James W. Heisig. — 6th ed.
    p. cm.
    Includes indexes.
    ISBN 978-0-8248-3592-7 (pbk. : alk. paper)
    1. Japanese language—Orthography and spelling. 2. Chinese characters—
    Japan—Textbooks. 3. Japanese language—Textbooks for foreign speakers—
    English. I. Title.
PL547.H4 2001
495.6'82421—dc22

                                  2010049981

The typesetting for this book was done at the Nanzan Institute for Religion and Culture.

University of Hawai'i Press books are printed on acid-free paper and meet the guidelines
for permanence and durability of the Council on Library Resources.

Contents

Introduction 1

    PART ONE: *Stories* (Lessons 1–12) 13

    PART TWO: *Plots* (Lessons 13–19) 119

    PART THREE: *Elements* (Lessons 20–56) 187

Indexes

    I. Kanji 431

    II. Primitive Elements 450

    III. Kanji in Stroke Order 453

    IV. Key Words and Primitive Meanings 465

Introduction

THE AIM OF THIS BOOK is to provide the student of Japanese with a simple method for correlating the writing and the meaning of Japanese characters in such a way as to make them both easy to remember. It is intended not only for the beginner, but also for the more advanced student looking for some relief to the constant frustration of forgetting how to write the kanji and some way to systematize what he or she already knows. By showing how to break down the complexities of the Japanese writing system into its basic elements and suggesting ways to reconstruct meanings from those elements, the method offers a new perspective from which to learn the kanji.

There are, of course, many things that the pages of this book will not do for you. You will read nothing about how kanji combine to form compounds. Nor is anything said about the various ways to pronounce the characters. Furthermore, all questions of grammatical usage have been omitted. These are all matters that need specialized treatment in their own right. Meantime, remembering the meaning and the writing of the kanji—perhaps the single most difficult barrier to learning Japanese—can be greatly simplified if the two are isolated and studied apart from everything else.

FORGETTING KANJI, REMEMBERING KANJI

What makes forgetting the kanji so natural is their *lack of connection with normal patterns of visual memory*. We are used to hills and roads, to the faces of people and the skylines of cities, to flowers, animals, and the phenomena of nature. And while only a fraction of what we see is readily recalled, we are confident that, given proper attention, anything we choose to remember, we can. That confidence is lacking in the world of the kanji. The closest approximation to the kind of memory patterns required by the kanji is to be seen in the various alphabets and number-systems we know. The difference is that while these symbols are very few and often sound-related, the kanji number in the thousands and have no consistent phonetic value. Nonetheless, traditional methods for learning the characters have been the same as those for learning alphabets: drill the shapes one by one, again and again, year after year. Whatever ascetic value there is in such an exercise, the more efficient way would be to relate the characters to something other than their sounds

in the first place, and so to break ties with the visual memory we rely on for learning our alphabets.

The origins of the Japanese writing system can be traced back to ancient China and the eighteenth century before the Christian era. In the form in which we find Chinese writing codified some 1,000 years later, it was made up largely of pictographic, detailed glyphs. These were further transformed and stylized down through the centuries, so that by the time the Japanese were introduced to the kanji by Buddhist monks from Korea and started experimenting with ways to adapt the Chinese writing system to their own language (about the fourth to seventh centuries of our era), they were already dealing with far more ideographic and abstract forms. The Japanese made their own contributions and changes in time, as was to be expected. And like every modern Oriental culture that uses the kanji, they continue to do so, though now more in matters of usage than form.

So fascinating is this story that many recommend studying etymology as a way to remember the kanji. Alas, the student quickly learns the many disadvantages of such an approach. As charming as it is to see the ancient drawing of a woman etched behind its respective kanji, or to discover the rudimentary form of a hand or a tree or a house, when the character itself is removed, the clear visual memory of the familiar object is precious little help for recalling how to write it. Proper etymological studies are most helpful *after* one has learned the general-use kanji. Before that, they only add to one's memory problems. We need a still more radical departure from visual memory.

Let me paint the impasse in another, more graphic, way. Picture yourself holding a kaleidoscope up to the light as still as possible, trying to fix in memory the particular pattern that the play of light and mirrors and colored stones has created. Chances are you have such an untrained memory for such things that it will take some time; but let us suppose that you succeed after ten or fifteen minutes. You close your eyes, trace the pattern in your head, and then check your image against the original pattern until you are sure you have it remembered. Then someone passes by and jars your elbow. The pattern is lost, and in its place a new jumble appears. Immediately your memory begins to scramble. You set the kaleidoscope aside, sit down, and try to draw what you had just memorized, but to no avail. There is simply nothing left in memory to grab hold of. The kanji are like that. One can sit at one's desk and drill a half dozen characters for an hour or two, only to discover on the morrow that when something similar is seen, the former memory is erased or hopelessly confused by the new information.

Now the odd thing is not that this occurs, but rather that, instead of openly admitting one's distrust of purely visual memory, one accuses oneself of a

poor memory or lack of discipline and keeps on following the same routine. Thus, by placing the blame on a poor visual memory, one overlooks the possibility of another form of memory that could handle the task with relative ease: *imaginative memory.*

By imaginative memory I mean the faculty to recall images created purely in the mind, with no actual or remembered visual stimuli behind them. When we recall our dreams we are using imaginative memory. The fact that we sometimes conflate what happened in waking life with what occurred merely in a dream is an indication of how powerful those imaginative stimuli can be. While dreams may be broken up into familiar component parts, the composite whole is fantastical and yet capable of exerting the same force on perceptual memory as an external stimulus. It is possible to use imagination in this way also in a waking state and harness its powers for assisting a visual memory admittedly ill-adapted for remembering the kanji.

In other words, if we could discover a limited number of basic elements in the characters and make a kind of alphabet out of them, assigning each its own image, fusing them together to form other images, and so building up complex tableaux in imagination, the impasse created by purely visual memory might be overcome. Such an imaginative alphabet would be every bit as rigorous as a phonetic one in restricting each basic element to one basic value; but its grammar would lack many of the controls of ordinary language and logic. It would be a kind of dream-world where anything at all might happen, and happen differently in each mind. Visual memory would be used minimally, to build up the alphabet. After that, one would be set loose to roam freely inside the magic lantern of imaginative patterns according to one's own preferences.

In fact, most students of the Japanese writing system do something similar from time to time, devising their own mnemonic aids but never developing an organized approach to their use. At the same time, most of them would be embarrassed at the academic silliness of their own secret devices, feeling somehow that there is no way to refine the ridiculous ways their mind works. Yet if it *does* work, then some such irreverence for scholarship and tradition seems very much in place. Indeed, shifting attention from why one *forgets* certain kanji to why one *remembers* others should offer motivation enough to undertake a more thorough attempt to systematize imaginative memory.

THE STRUCTURE OF THIS BOOK

The basic alphabet of the imaginative world hidden in the kanji we may call, following traditional terminology, *primitive elements* (or simply *primitives*). These are not to be confused with the so-called "radicals" which form the basis of etymological studies of sound and meaning, and now are

used for the lexical ordering of the characters. In fact, most of the radicals are themselves primitives, but the number of primitives is not restricted to the traditional list of radicals.

The primitives, then, are the fundamental strokes and combinations of strokes from which all the characters are built up. Calligraphically speaking, there are only nine possible kinds of strokes in theory, seventeen in practice. A few of these will be given *primitive meanings;* that is, they will serve as fundamental images. Simple combinations will yield new primitive meanings in turn, and so on as complex characters are built up. If these primitives are presented in orderly fashion, the taxonomy of the most complex characters is greatly simplified and no attempt need be made to memorize the primitive alphabet apart from actually using it.

The number of primitives, as we are understanding the term, is a moot question. Traditional etymology counts some 224 of them. We shall draw upon these freely, and also ground our primitive meanings in traditional etymological meanings, without making any particular note of the fact as we proceed. We shall also be departing from etymology to avoid the confusion caused by the great number of similar meanings for differently shaped primitives. Wherever possible, then, the generic meaning of the primitives will be preserved, although there are cases in which we shall have to specify that meaning in a different way, or ignore it altogether, so as to root imaginative memory in familiar visual memories. Should the student later turn to etymological studies, the procedure we have followed will become more transparent, and should not cause any obstacles to the learning of etymologies. The list of elements that we have singled out as primitives proper (Index II) is restricted to the following four classes: basic elements that are not kanji, kanji that appear as basic elements in other kanji with great frequency, kanji that change their meaning when they function as parts of other kanji, and kanji that change their shape when forming parts of other kanji. Any kanji that keeps both its form and its meaning and appears as part of another kanji *functions* as a primitive, whether or not it occurs with enough frequency to draw attention to it as such.

The 2,200 characters chosen for study in these pages (given in the order of presentation in Index I and arranged according to the number of strokes in Index III) include the basic 1,945 general-use kanji established as standard by the Japanese Ministry of Education in 1981, another 60 or so used chiefly in proper names, and a handful of characters that are convenient for use as primitive elements. In 2010 another 196 kanji were added to the list of kanji approved for general use, 39 of which had already been incorporated into earlier editions of this book.

Each kanji is assigned a *key word* that represents its basic meaning, or one of its basic meanings. The key words have been selected on the basis of how a given kanji is used in compounds and on the meaning it has on its own. (A total of 190 of the kanji that appear in this book are used commonly in family and personal names, and some of them have no other use in standard Japanese. Nevertheless, each of them has been assigned its own key word.) There is no repetition of key words, although many are nearly synonymous. In these cases, it is important to focus on the particular flavor that that word enjoys in English, so as to evoke connotations distinct from similar key words. To be sure, many of the characters carry a side range of connotations not present in their English equivalents, and vice versa; many even carry several ideas not able to be captured in a single English word. By simplifying the meanings through the use of key words, however, one becomes familiar with a kanji and at least one of its principal meanings. The others can be added later with relative ease, in much the same way as one enriches one's understanding of one's native tongue by learning the full range of feelings and meanings embraced by words already known.

Given the primitive meanings and the key word relevant to a particular kanji (cataloged in Index IV), the task is to create a composite ideogram. Here is where fantasy and memory come into play. The aim is to shock the mind's eye, to disgust it, to enchant it, to tease it, or to entertain it in any way possible so as to brand it with an image intimately associated with the key word. That image, in turn, inasmuch as it is composed of primitive meanings, will dictate precisely how the kanji is to be penned—stroke for stroke, jot for jot. Many characters, perhaps the majority of them, can be so remembered on a first encounter, provided sufficient time is taken to fix the image. Others will need to be reviewed by focusing on the association of key word and primitive elements. In this way, mere drill of visual memory is all but entirely eliminated.

Since the goal is not simply to remember a certain number of kanji, but also to learn *how* to remember them (and others not included in this book), the course has been divided into three parts. Part One provides the full associative story for each character. By directing the reader's attention, at least for the length of time it takes to read the explanation and relate it to the written form of the kanji, most of the work is done for the student, even as a feeling for the method is acquired. In Part Two, only the skeletal plots of the stories are presented, and the individual must work out his or her own details by drawing on personal memory and fantasy. Part Three, which comprises the major portion of the course, provides only the key word and the primitive meanings, leaving the remainder of the process to the student.

It will soon become apparent that the most critical factor is the *order of*

learning the kanji. The actual method is simplicity itself. Once more basic characters have been learned, their use as primitive elements for other kanji can save a great deal of effort and enable one to review known characters at the same time as one is learning new ones. Hence, to approach this course haphazardly, jumping ahead to the later lessons before studying the earlier ones, will entail a considerable loss of efficiency. If one's goal is to learn to write the entire list of general-use characters, then it seems best to learn them in the order best suited to memory, not in order of frequency or according to the order in which they are taught to Japanese children. Should the individual decide to pursue some other course, however, the indexes should provide all the basic information for finding the appropriate frame and the primitives referred to in that frame.

It may surprise the reader casually leafing through these pages not to find a single drawing or pictographic representation. This is fully consistent with what was said earlier about placing the stress on imaginative memory. For one thing, pictographs are an unreliable way to remember all but very few kanji; and even in these cases, the pictograph should be *discovered* by the student by toying with the forms, pen in hand, rather than *given* in one of its historical graphic forms. For another, the presentation of an image actually inhibits imagination and restricts it to the biases of the artist. This is as true for the illustrations in a child's collection of fairy tales as it is for the various phenomena we shall encounter in the course of this book. The more original work the individual does with an image, the easier will it be to remember a kanji.

Admonitions

Before setting out on the course plotted in the following pages, attention should be drawn to a few final points. In the first place, one must be warned about setting out too quickly. It should not be assumed that, because the first characters are so elementary, they can be skipped over hastily. The method presented here needs to be learned step by step, lest one find oneself forced later to retreat to the first stages and start over; 20 or 25 characters per day would not be excessive for someone who has only a couple of hours to give to study. If one were to study them full-time, there is no reason why the entire course could not be completed successfully in four to six weeks. By the time Part One has been traversed, the student should have discovered a rate of progress suitable to the time available.

Second, repeated instruction to study the characters with pad and pencil should be taken seriously. Remembering the characters demands that they be written, and there is really no better way to improve the aesthetic appearance of one's writing and acquire a "natural feel" for the flow of the kanji than by

writing them. The method may spare one from having to write the same character over and over in order to learn it, but it does not give one the fluency at writing that comes only with constant practice. If pen and paper are inconvenient, one can always make do with the palm of the hand, as the Japanese do. It provides a convenient square space for jotting on with one's index finger when riding in a bus or walking down the street.

Third, the kanji are best reviewed by beginning with the key word, progressing to the respective story, and then writing the character itself. Once one has been able to perform these steps, reversing the order follows as a matter of course. More will be said about this later in the book.

In the fourth place, it is important to note that the best order for *learning* the kanji is by no means the best order for *remembering* them. They need to be recalled when and where they are met, not in the sequence in which they are presented here. For that purpose, recommendations are given in Lesson 5 for designing flash cards for random review.

Finally, it seems worthwhile to give some brief thought to any ambitions one might have about "mastering" the Japanese writing system. The idea arises from, or at least is supported by, a certain bias about learning that comes from overexposure to schooling: the notion that language is a cluster of skills that can be rationally divided, systematically learned, and certified by testing. The kanji, together with the wider structure of Japanese—and indeed of *any* language for that matter—resolutely refuse to be mastered in this fashion. The rational order brought to the kanji in this book is only intended as an aid to get you close enough to the characters to befriend them, let them surprise you, inspire you, enlighten you, resist you, and seduce you. But they cannot be mastered without a full understanding of their long and complex history and an insight into the secret of their unpredictable vitality—all of which is far too much for a single mind to bring to the tip of a single pen.

That having been said, the goal of this book is still to attain native proficiency in writing the Japanese characters and associating their meanings with their forms. If the logical systematization and the playful irreverence contained in the pages that follow can help spare even a few of those who pick the book up the grave error of deciding to pursue their study of the Japanese language without aspiring to such proficiency, the efforts that went into it will have more than received their reward.

Self-study and classroom study

As this book went through one reprint after the other, I was often tempted to rethink many of the key words and primitive meaning. After careful consideration and review of the hundred of letters I received from students

all over the world, and in the light of the many adjustments required for versions in other languages, I decided to let it stand with only minor alterations. There are, however, two related questions that come up with enough frequency to merit further comment at the outset: the use of this book in connection with formal courses of Japanese, and the matter of pronunciation or "readings" of the kanji.

The reader will not have to finish more than a few lessons to realize that this book was designed for self-learning. What may not be so apparent is that *using it to supplement the study of kanji in the classroom or to review for examinations has an adverse influence on the learning process.* The more you try to combine the study of the written kanji through the method outlined in these pages with traditional study of the kanji, the less good this book will do you. I know of no exceptions.

Virtually all teachers of Japanese, native and foreign, would agree with me that learning to write the kanji with native proficiency is the greatest single obstacle to the foreign adult approaching Japanese—indeed so great as to be *presumed* insurmountable. After all, if even well-educated Japanese study the characters formally for nine years, use them daily, and yet frequently have trouble remembering how to reproduce them, much more than English-speaking people have with the infamous spelling of their mother tongue, is it not unrealistic to expect that even with the best of intentions and study methods those not raised with the kanji from their youth should manage the feat? Such an attitude may never actually be spoken openly by a teacher standing before a class, but as long as the teacher believes it, it readily becomes a self-fulfilling prophecy. This attitude is then transmitted to the student by placing greater emphasis on the supposedly simpler and more reasonable skills of learning to speak and read the language. In fact, as this book seeks to demonstrate, nothing could be further from the truth.

To begin with, the writing of the kanji is the most completely rational part of the language. Over the centuries, the writing of the kanji has been simplified many times, always with rational principles in mind. Aside from the Korean *hangul,* there may be no writing system in the world as logically structured as the Sino-Japanese characters are. The problem is that the usefulness of this inner logic has not found its way into learning the kanji. On the contrary, it has been systematically ignored. Those who have passed through the Japanese school system tend to draw on their own experience when they teach others how to write. Having begun as small children in whom the powers of abstraction are relatively undeveloped and for whom constant repetition is the only workable method, they are not likely ever to have considered reor-

ganizing their pedagogy to take advantage of the older student's facility with generalized principles.

So great is this neglect that I would have to say that I have never met a Japanese teacher who can claim to have taught a foreign adult to write the basic general-use kanji that all high-school graduates in Japan know. Never. Nor have I ever met a foreign adult who would claim to have learned to write at this level from a native Japanese teacher. I see no reason to assume that the Japanese are better suited to teach writing because it is, after all, their language. Given the rational nature of the kanji, precisely the opposite is the case: the Japanese teacher is an impediment to learning to associate the meanings of the kanji with their written form. The obvious victim of the conventional methods is the student, but on a subtler level the reconfirmation of unquestioned biases also victimizes the Japanese teachers themselves, the most devoted of whom are prematurely denied the dream of fully internationalizing their language.

There are additional problems with using this book in connection with classroom study. For one thing, as explained earlier in the Introduction, the efficiency of the study of the kanji is directly related to the order in which they are learned. Formal courses introduce kanji according to different principles that have nothing to do with the writing. More often than not, the order in which Japan's Ministry of Education has determined children should learn the kanji from primary through middle school, is the main guide. Obviously, learning the writing is far more important than being certified to have passed some course or other. And just as obviously, one needs to know *all* the general-use kanji for them to be of any use for the literate adult. When it comes to reading basic materials, such as newspapers, it is little consolation to know half or even three-quarters of them. The crucial question for pedagogy, therefore, is not what is the best way to qualify at some intermediate level of proficiency, but simply how to learn all the kanji in the most efficient and reliable manner possible. For this, the traditional "levels" of kanji proficiency are simply irrelevant. The answer, I am convinced, lies in self-study, following an order based on learning all the kanji.

I do not myself know of any teacher of Japanese who has attempted to use this book in a classroom setting. My suspicion is that they would soon abandon the idea. The book is based on the idea that the writing of the kanji can be learned on its own and independently of any other aspect of the language. It is also based on the idea that the pace of study is different from one individual to another, and for each individual, from one week to the next. Organizing study to the routines of group instruction runs counter to those ideas.

This brings us to our second question. The reasons for isolating the writing

of the kanji from their pronunciation follow more or less as a matter of course from what has been said. The reading and writing of the characters are taught simultaneously on the grounds that one is useless without the other. This only begs the basic question of why they could not better, and more quickly, be taught one *after* the other, concentrating on what is for the foreigner the simpler task, writing, and later turning to the more complicated, the reading.

One has only to look at the progress of non-Japanese raised with kanji to see the logic of the approach. When Chinese adult students come to the study of Japanese, they already know what the kanji mean and how to write them. They have only to learn how to read them. The progress they make in comparison with their Western counterparts is usually attributed to their being "Oriental." In fact, Chinese grammar and pronunciation have about as much to do with Japanese as English does. It is their knowledge of the meaning and writing of the kanji that gives the Chinese the decisive edge. My idea was simply to learn from this common experience and give the kanji an English reading. Having learned to write the kanji in this way—which, I repeat, is the most logical and rational part of the study of Japanese—one is in a much better position to concentrate on the often irrational and unprincipled problem of learning to pronounce them.

In a word, it is hard to imagine a *less* efficient way of learning the reading and writing of the kanji than to study them simultaneously. And yet this is the method that all Japanese textbooks and courses follow. The bias is too deeply ingrained to be rooted out by anything but experience to the contrary.

Many of these ideas and impressions, let it be said, only developed after I had myself learned the kanji and published the first edition of this book. At the time I was convinced that proficiency in writing the kanji could be attained in four to six weeks if one were to make a full-time job of it. Of course, the claim raised more eyebrows than hopes among teachers with far more experience than I had. Still, my own experience with studying the kanji and the relatively small number of individuals I have directed in the methods of this book, bears that estimate out, and I do not hesitate to repeat it here.

THE STORY BEHIND THIS BOOK

A word about how the book came to be written. I began my study of the kanji one month after coming to Japan with absolutely no previous knowledge of the language. Because travels through Asia had delayed my arrival by several weeks, I took up residence at a language school in Kamakura and began studying on my own without enrolling in the course already in progress. A certain impatience with my own ignorance compared to everyone around me, coupled with the freedom to devote myself exclusively to language stud-

ies, helped me during those first four weeks to make my way through a basic introductory grammar. This provided a general idea of how the language was constructed but, of course, almost no facility in using any of it.

Through conversations with the teachers and other students, I quickly picked up the impression that I had best begin learning the kanji as soon as possible, since this was sure to be the greatest chore of all. Having no idea at all how the kanji "worked" in the language, yet having found my own pace, I decided—against the advice of nearly everyone around me—to continue to study on my own rather than join one of the beginners' classes.

The first few days I spent poring over whatever I could find on the history and etymology of the Japanese characters, and examining the wide variety of systems on the market for studying them. It was during those days that the basic idea underlying the method of this book came to me. The following weeks I devoted myself day and night to experimenting with the idea, which worked well enough to encourage me to carry on with it. Before the month was out I had learned the meaning and writing of some 1,900 characters and had satisfied myself that I would retain what I had memorized. It was not long before I became aware that something extraordinary had taken place.

For myself, the method I was following seemed so simple, even childish, that it was almost an embarrassment to talk about it. And it had happened as such a matter of course that I was quite unprepared for the reaction it caused. On the one hand, some at the school accused me of having a short-term photographic memory that would fade with time. On the other hand, there were those who pressed me to write up my "methods" for their benefit. But it seemed to me that there was too much left to learn of the language for me to get distracted by either side. Within a week, however, I was persuaded at least to let my notes circulate. Since most everything was either in my head or jotted illegibly in notebooks and on flash cards, I decided to give an hour each day to writing everything up systematically. One hour soon became two, then three, and in no time at all I had laid everything else aside to complete the task. By the end of that third month I brought a camera-ready copy to Nanzan University in Nagoya for printing. During the two months it took to prepare it for printing I added an Introduction.

Through the kind help of Mrs. Iwamoto Keiko of Tuttle Publishing Company, most of the 500 copies were distributed in Tokyo bookstores, where they sold out within a few months. After the month I spent studying how to write the kanji, I did not return to any formal review of what I had learned. (I was busy trying to devise another method for simplifying the study of the reading of the characters, which was later completed and published as a companion volume to this one.) When I would meet a new character, I would learn it as I

had the others, but I have never felt the need to retrace my steps or repeat any of the work. Admittedly, the fact that I now use the kanji daily in my teaching, research, and writing is a distinct advantage. But I remain convinced that whatever facility I have I owe to the procedures outlined in this book.

Perhaps only one who has seen the method through to the end can appreciate both how truly uncomplicated and obvious it is, and how accessible to any average student willing to invest the time and effort. For while the method is *simple* and does eliminate a great deal of wasted effort, the task is still not an *easy* one. It requires as much stamina, concentration, and imagination as one can bring to it.

PART ONE

Stories

Lesson 1

LET US BEGIN with a group of 15 kanji, all of which you probably knew before you ever cracked the covers of this book. Each kanji has been provided with a single *key word* to represent the basic meaning. Some of these characters will also serve later as *primitive elements* to help form other kanji, when they will take a meaning different from the meaning they have as kanji. Although it is not necessary at this stage to memorize the special primitive meaning of these characters, a special remark preceded by a star (*) has been appended to alert you to the change in meaning.

The *number of strokes* of each character is given in square brackets at the end of each explanation, followed by the stroke-by-stroke *order of writing*. It cannot be stressed enough how important it is to learn to write each kanji in its proper order. As easy as these first characters may seem, study them all with a pad and pencil to get into the habit from the very start.

Finally, note that each key word has been carefully chosen and should not be tampered with in any way if you want to avoid confusion later on.

1	one

─── In Chinese characters, the number **one** is laid on its side, unlike the Roman numeral I which stands upright. As you would expect, it is written from left to right. [1]

─

* As a primitive element, the key-word meaning is discarded, since it is too abstract to be of much help. Instead, the single horizontal stroke takes on the meaning of *floor* or *ceiling*, depending on its position: if it stands above another primitive, it means *ceiling*; if below, *floor*.

2

一

two

Like the Roman numeral II, which reduplicates the numeral I, the kanji for **two** is a simple reduplication of the horizontal stroke that means *one*. The order of writing goes from above to below, with the first stroke slightly shorter. [2]

一 二

3

三

three

And like the Roman numeral III, which triples the numeral I, the kanji for **three** simply triples the single horizontal stroke. In writing it, think of "1 + 2 = 3" ($一 + 二 = 三$) in order to keep the middle stroke shorter. [3]

一 二 三

4

四

four

This kanji is composed of two primitive elements, *mouth* 口 and *human legs* 儿, both of which we will meet in the coming lessons. Assuming that you already knew how to write this kanji, we will pass over the "story" connected with it until later.

Note how the second stroke is written left-to-right and then top-to-bottom. This is consistent with what we have already seen in the first three numbers and leads us to a general principle that will be helpful when we come to more complicated kanji later on: WRITE NORTH-TO-SOUTH, WEST-TO-EAST, NORTHWEST-TO-SOUTHEAST. [5]

丨 冂 冂 冈 四

5

五

five

As with *four,* we shall postpone learning the primitive elements that make up this character. Note how the general principle we just learned in the preceding frame applies to the writing of the character for **five**. [4]

一 丁 开 五

| 6 | six |

六

The primitives here are *top hat* and *animal legs*. Once again, we glide over them until later. [4]

     ノ   亠   亠   六

| 7 | seven |

七

Note that the first stroke "cuts" through the second. This distinguishes **seven** from the character for *spoon* 匕 (FRAME 476), in which the horizontal stroke stops short. [2]

     一   七

* As a primitive, this form takes on the meaning of *diced,* i.e., "cut" into little pieces, consistent both with the way the character is written and with its association with the kanji for *cut* 切 to be learned in a later lesson (FRAME 89).

| 8 | eight |

八

Just as the Arabic numeral "8" is composed of a small circle followed by a larger one, so the kanji for **eight** is composed of a short line followed by a longer line, slanting towards it but not touching it. And just as the "lazy 8" ∞ is the mathematical symbol for "infinity," so the expanse opened up below these two strokes is associated by the Japanese with the sense of an infinite expanse or something "all-encompassing." [2]

     ノ   八

| 9 | nine |

九

If you take care to remember the stroke order of this kanji, you will not have trouble later keeping it distinct from the kanji for *power* 力 (FRAME 922). [2]

     ノ   九

REMEMBERING THE KANJI 1

* As a primitive, we shall use this kanji to mean *baseball team* or simply *baseball*. The meaning, of course, is derived from the *nine* players who make up a team.

10

ten

十

Turn this character 45° either way and you have the x used for the Roman numeral **ten**. [2]

$$一 \quad 十$$

* As a primitive, this character sometimes keeps its meaning of *ten* and sometimes signifies *needle,* this latter derived from the kanji for *needle* 針 (FRAME 292). Since the primitive is used in the kanji itself, there is no need to worry about confusing the two. In fact, we shall be following this procedure regularly.

11

mouth

口

Like several of the first characters we shall learn, the kanji for **mouth** is a clear pictograph. Since there are no circular shapes in the kanji, the square must be used to depict the circle. [3]

$$｜ \quad 冂 \quad 口$$

* As a primitive, this form also means *mouth.* Any of the range of possible images that the word suggests—an opening or entrance to a cave, a river, a bottle, or even the largest hole in your head—can be used for the primitive meaning.

12

day

日

This kanji is intended to be a pictograph of the sun. Recalling what we said in the previous frame about round forms, it is easy to detect the circle and the big smile that characterize our simplest drawings of the sun—like those yellow badges with the words, "Have a nice **day**!" [4]

$$｜ \quad 冂 \quad 日 \quad 日$$

* Used as a primitive, this kanji can mean *sun* or *day* or a *tongue wagging in the mouth*. This latter meaning, incidentally, derives from an old character outside the standard list meaning something like "sayeth" and written almost exactly the same, except that the stroke in the middle does not touch the right side (曰, FRAME 620).

13　　　　　　　　　　　　　　　　　　　　　　　　　　**month**

月

This character is actually a picture of the moon, with the two horizontal lines representing the left eye and mouth of the mythical "man in the moon." (Actually, the Japanese see a hare in the moon, but it is a little farfetched to find one in the kanji.) And one **month**, of course, is one cycle of the moon. [4]

丿　丿　月　月

* As a primitive element, this character can take on the sense of *moon, flesh,* or *part of the body*. The reasons for the latter two meanings will be explained in a later chapter.

14　　　　　　　　　　　　　　　　　　　　　　　　　　**rice field**

田

Another pictograph, this kanji looks like a bird's-eye view of a **rice field** divided into four plots. Be careful when writing this character to get the order of the strokes correct. You will find that it follows perfectly the principle stated in FRAME 4. [5]

丨　冂　冂　田　田

* When used as a primitive element, the meaning of *rice field* is most common, but now and again it will take the meaning of *brains* from the fact that it looks a bit like that tangle of gray matter nestled under our skulls.

15　　　　　　　　　　　　　　　　　　　　　　　　　　**eye**

目

Here again, if we round out the corners of this kanji and curve the middle strokes upwards and downwards respectively, we get something resembling an **eye**. [5]

| 冂 冃 冃 目

* As a primitive, the kanji keeps its sense of *eye,* or to be more specific, an *eyeball.* When placed in the surroundings of a complex kanji, the primitive will sometimes be turned on its side like this: ⮡.

Although only 9 of the 15 kanji treated in this lesson are formally listed as primitives—the elements that join together to make up other kanji—some of the others may also take on that function from time to time, only not with enough frequency to merit learning them as separate primitive elements and attaching special meanings to them. In other words, whenever one of the kanji already learned is used in another kanji, it will retain its key-word meaning unless we have assigned it a special primitive meaning.

Lesson 2

IN THIS LESSON we learn what a "primitive element" is by using the first 15 characters as pieces that can be fitted together to form new kanji—19 of them to be exact. Whenever the primitive meaning differs from the key-word meaning, you may want to go back to the original frame to refresh your memory. From now on, though, you should learn *both* the key word and the primitive meaning of new kanji as they appear. An INDEX OF PRIMITIVE ELEMENTS has been added at the end of the book.

16		old

古

The primitive elements that compose this character are *ten* and *mouth,* but you may find it easier to remember it as a pictograph of a tombstone with a cross on top. Just think back to one of those graveyards you have visited, or better still, used to play in as a child, with **old** inscriptions on the tombstones.

This departure from the primitive elements in favor of a picto-

graph will take place now and again at these early stages, and almost never after that. So you need not worry about cluttering up your memory with too many character "drawings." [5]

* Used as a primitive element, this kanji keeps its key-word sense of *old*, but care should be taken to make that abstract notion as graphic as possible.

17

I

There are a number of kanji for the word I, but the others tend to be more specific than this one. The key word here should be taken in the general psychological sense of the "perceiving subject." Now the one place in our bodies that all *five* senses are concentrated in is the head, which has no less than *five mouths*: 2 nostrils, 2 ears, and 1 mouth. Hence, *five mouths* = I. [7]

一 丁 开 五 五 吾 吾

18

冒

risk

Remember when you were young and your mother told you never to look directly into the *sun* for fear you might burn out your *eyes*? Probably you were foolish enough to **risk** a quick glance once or twice; but just as probably, you passed that bit of folk wisdom on to someone else as you grew older. Here, too, the kanji that has a *sun* above and an *eye* right below looking up at it has the meaning of **risk** (see FRAME 12). [9]

丶 冂 冖 冃 冒

19

朋

companion

The first **companion** that God made, as the Bible story goes, was Eve. Upon seeing her, Adam exclaimed, "*Flesh* of my *flesh!*" And that is precisely what this kanji says in so many strokes. [8]

丿 刀 月 月 朋

20　　　　　　　　　　　　　　　　　　　　　**bright**

明

Among nature's **bright** lights, there are two that the biblical myth has God set in the sky: the *sun* to rule over the day and the *moon* to rule the night. Each of them has come to represent one of the common connotations of this key word: the *sun*, the **bright** insight of the clear thinker, and the *moon*, the **bright** intuition of the poet and the seer (see FRAME 13). [8]

日　明

21　　　　　　　　　　　　　　　　　　　　　**chant**

唱

This one is easy! You have one *mouth* making no noise (the choirmaster) and two *mouths with wagging tongues* (the minimum for a chorus). So think of the key word, **chant**, as monastery singing and the kanji is yours forever (see FRAME 11). [11]

口　唱　唱

22　　　　　　　　　　　　　　　　　　　　　**sparkle**

晶

What else can the word **sparkle** suggest if not a diamond? And if you've ever held a diamond up to the light, you will have noticed how every facet of it becomes like a miniature *sun*. This kanji is a picture of a tiny *sun* in three places (that is, "everywhere"), to give the sense of something that **sparkles** on all sides. Just like a diamond. In writing the primitive elements three times, note again how the rule for writing given in FRAME 4 holds true not only for the strokes in each individual element but also for the disposition of the elements in the character as a whole. [12]

日　晶　晶

23　　　　　　　　　　　　　　　　　　　　　**goods**

品

As in the character for *sparkle*, the triplication of a single element in this character indicates "everywhere" or "heaps of." When we think of **goods** in modern industrial society, we think of what has been mass-produced—that is to say, produced for

the "masses" of open *mouths* waiting like fledglings in a nest to "consume" whatever comes their way. [9]

口 口口 品

---

24 spine

This character is rather like a picture of two of the vertebrae in the **spine** linked by a single stroke. [7]

丶 冖 口 𠮥 𠮷 呂 呂

---

25 prosperous

What we mentioned in the previous two frames about 3 of something meaning "everywhere" or "heaps of" was not meant to be taken lightly. In this kanji we see *two suns,* one atop the other, which, if we are not careful, is easily confused in memory with the *three suns* of *sparkle*. Focus on the number this way: since we speak of **prosperous** times as *sunny,* what could be more **prosperous** than a sky with *two suns* in it? Just be sure to actually SEE them there. [8]

日 昌

---

26 early

This kanji is actually a picture of the first flower of the day, which we shall, in defiance of botanical science, call the *sun-flower,* since it begins with the element for *sun* and is held up on a stem with leaves (the pictographic representation of the final two strokes). This time, however, we shall ignore the pictograph and imagine *sun*flowers with *needles* for stems, which can be plucked and used to darn your socks.

The sense of **early** is easily remembered if one thinks of the *sun*flower as the **early** riser in the garden, because the *sun,* showing favoritism towards its namesake, shines on it before all the others (see FRAME 10). [6]

日 早 早

* As a primitive element, this kanji takes the meaning of *sunflower,* which was used to make the abstract key word *early* more graphic.

---

27   **rising sun**

旭

This character is a sort of nickname for the Japanese flag with its well-known emblem of the **rising sun**. If you can picture two seams running down that great red *sun,* and then imagine it sitting on a *baseball* bat for a flagpole, you have a slightly irreverent—but not altogether inaccurate—picture of how the sport has caught on in the Land of the **Rising Sun**. [6]

丿　九　九　旭　旭　旭

---

28   **generation**

世

We generally consider one **generation** as a period of thirty (or *ten* plus *ten* plus *ten*) years. If you look at this kanji in its completed form—not in its stroke order—you will see three *tens.* When writing it, think of the lower horizontal lines as "addition" lines written under numbers to add them up. Thus: *ten* "plus" *ten* "plus" *ten* = thirty. Actually, it's a lot easier doing it with a pencil than reading it in a book. [5]

一　十　卅　卅　世

---

29   **stomach**

胃

You will need to refer back to FRAMES 13 and 14 here for the special meaning of the two primitive elements that make up this character: *flesh (part of the body)* and *brain.* What the kanji says, if you look at it, is that the *part of the body* that keeps the *brain* in working order is the **stomach**. To keep the elements in proper order, when you write this kanji think of the *brain* as being "held up" by the *flesh.* [9]

田　胃

30   **nightbreak**

旦

While we normally refer to the start of the day as "daybreak,"
Japanese commonly refers to it as the "opening up of night" into
day. Hence the choice of this rather odd key word, **nightbreak**.
The single stroke at the bottom represents the *floor* (have a peek
again at FRAME 1) or the horizon over which the *sun* is poking
its head. [5]

日   旦

---

31   **gall bladder**

胆

The pieces in this character should be easily recognizable: on
the left, the element for *part of the body*, and on the right, the
character for *nightbreak*, which we have just met. What all of
this has to do with the **gall bladder** is not immediately clear. But
all we need to do is give a slight twist to the traditional biblical advice about not letting the sun set on your anger (which
ancient medicine associated with the choler or bile that the
gall bladder is supposed to filter out), and change it to "not
letting the *night break* on your anger" (or your **gall**)—and the
work of remembering the kanji is done. And the improvement
is not a bad piece of advice in its own right, since anger, like so
many other things, can often be calmed by letting the sun set
on it and then "sleeping it off." [9]

月   胆

---

32   **span**

亘

"Sunrise, sunset, sunrise, sunset…" goes the song of the Fiddler
on the Roof. You can almost see the journey of the *sun* as it
moves from one horizon (the *floor*) to its noonday heights in
the sky overhead *(ceiling)* and then disappears over the other
horizon—day after day, marking the **span** of our lives. [6]

一   百   亘

We end this lesson with two final pictographic characters that happen to be among the easiest to recognize for their form, but among the most difficult to write. We introduce them here to run an early test on whether or not you have been paying close attention to the stroke order of the kanji you have been learning.

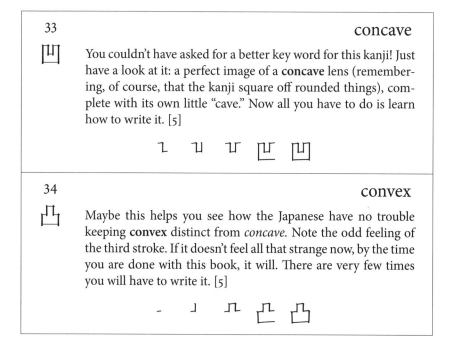

33	concave
凹	You couldn't have asked for a better key word for this kanji! Just have a look at it: a perfect image of a **concave** lens (remembering, of course, that the kanji square off rounded things), complete with its own little "cave." Now all you have to do is learn how to write it. [5]

34	convex
凸	Maybe this helps you see how the Japanese have no trouble keeping **convex** distinct from *concave*. Note the odd feeling of the third stroke. If it doesn't feel all that strange now, by the time you are done with this book, it will. There are very few times you will have to write it. [5]

Lesson 3

AFTER LESSON 2, you should now have some idea of how an apparently complex and difficult kanji can be broken down into simple elements that make remembering it a great deal easier. After completing this lesson you should have a clearer idea of how the course is laid out. We merely add a couple of primitive elements to the kanji we already know and see how many new kanji we can form—in this case, 18 in all—and when we run out, add more primitives. And so on, until there are no kanji left.

In Lesson 3 you will also be introduced to primitive elements that are not themselves kanji but only used to construct other kanji. These are marked with a star [*] instead of a number. There is no need to make a special effort to memorize them. The sheer frequency with which most of them show up should make remembering them automatic.

---

* | **walking stick**

This primitive element is a picture of just what it looks like: a cane or **walking stick**. It carries with it the connotations of lameness and whatever else one associates with the use of a cane. Rarely—but very rarely—it will be laid on its side. Whenever this occurs, it will ALWAYS be driven through the middle of some other primitive element. In this way, you need not worry about confusing it with the primitive meanings of *one*. [1]

|

---

* ∕ **a drop of**

The meaning of this primitive is obvious from the first moment you look at it, though just what it will be **a drop of** will differ from case to case. The important thing is not to think of it as something insignificant like a "drop in the bucket" but as something so important that it can change the whole picture—like **a drop of** arsenic in your mother-in-law's coffee. [1]

∕

* In general, it is written from right to left, but there are times when it can be slanted left to right. At other times it can be stretched out a bit. (In cases where you have trouble remembering this, it may help to think of it as an *eyedropper* dripping drops of something or other.) Examples will follow in this lesson.

---

35 旧 **olden times**

A *walking stick* is needed for *days* of **olden times**, since *days*, too, get old—at least insofar as we refer to them as the "good old

days." The main thing here is to think of "good old days" when you hear the key word **olden times**. The rest will take care of itself. [5]

丨 旧

---

36 oneself

自

You can think of this kanji as a stylized pictograph of the nose, that little *drop* that Mother Nature set between your *eyes*. The Japanese refer to themselves by pointing a finger at their nose—giving us an easy way to remember the kanji for **oneself**. [6]

′ 丨′ 冂 白 自 自

* The same meaning of *oneself* can be kept when this kanji is used as a primitive element, but you will generally find it better to give it the meaning of *nose* or *nostrils,* both because it accords with the story above and because it is the first part of the kanji for *nose* (FRAME 733).

---

37 white

白

The color **white** is a mixture of all the primary colors, both for pigments and for light, as we see when a prism breaks up the rays of the *sun*. Hence, a single *drop* of *sun* spells **white**. [5]

′ 丨′ 冂 白 白

* As a primitive, this character can either retain its meaning of *white* or take the more graphic meaning of a *white bird* or *dove*. This latter stems from the fact that it appears at the top of the kanji for *bird*, which we shall get to later (FRAME 2091).

---

38 hundred

百

The Japanese refer to a person's 99th birthday as a "*white* year" because *white* is the kanji you are left with if you subtract *one* from a **hundred**. [6]

一 一 厂 厂 万 百 百

---

39   **in**

中

The elements here are a *walking stick* and a *mouth*. Remember the trouble your mother had getting medicine **in** your *mouth*? Chances are it crossed her mind more than once to grab something handy, like your grandfather's *walking stick,* to pry open your jaws while she performed her duty. Keep the image of getting something **in** from the outside, and the otherwise abstract sense of this key word should be a lot easier than trying to spoon castor oil **in**to a baby's mouth. [4]

丨 冂 口 中

---

40   **thousand**

千

This kanji is almost too simple to pull apart, but for the sake of practice, have a look at the *drop* above and the *ten* below. Now put the elements together by thinking of squeezing two more zeros out of an *eyedropper* alongside the number *ten* to make it a **thousand.** [3]

丿 二 千

---

41   **tongue**

舌

The primitive for *mouth* and the character for *thousand* naturally form the idea of **tongue** if one thinks of a *thousand mouths* able to speak the same language, or as we say, "sharing a common **tongue.**" It is easy to see the connection between the idiom and the kanji if you take its image literally: a single **tongue** being passed around from *mouth* to *mouth.* [6]

丿 二 千 千 舌 舌

---

42   **measuring box**

升

This is the character for the little wooden box that the Japanese use for measuring things, as well as for drinking saké out of.

Simply imagine the outside as spiked with a *thousand* sharp *needles*, and the quaint little **measuring box** becomes a drinker's nightmare!

Be very careful when you write this character not to confuse it with the writing of *thousand*. The reason for the difference gives us a chance to clarify another general principle of writing that supersedes the one we mentioned in FRAME 4: WHEN A SINGLE STROKE RUNS VERTICALLY THROUGH THE MIDDLE OF A CHARACTER, IT IS WRITTEN LAST. [4]

丿 丿 チ 升

43		rise up

昇

Our image here is made up of two primitive elements: a *sun* and a *measuring box*. Just as the *sun* can be seen **rising up** in the morning from—where else—the Land of the Rising Sun, this kanji has the *sun* **rising up** out of a Japanese *measuring box*—the "*measuring box* of the **rising-up** *sun*." [8]

44		round

丸

We speak of "**round** numbers," or "**rounding** a number off," meaning to add an insignificant amount to bring it to the nearest 10. For instance, if you add just a wee bit, the tiniest *drop*, to *nine*, you end up with a **round** number. [3]

丿 九 丸

* As a primitive, this element takes the meaning of a *fat man*. Think of a grotesquely *fat man* whose paunch so covers the plate that he is always getting hit by the pitch. Hence a *round baseball player* becomes a *fat man*.

45		measurement

寸

This kanji actually stood for a small **measurement** used prior to the metric system, a bit over an inch in length, and from there acquired the sense of **measurement**. In the old system, it was

one-*tenth* of a *shaku* (whose kanji we shall meet in FRAME 1151). The picture, appropriately, represents one *drop* of a *ten* (with a hook!). [3]

* As a primitive, we shall use this to mean *glue* or *glued to*. There is no need to devise a story to remember this, since the primitive will appear so often you would have to struggle hard NOT to remember it.

---

46 肘	**elbow**

Instead of the familiar "grease" we usually associate with the **elbow** of someone hard at work, the kanji gives us a *part of the body* that has been *glued to* its task. [7]

月 肘

---

47 専	**specialty**

Ten . . . rice fields . . . glue. That is how one would read the primitive elements of this kanji from top to bottom. Now if we make a simple sentence out of these elements, we get: "*Ten rice fields glued* together."

A **specialty**, of course, refers to one's special "*field*" of endeavor or competence. In fact, few people remain content with a single **specialty** and usually extend themselves in other *fields* as well. This is how we come to get the picture of *ten fields glued* together to represent a **specialty**. [9]

一 厂 冂 厅 百 車 重 専 専

---

48 博	**Dr.**

At the left we have the *needle;* at the right, the kanji for *specialty*, plus an extra *drop* at the top. Think of a **Dr.** who is a *specialist* with a *needle* (an acupuncturist) and let the *drop* at the top represent the period at the end of **Dr.**

In principle we are trying to avoid this kind of device, which plays on abstract grammatical conventions; but I think you will

agree, after you have had occasion to use the right side of this kanji in forming other kanji, that the exception is merited in this case. [12]

* The primitive form of this kanji eliminates the *needle* on the left and gets the meaning of an *acupuncturist*.

We have already seen one example of how to form primitives from other primitives, when we formed the *nightbreak* out of *sun* and *floor* (FRAME 30). Let us take two more examples of this procedure right away, so that we can do so from now on without having to draw any particular attention to the fact.

*	divining rod

This is a picture of a **divining rod**, composed of *a drop* and a *walking stick*, but easy enough to remember as a pictograph. Alternately, you can think of it as a **magic wand**. In either case, it should suggest images of magic or fortune-telling.

Nowadays it is written in the stroke order given here when it appears as a primitive, but until recently the order was often reversed (in order to instill correct habits for more stylized calligraphy). [2]

* Although it falls outside of the list of general-use kanji, this element is actually a kanji in its own right, having virtually the same meaning as the kanji in the next frame.

49	fortune-telling

This is one of those kanji that is a real joy of simplicity: a *divining rod* with a *mouth*—which translate directly into **fortune-telling**.

Note how the movement from top to bottom (the movement in which the kanji are written) is also the order of the elements which make up our story and of the key word itself: first *divining rod,* then *mouth.* This will not always be possible, but where it is, memory has almost no work at all to do. [5]

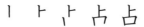

50

上

above

The two directions, **above** and below, are usually pointed at with the finger. But the characters do not follow that custom, so we have to choose something else, easily remembered. The primitives show a *magic wand* standing *above* a *floor*—"magically," you might say. Anyway, go right on to the next frame, since the two belong together and are best remembered as a unit, just as the words **above** and *below* suggest each other. [3]

丨　卜　上

51

下

below

Here we see our famous miraculous *magic wand* hanging, all on its own, **below** the *ceiling,* as you probably already guessed would happen. In addition to giving us two new kanji, the two shapes given in this and the preceding frame also serve to fix the use of the primitives for *ceiling* and *floor,* by drawing our attention successively to the line standing above and **below** the primitive element to which it is related. [3]

一　丁　下

52

卓

eminent

The word **eminent** suggests a famous or well-known person. So all you need to do—given the primitives of a *magic wand* and a *sunflower*—is to think of the world's most **eminent** magician as one who uses a *sunflower* for a *magic wand* (like a flower-child who goes around turning the world into peace and love). [8]

丶　ﾄ　ﾄ　占　卢　卣　卣　卓

* 　　　　　　　　　　　　　　　　　　mist

卓　Here is our second example of a primitive composed of other primitives but not itself a kanji. At the bottom is the primitive (also a kanji) for *early* or *sunflower*. At the top, a *needle*. Conveniently, **mist** falls *early* in the morning, like little *needles* of rain, to assure that the *sunflower* blooms *early* as we have learned it should. [8]

一　十　ﾅ　占　吉　吉　直　卓

53　　　　　　　　　　　　　　　　　morning

朝　On the right we see the *moon* fading off into the first light of **morning**, and to the left, the *mist* that falls to give nature a shower to prepare it for the coming heat. If you can think of the *moon* tilting over to spill *mist* on your garden, you should have no trouble remembering which of all the elements in this story are to serve as primitives for constructing the character. [12]

卓　朝

54　　　　　　　　　　　　　　　　　derision

嘲　The bad feeling created by words spoken in **derision** often leaves a bad taste in the *mouth* of the one who speaks them, kind of like the foul aftertaste that follows a night before of too much of the wrong stuff—or what we call *morning mouth*. [15]

口　嘲

Lesson 4

AT THE RISK OF going a little bit too fast, we are now going to introduce five new primitive elements, all of which are very easy to remember, either because of their frequency or because of their shape. But remember: there is no reason to study the primitives by themselves. They are being presented systematically to make their learning automatic.

⋆	animal legs

ノ丶

Like the four that follow it, this primitive is not a kanji in its own right, though it is said to be derived from 八, the character we learned earlier for *eight*. It ALWAYS comes at the bottom of the primitive to which it is related. It can mean the **legs** of any kind of **animal**: from a grizzly bear's paws to an octopus's tentacles to the spindle shanks of a spider. (The one animal not allowed is our friend homo sapiens, whose legs figure in the next frame.) Even where the term "legs" will apply metaphorically to the legs of pieces of furniture, it is best to keep the association with **animal legs**. (You may review FRAME 6 here.) [2]

ノ　ノ丶

⋆	human legs

儿

Notice how these **human legs** are somewhat shapelier and more highly evolved than those of the so-called "lower animals." The one on the left, drawn first, is straight; while the one on the right bends gracefully and ends with a hook. Though they are not likely to suggest the **legs** of any **human** you know, they do have something of the look of someone out for a stroll, especially if you compare them to *animal legs*.

If you had any trouble with the kanji for the number *four*, now would be the time to return to it (FRAME 4). [2]

丿　儿

*

wind

This primitive gets its name from the full kanji for the **wind** (FRAME 563). It is called an "enclosure" because other elements are often drawn in the middle of it, though it can also be compressed together so that there is no room for anything in it. The main thing to remember when writing this element is that the second stroke bends OUTWARDS, like a gust of **wind** blown from above. In addition to the basic meaning of **wind**, we shall also have occasion to use the image of a **weather vane**. The derivation is obvious. [2]

*

bound up

Like *wind,* the element meaning **bound up** is also an enclosure that can wrap itself around other elements or be compressed when there is nothing to enclose. When this latter happens— usually because there is not enough room—and it is set on top, the little hook at the end is dropped off, like this: ʹ.

The sense of **bound up** is that of being "tied and gagged" or wrapped up tightly. If you have trouble remembering when it serves as an enclosure (with the hook) and when not (without the hook), you might think of the former as a **chain** and the latter as a **rope**. [2]

*

horns

This primitive element ALWAYS appears at the top of the element to which it is related, and is always attached, or almost attached, to the first horizontal line to come under it. The **horns** can never simply be left hanging in the air. When there is no line available, an extra horizontal stroke (like a *one*) is added. The final kanji of this lesson gives an example.

The meaning of this element is wide enough to embrace the **horns** of bulls, rams, billy goats, and moose, but not the family of musical instruments. As with other elements with such

"open" meanings, it is best to settle on one that you find most vivid and stick with that image consistently. [2]

丶　丶丿

---

55   only

只

When we run across abstract key words like this one, the best way to get an image it to recall some common but suggestive phrase in which the word appears. For instance, we can think of the expression "it's the **only** one of its kind." Then we imagine a barker at a side-show advertising some strange pac-man like creature he has inside his tent, with only a gigantic *mouth* and two wee *animal legs*. [5]

丨　冂　口　尸　只

---

56   shellfish

貝

To remember the primitive elements that make up this kanji, an *eye* and *animal legs,* you might be tempted to think of it as a pictograph of a **shellfish** with its ridged shell at the top and two little *legs* sticking out of the bottom. But that might not help you recall later just how many ridges to put on the shell. Better to imagine a freakish **shellfish** with a single, gigantic *eye* roaming the beaches on its slender little *legs,* scaring the wits out of the sunbathers. [7]

丨　冂　冊　月　目　貝　貝

* When used as a primitive, in addition to *shells,* the meanings *oyster* and *clam* will often come in handy.

---

57   pop song

唄

There is a lot of money to be made if one's **songs** are "**pop**ular." This is depicted here as a stream of *clams* spewing out of the *mouth* of someone performing a **pop song**. [10]

口　唄

58

貞

upright

Now take the last primitive, the *shellfish*, and set a *magic wand* over it, and you have the kanji for **upright**. After all, the *clam* and the *oyster* are incapable of walking **upright**. It would take a magician with his *wand* to pull off such a feat—which is precisely what we have in this kanji. [9]

ト 貞

59

員

employee

How do we get a *mouth* over a *shellfish* to mean an **employee**? Simple. Just remember the advice new **employees** get about keeping their *mouths* shut and doing their job, and then make that more graphic by picturing an office building full of white-collar workers scurrying around with *clams* pinched to their *mouths*. [10]

ロ 員

60

貼

post a bill

The key word in this frame has do with **posting bills** to a bill-board. In this case, the billboard is standing at the exit to a Chinese restaurant displaying the latest alternative to the traditional *fortune-telling* cookies. Look closely and you will see rows of leftover shells of *clams* with little slips of paper sticking out of them **posted** to the billboard.[12]

貝 貼

61

見

see

The elements that compose the character for **see** are the *eye* firmly fixed to a pair of *human legs*. Surely, somewhere in your experience, there is a vivid image just waiting to be dragged up to help you remember this character.... [7]

｜ 冂 冃 目 見 見

---

62   newborn babe

児

The top part of the kanji in this frame, you will remember, is the character for *olden times*, those *days* so old they needed a *walking stick* to get around. Western mythical imagination has old "Father Time" leaning on his sickle with a **newborn babe** crawling around his *legs*, the idea being that the circle of birth-and-death goes on.

This is the first of three times that the kanji for *olden times* will appear in this book as a primitive element in another kanji, so try to make the most of it. [7]

丨 旧 旧 児

63   beginning

元

"In the **beginning**…" starts that marvelous shelf of books we call the Bible. It talks about how all things were made, and tells us that when the Creator came to humanity she made *two* of them, man and woman. While we presume she made *two* of every other animal as well, we are not told as much. Hence we need only *two* and a pair of *human legs* come to the kanji that means **beginning**. [4]

一 二 テ 元

64   page

頁

What we have to do here is turn a *shellfish* into a **page** of a book. The *one* at the top tells us that we only get a rather short book, in fact a book of only *one* **page**. Imagine a title printed on the shell of an *oyster*, let us say "Pearl of Wisdom," and then open the quaint book to its *one* and only **page**, on which you find a single, radiant *drop of* wisdom, one of the masterpiece poems of nature. [9]

一 丆 厂 丆 百 百 百 頁 頁

* As a primitive, this kanji takes the unrelated meaning of a *head* (preferably one detached from its body), derived from the character for *head* (FRAME 1549).

65	stubborn

頏

This character refers to the block*headed*, persistent **stubbornness** of one who sticks to an idea or a plan just the way it was at the *beginning*, without letting anything that comes up along the way alter things in the least. The explanation makes "sense," but is hard to remember because the word *"beginning"* is too abstract. Back up to the image we used two frames ago—Adam and Eve in their Eden—and try again: The root of all **stubbornness** goes back to the *beginning*, with two brothers each **stubbornly** defending his own way of life and asking their God to bless it favorably. Abel stuck to agriculture, Cain to animal-raising. Picture these two with their giant, swelled *heads*, each vying for the favors of heaven, a **stubborn** grimace on their faces. No wonder something unfortunate happened! [13]

兀　頏

66	mediocre

凡

While we refer to something insignificant as a "*drop* in the bucket," the kanji for **mediocre** suggests the image of a "*drop* in the *wind*." [3]

丿　几　凡

67	defeat

負

Above we have the condensed form of *bound up*, and below the familiar *shellfish*. Now imagine two *oysters* engaged in *shell*-to-*shell* combat, the one who is **defeated** being *bound and gagged* with seaweed, the victor towering triumphantly over it. The *bound shellfish* thus becomes the symbol for **defeat**. [9]

勹　負

68	ten thousand

万

Japanese counts higher numbers in units of **ten thousand**, unlike the West, which advances according to units of one thousand. (Thus, for instance, 40,000 would be read "four **ten-thousands**"

by a Japanese.) Given that the comma is used in larger numbers to *bind up* a numerical unit of one thousand, the elements for *one* and *bound up* naturally come to form **ten thousand**.

The order of strokes here needs special attention, both because it falls outside the general principles we have learned already, and because it involves writing the element for *bound up* in an order opposite to the one we learned. If it is any consolation, this happens every time these three strokes come together. [3]

一 丁 万

| 69 | phrase |

句

By combining the two primitives *bound up* and *mouth*, it is easy to see how this character can get the meaning of a **phrase**. After all, a **phrase** is nothing more than a number of words *bound up* tightly and neatly so that they will fit in your *mouth*. [5]

丿 勹 勹 句 句

| 70 | texture |

肌

Ever notice how the **texture** of your face and hands is affected by the *wind*? A day's skiing or sailing makes them rough and dry, and in need of a good soft cream to soothe the burn. So whenever a *part of the body* gets exposed to the *wind*, its **texture** is affected. (If it is any help, the Latin word hiding inside **texture** connotes how something is "to the touch.") [6]

月 肌

| 71 | decameron |

旬

There simply is not a good phrase in English for the block of ten days which this character represents. So we resurrect the classical phrase, **decameron**, whose connotations the tales of Boccaccio have done much to enrich. Actually, it refers to a journey of ten *days* taken by a band of people—that is, a group of people *bound together* for the *days* of the **decameron**. [6]

勹 旬

72 ladle

勺

If you want to *bind up drops* of anything—water, soup, lemonade—you use something to scoop these *drops* up, which is what we call a **ladle**. See the last *drop* left inside the **ladle**? [3]

勹 勺

73 bull's eye

的

The elements *white bird* and *ladle* easily suggest the image of a **bull's eye** if you imagine a rusty old *ladle* with a **bull's eye** painted on it in the form of a tiny *white bird*, who lets out a little "peep" every time you hit the target. [8]

白 的

74 neck

首

Reading this kanji from the top down, we have: *horns . . . nose*. Together they bring to mind the picture of a moose-head hanging on the den wall, with its great *horns* and long *nose*. Now while we would speak of cutting off a moose's "head" to hang on the wall, the Japanese speak of cutting off its **neck**. It's all a matter of how you look at it. Anyway, if you let the word **neck** conjure up the image of a moose with a very l-o-n-g **neck** hanging over the fireplace, whose *horns* you use for a coat-rack and whose *nose* has spigots left and right for scotch and water, you should have no trouble with the character.

Here we get a good look at what we mentioned when we first introduced the element for *horns*: that they can never be left floating free and require an extra horizontal stroke to prevent that from happening, as is the case here. [9]

丶 丷 丷 丷 丷 芐 苩 首 首

Lesson 5

THAT IS ABOUT all we can do with the pieces we have accumulated so far, but as we add each new primitive element to those we already know, the number of kanji we will be able to form will increase by leaps and bounds.

If we were to step outside of the standard list, we would see that there are still a handful of more characters we could make with the pieces at hand, though none of them is very useful

While many of the stories you have learned in the previous lessons are actually more complex than the majority you will learn in the later chapters, they are the *first* stories you have learned, and for that reason are not likely to cause you much difficulty. By now, however, you may be wondering just how to go about reviewing what you have learned. Obviously it won't do simply to flip through the pages you have already studied, because the order already gives them away. The best method is to design for yourself a set of flash cards that you can add to as you go through the book.

If you have not already started doing this on your own, you might try it this way: Buy heavy paper (about twice the thickness of normal index cards), unlined and with a semigloss finish. Cut it into cards of about 9 cm. long and 6 cm. wide. On one side, make a large ball-pen drawing of one kanji in the top two-thirds of the card. (Writing done with fountain pens and felt-tip pens tends to smear with the sweat that comes from holding them in your hands for a long time.) On the bottom right-hand corner, put the number of the frame in which the kanji appeared. On the back side, in the upper left-hand corner, write the key-word meaning of the character. Then draw a line across the middle of the card and another line about 2 cm. below it. The space between these two lines can be used for any notes you may need later to remind you of the primitive elements or stories you used to remember the character. *Only fill this in when you need to, but make a card for every kanji* as soon as you have learned it.

The rest of the space on the card you will need later; when you study the readings of the characters, you might use the space above the double lines. The bottom half of the card, on both sides, can be left free for inserting kanji compounds (front side) and their readings and meanings (back side).

50

BELOW

wand BELOW

floor with magic

A final note about reviewing. You have probably gotten yourself into the habit of writing the character several times when memorizing it, whether you need to or not; and then writing it MORE times for kanji that you have trouble remembering. There is really no need to write the kanji more than once, unless you have trouble with the stroke order and want to get a better "feel" for it. If a kanji causes you trouble, spend time clarifying the imagery of its story. Simply rewriting the character will reinforce any latent suspicions you still have that the "tried and true method" of learning by repeating is the only reliable one—the very bias we are trying to uproot. Also, when you review, REVIEW ONLY FROM THE KEY WORD TO THE KANJI, NOT THE OTHER WAY AROUND. The reasons for this, along with further notes on reviewing, will come later.

We are now ready to return to work, adding a few new primitives one by one, and seeing what new characters they allow us to form. We shall cover 24 new kanji in this lesson.

| 75 | fish guts |

乙

The kanji shown here actually represents the "second" position in the old Chinese zodiac, which the Japanese still use as an alternate way of enumeration, much the same way that English will revert to Roman numerals. Among its many other meanings are "pure," "tasteful," "quaint," and—get this!—**fish guts**. Since it is a pictograph of a fishhook, it should not be hard to associate it with the key word. [1]

乙

* We will keep *fishhook* as the primitive meaning. Its shape will rarely be quite the same as that of the kanji. When it appears at the bottom of another primitive, it is straightened out, almost as if the weight of the upper element had bent it out of shape: ∟. And when it appears to the right of another element, the short horizontal line that gets the shape started is omitted and it is stretched out and narrowed, all for reasons of space and aesthetics: L. Examples follow.

| 76 | riot |

乱

In a **riot**, manners are laid aside and tempers get short, even in so courtesy-conscious a land as Japan. This kanji shows what

happens to a **rioting** *tongue*: it gets "barbed" like a *fishhook*, and sets to attacking the opposition, to *hook* them as it were. [7]

舌　乱

77　　　　　　　　　　　　　　　　　　straightaway

直

Begin with the top two primitives, *needle* and *eye*. Together they represent the *eye of a needle*. Below them is a *fishhook* that has been **straightened out** and its barb removed so that it can pass through the *eye of the needle*. [8]

一　十　广　市　肯　肻　眗　直

⁎　　　　　　　　　　　　　　　　　　　　　tool

灬

Although this primitive is not very common, it is useful to know, as the following examples will show. Conveniently, it is always drawn at the very bottom of any kanji in which it figures. The first stroke, the horizontal one, is detached from anything above it, but is necessary to distinguish **tool** from *animal legs*. The sense of the element is a carpenter's **tool**, which comes from its pictographic representation of a small table with legs (make them *animal legs* if you need a more graphic image), so that any element lying on top of it will come to be viewed as a **tool** in the hands of a carpenter. [3]

一　ノ　灬

78　　　　　　　　　　　　　　　　　　　　tool

具

Here is the full kanji on which the last frame is based. If you can think of a table full of carpenter's **tools** of all sorts, each equipped with its own *eye* so that it can keep a watch over what you are doing with it, you won't have trouble later keeping the primitive and the kanji apart. [8]

目　且　具　具

79

真

true

Here again we meet the composite element, *eye of the needle*, which here combines with *tool* to give us a measure of what is **true** and what is not. [10]

一　十　直　真

---

*

ナ

by one's side

This primitive has the look of *ten*, except that the left stroke is bent down toward the left. It indicates where your hands (your *ten* fingers) fall when you let them droop: **by your side**.

The stroke order of this character can be reversed; but whichever stroke is written second, that stroke should be drawn longer than the other. The difference is slight, and all but unnoticeable in printed characters, but it should be learned all the same. [2]

一　ナ　・　ノ　ナ

80

工

craft

The pictograph of an I beam, like the kind that is used in heavy construction work on buildings and bridges, gives us the character for **craft** in general. [3]

一　丁　工

* As a primitive element, the key word retains the meaning of *craft* and also takes on the related meanings of *I beam* and *artificial*.

81

左

left

By combining the primitive and the kanji of the last two frames and reading the results, we get: *by one's side . . . craft*. Conveniently, the **left** has traditionally been considered the "sinister" *side*, where dark and occult *crafts* are cultivated. Note how the second stroke droops over to the **left** and is longer than the first. [5]

一 ナ ナ 右 左

82　　　　　　　　　　　　　　　　　　　　right

右

When thinking of the key word **right**, in order to avoid confusion with the previous frame, take advantage of the double-meaning here, too. Imagine a little *mouth* hanging down by your *side*—like a little voice of conscience—telling you the **right** thing to do. Here the second stroke should reach out to the **right** and be drawn slightly longer than the first. [5]

ノ ナ 大 右 右

83　　　　　　　　　　　　　　　　　　　possess

有

The picture here is of someone with a slab of *meat* dangling *by the side*, perhaps from a belt or rope tied around the waist. Think of it as an evil spirit in **possession** of one's soul, who can be exorcized only by allowing fresh *meat* to hang *by one's side* until it begins to putrefy and stink so bad that the demon departs. Take careful note of the stroke order. [6]

ノ ナ 大 右 有 有

84　　　　　　　　　　　　　　　　　　　　bribe

賄

To the left we have the primitive for a *shellfish*, and to the right the kanji we just learned for *possess*. Keep the connotation of the last frame for the word *possess*, and now expand your image of *shells* to include the ancient value they had as money (a usage that will come in very helpful later on). Now one who is *possessed* by *shells* is likely to abandon any higher principles to acquire more and more wealth. These are the easiest ones to **bribe** with a few extra *shells*. [13]

貝 賄

85   tribute

貢

A **tribute** has a kind of double-meaning in English: honor paid freely and *money* collected by coercion. Simply because a ruler bestows a noble name on a deed is hardly any consolation to the masses who must part with their hard-earned *money*. Little wonder that this ancient *craft* of getting *money* by calling it a **tribute** has given way to a name closer to how it feels to those who pay it: a tax. [10]

一 工 貢

86   paragraph

項

To the right we see a *head* and to the left an element that means *craft*. When we think of a **paragraph**, we immediately think of a *heading* device to break a text into parts. (Think of the elaborate *heads* often seen at the start of medieval manuscripts and the task becomes easier still.) Just where and how to do it belongs to the writer's *craft*. Hence, we define **paragraphing** as the *"heading craft"* to remember this character. [12]

工 項

87   sword

刀

Although this kanji no longer looks very much like a **sword**, it does have some resemblance to the handle of the **sword**. This is to our advantage, in that it helps us make a distinction between two primitive elements based on this kanji. [2]

フ 刀

* In the form of the kanji, this primitive means a *dagger*. When it appears to the right of another element, it is commonly stretched out like this 刂 and takes the sense of a great and flashing *saber*, a meaning it gets from a character we shall learn later (FRAME 1801).

88	blade

刃

Think of using a *dagger* as a razor **blade**, and it shouldn't be hard to imagine cutting yourself. See the little *drop of* blood clinging to the **blade**? [3]

$$\text{フ 刀 刃}$$

89	cut

切

To the right we see the *dagger* and next to it the number *seven* whose primitive meaning we decided would be *diced* (FRAME 7). It is hard to think of **cutting** anything with a knife without imagining one of those skillful Japanese chefs. Only let us say that he has had too much to drink at a party, grabs a *dagger* lying on the mantelpiece and starts *dicing* up everything in sight, starting with the hors d'oeuvres and going on to the furniture and the carpets…. [4]

$$\text{一 七 切 切}$$

90	seduce

召

A *sword* or *dagger* posed over a *mouth* is how the character for "beckoning" is written. The related but less tame key word **seduce** was chosen because it seemed to fit better with the—how shall we put it?—Freudian implications of the kanji. (Observe if you will that it is not sure whether the long slender object is **seducing** the small round one or vice versa.) [5]

$$\text{刀 召}$$

* The primitive meaning remains the same: *seduce*. Just be sure to associate it with a very concrete image.

91	shining

昭

Let the key word suggest **shining** one's shoes, the purpose of which is to *seduce* the *sun* down on them for all to see. [9]

$$\text{日 昭}$$

92 則 rule

The character depicts a *clam* alongside a great and flashing *saber*. Think of digging for *clams* in an area where there are gaming **rules** governing how large a find has to be before you can keep it. So you take your trusty *saber*, which you have carefully notched like a yardstick, crack open a *clam*, and then measure the poor little beastie to see if it is as long as the **rules** say it has to be. [9]

* 畐 wealth

To prepare for following frame, we introduce here a somewhat rare primitive meaning **wealth**. It takes its meaning from the common image of the overwealthy as also being overfed. More specifically, the kanji shows us *one* single *mouth* devouring all the harvest of the *fields*, presumably while those who labor in them go hungry. Think of the phrase exactly as it is written when you draw the character, and the disposition of the elements is easy. [9]

93 副 vice-

The key word **vice** has the sense of someone second-in-command. The great and flashing *saber* to the right (its usual location, so you need not worry about where to put it from now on) and the *wealth* on the left combine to create an image of dividing one's property to give a share to one's **vice**-*wealth*-holder. [11]

畐 副 副

94 別 separate

In the Old East, the samurai and his *saber* were never **separated**. They were constant companions, like the cowboy of the Old West and his six-shooter. This character depicts what must

have been the height of **separation**-anxiety for a samurai: to be *bound up with a rope* and unable to get at his *saber* leaning only a few feet away from him. Look at that *mouth* bellowing out for shame and sorrow!

Note the order in which the element for *tied up* is written—just as it had been with the character for *ten thousand*. [7]

口　弓　另　別

95　　　　　　　　　　　　　　　　　　　　　street

丁

The picture here is of a **street** sign on a long pole: Hollywood and Vine, if you please, or any *street* that immediately conjures up the image of a **street** sign to you. [2]

一　丁

* Used as a primitive, we change the meaning of the key word and take the shape to signify a *nail* or a *spike*. Should it happen, on reviewing, that you find the pictographs get jumbled, then think of jerking a *street* sign out of the ground and using it as a *nail* to repair your garage roof.

96　　　　　　　　　　　　　　　　　　　　　village

町

Street signs standing at the corner of the *rice fields* depict the **village** limits. (Remember what was said earlier: when used as a primitive, a kanji may either take its primitive meaning or revert to the original meaning of its key word.) [7]

丨　冂　冂　冊　田　田　町

97　　　　　　　　　　　　　　　　　　　　　　can

可

Remember the story about the "Little Engine that **Could**" when you hear this key word, and the rest is simple. See the determined little locomotive huffing and puffing up the mountain—"I think I **can**, I think I **can**..."—spitting railroad *spikes* out of its *mouth* as it chews up the line to the top. [5]

一　丁　冂　可　可

98　　　　　　　　　　　　　　　　　　　　place on the head

頂　The key word is actually a formal metaphor meaning "humble
acceptance." Reading off the two primitive elements in the order
of their writing, we have: *nail . . . head*. As in "hitting the *nail*
on the *head*." Now one presumes that most people can handle
metaphors, but if you were to run into a dimwit working in a
hardware store who only knew the literal meaning of things,
and were to ask him, in your best Japanese, to **place on your
head** a nail, he might miss the point and cause you considerable
torment. [11]

丁　頂

Lesson 6

THE LAST GROUP OF primitives took us pretty far, and probably forced you to
pay more attention to the workings of imagination. In this lesson we shall concentrate on primitives that have to do with people.

As you were reminded in FRAME 96, even those kanji that are given special
meanings as primitives may also retain their key word meaning when used as
primitives. Although this may sound confusing, in fact it turns out to be convenient for making stories and, in addition, helps to reinforce the original meaning of the character.

99　　　　　　　　　　　　　　　　　　　　　　　　　child

　This kanji is a pictograph of a **child** wrapped up in one of those
handy cocoons that Japanese mothers fix to their backs to carry
around young **children** who cannot get around by themselves.
The first stroke is like a wee head popping out for air; the second
shows the body and legs all wrapped up; and the final stroke
shows the arms sticking out to cling to the mother's neck. [3]

ㄱ 了 子

* As a primitive, the meaning of *child* is retained, though you might imagine a little older *child,* able to run around and get into more mischief.

---

100   cavity

孔

Probably the one thing most *children* fear more than anything else is the dentist's chair. Once a *child* has seen a dentist holding the x-rays up to the light and heard that ominous word **cavity**, even though it is not likely to know that the word means "hole" until it is much older, it will not be long before those two syllables get associated with the drill and that row of shiny *hooks* the dentist uses to torture people who are too small to fight back. [4]

ㄱ 了 孑 孔

---

101   complete

了

Learn this character by returning to FRAME 99 and the image given there. The only difference is that the "arms" have been left off (actually, only tucked inside). Thus a *child* with its arms wrapped up into the back-sack is the picture of a job successfully **completed**. [2]

ㄱ 了

---

102   woman

女

You have probably seen somewhere the form of a squatting **woman** drawn behind this character, with two legs at the bottom, two arms (the horizontal line) and the head poking out the top. A little farfetched, until you draw the character and feel the grace and flow of the three simple strokes. Remembering the kanji is easy; being able to write it beautifully is another thing. [3]

く 女 女

* The primitive meaning is the same: *woman*.

---

103 **fond**

好

The phrase "to be **fond** of someone" has a natural gentleness about it, and lends a tenderness to the sense of touching by giving us the related term "to **fondle**." The character likens it to a *woman* **fondling** her *child*. [6]

女　好

---

104 **likeness**

如

Pardon me if I revert to the venerable old Dr. Freud again, but his eye for symbolism is often helpful to appreciate things that more earthy imaginations once accepted more freely but that we have learned to cover over with a veneer of etiquette. For instance, the fact that things like the *mouth* of a cave served as natural ritual substitutes for the opening through which a *woman* gives birth. Hence, in order to be reborn as an adult, one may have to pass through the psychological equivalent of the womb, that is, something that bears a **likeness** to the *opening* of the *woman* from whom you were born. [6]

女　如

---

105 **mama**

母

Look closely at this kanji and you will find the outline of the kanji for *woman* in it, the second stroke of which has been expanded to make space for the two breasts that make her a **mama**. Likening this sound to a baby nursing at its mother's breast has afforded some scholars of comparative linguistics a way to explain the presence of the same word across a wide range of language-groups. [5]

乚　口　口　口　母

* As a primitive we shall add the meaning of *breasts* in accord with the explanation given above. Take careful note of the fact that the form is altered slightly when this kanji serves as a

primitive, the final two dots joining together to form a longer stroke. An example follows in the next frame.

| 106 | pierce |

貫

If one is asked to think of associations for the word **pierce**, among the first to come to mind is that of **piercing** one's ears to hold earrings, a quite primitive form of self-mutilation that has survived into the 21st century. The kanji here is read, top to bottom: *mama . . . oyster*. All you need to do is imagine **piercing** an ear so that it can hold a mother-of-pearl (actually, a *mama-of-pearl*) you have just wrested from an *oyster*. [11]

| 107 | elder brother |

兄

By now kanji like this one should "look like" something to you even though it is more of an "ideogram" than a "pictograph." The large *mouth* on top and the *human legs* below almost jump off the page as a caricature of **elder brother**, the one with the big *mouth* (or if you prefer a kinder image, the one who "has the say" among all the children). [5]

口　兄

* As a primitive this character will take the meaning of *teenager*, in accord with the familiar image of the big *mouth* and the gangling, clumsy *legs*.

| 108 | curse |

呪

For some reason, the inventor of this kanji associated a **curse** with the *mouth* of an *older brother*. I leave it to you to decide if he is on the giving or receiving end of the sorcery. [8]

口　呪

---

109   **overcome**

克   In this frame we get a chance to use the kanji we just learned in
     its primitive meaning of *teenager*. The *needle* on top indicates
     one of the major problems confronting the *teenager* growing
     up in today's world: drugs. Many of them will fall under the
     shadow of the *needle* at some time during those tender years,
     but only when a whole generation rises up and decides that "We
     Shall **Overcome**" the plague, will the *needle* cease to hang over
     their heads, as it does in this character. [7]

Lesson 7

IN THIS LESSON we turn to primitive elements having to do with quantity. We
will also introduce a form known as a "roof," a sort of overhead "enclosure" that
comes in a variety of shapes. But let us begin slowly and not get ahead of ourselves, for it is only after you have mastered the simple forms that the apparently impenetrable complexities of later primitives will dissolve. The primitives
we give here will immediately suggest others, on the basis of what we have
already learned. Hence the somewhat haphazard order among the frames of
this lesson.

---

110   **little**

小   The sense of **little** in this character is not the same as "a little
     bit." That meaning comes in the next frame. Here **little** means
     "small" or "tiny." The image is one of three **little** *drops*, the first of
     which (the one in the middle) is written larger so that the kanji
     has some shape to it. The point of writing it three times is to rub
     the point in: **little**, **little**, nothing but **little**. [3]

         亅   小   小

* The primitive of the same shape keeps the same meaning. Written above a horizontal line, its form is slightly altered, the last two strokes turning inwards like this: ⅈⅈ.

---

111   **few**

少

First we need to look at the fourth stroke, the *drop* at the bottom that has been extended into a longer diagonal stroke leaning left. This happens because a single, isolated drop will NEVER appear beneath its relative primitive in its normal size, for fear it would drop off and get lost. As for the meaning, let the tiny *drop* indicate a further belittling of what is already *little*—thus making it a **few** of something *little*. [4]

---

112   **large**

大

Here we have a simple pictograph of a person, taking up the space of an entire character and giving it the sense of **large**. It should not be too hard to locate the two legs and outstretched arms. [3]

一　ナ　大

* As a primitive, we need a different meaning, since the element representing the human person will come up later. Therefore, this shape will become a *large dog* or, if you prefer, a *St. Bernard dog*. In FRAME 253 we will explain why this choice was made.

---

113   **many**

多

"**Many** *moons* ago," begins much of Amerindian folklore—a colorful way of saying "Once upon a time" and a great deal of help for remembering this kanji. Here we have two *moons* (three of them would take us back to the beginning of time, which is further than we want to go), lacking the final stroke because they are partially hidden behind the clouds of time. [6]

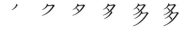

| 114 | evening |

Just as the word **evening** adds a touch of formality or romanticism to the ordinary word "night," so the kanji for **evening** takes the ordinary looking *moon* in the night sky and has a cloud pass over it (as we saw in the last frame). [3]

ノ　ク　タ

* The primitive keeps the same meaning and connotation as the kanji.

| 115 | eventide |

In the next lesson we will meet the character for morning-*tide* and the element for *drops of water*. Meantime we have a perfect blend of picture and idea in this kanji to play on the English word for nightfall, **eventide**: *drops of water* inching their way up the shore in the *evening*. [6]

ヽ　ゝ　氵　氵　汐　汐

| 116 | outside |

On the left, the primitive for *evening*, and on the right, that for the *magic wand*. Now, as every magician worth his abracadabra knows, bringing your *magic wand* out into the *evening* air makes your magic much more powerful than if you were to stay indoors. Hence, *evening* and *magic wand* takes you naturally **outside**. [5]

夕　外

| 117 | name |

Perhaps you have heard of the custom, still preserved in certain African tribes, of a father creeping into the tent or hut of his newborn child on the night of the child's birth, to whisper into its ear the **name** he has chosen for it, before making his choice public. It is an impressive **naming** custom and fits in tidily with

the way this character is constructed: *evening . . . mouth.* At *evening* time, a *mouth* pronounces the **name** that will accompany one throughout life. [6]

夕 名

---

*   **cliff**

厂

This primitive means precisely what it looks like: a steep **cliff**. You can almost see someone standing at the top looking down into the abyss below. [2]

一 厂

---

118   **stone**

石

With a *mouth* under a *cliff*, what else could we have here but the entrance to a secret cavern, before which a great **stone** has been rolled so that none may enter. Perhaps it is the hiding place where Ali Baba and his band of thieves have stored their treasures, in which case that magic word known to every school child who ever delighted over the tales of the *Arabian Nights* should be enough to push the **stone** aside. But take care—the *cliff* is steep, and one slip will send you tumbling down into the ravine below. [5]

This is the one and only time that the second stroke in *cliff* will reach over to the middle of the horizontal stroke. If you think of the edge jutting outwards (in keeping with the story above), the problem should be taken care of.

一 厂 不 石 石

* The *stone* is a quite common primitive element, which is not restricted to great boulders but used of *stones* or *rocks* of any size or shape.

---

119   **resemblance**

肖

The word **resemblance** should suggest, among other things, a son's **resemblance** to his father. A "chip off the old block" is the

way we often put it, but the character is more simple. It speaks of a *little* bit of *flesh*. [7]

ソ 肖

* When used as a primitive, the sense of *resemblance* is replaced by that of *spark* or *candle*. (If you want an explanation: the kanji for *moon* also carries a secondary sense of *fire*, which we omitted because we are keeping that meaning for other primitives.)

---

120   **nitrate**

硝

The word **nitrate** should immediately suggest a beaker of **nitric** acid, which, as every high-school chemistry student knows, can eat its way through some pretty tough substances. Here we imagine pouring it over a *rock* and watching the *sparks* fly as it bores a hole through the rock. [12]

石　硝

---

121   **smash**

砕

We begin with the two elements on the right, *baseball* and *needle*. Since they will be coming together from time to time, let us give the two of them the sense of a *game of cricket* in which a *needle* is laid across the wicket. Then imagine using a *rock* for a ball. A **smash** hit would probably splinter the bat in all directions, and a **smashing** pitch would do the same with the *needle* wicket. [9]

石　矴　砕

---

122   **sand**

砂

Good **sand** for beaches has *few* or no *stones* in it. That means that all of us whose feet have been spoiled by too much time in shoes don't have to watch our step as we cavort about. [9]

石　砂

123	jealous

妬

It should not be hard to leap from the key word to the image of a *woman* who is **jealous** of the *rock* that another *woman* is sporting on the third finger of her left hand. [8]

女　妬

124	plane

削

Long before the invention of the carpenter's **plane**, people used knives and machetes (or here, *sabers*) to smooth out their woodwork. If you have ever seen the process, you will have been amazed at the speed and agility with which the adept can **plane** a hunk of wood into shape. Indeed, you can almost see the *sparks* fly from their *sabers*. [9]

肖　削

125	ray

光

There are really only 2 primitives here, *little* and *human legs*. The 4th stroke that separates them is added for reasons of aesthetics. (If that doesn't make sense, try writing the kanji without it and see how ugly the results look, even to your beginner's eye.)

Now if you have wondered what those little particles of "dust" are that dance around in the light-**rays** that come through the window and fall on your desk, try imagining them as *little* and disembodied *human legs*, and you should have no trouble with this character. [6]

丨　丶丨　丷丨　业　と　光

126	plump

太

"**Plump**" is one of those delightful English words that almost sound like their meaning. No sooner do you hear it than you think of a round and ample-bodied person falling into a sofa like a *large drop* of oil plopping into a fishbowl—kerrrr-**plump**! [4]

一 ナ 大 太

127

器

utensil

The picture in this kanji is not a pleasant one. It shows a large and fluffy *St. Bernard dog* stretched out on a table all stuffed and stewed and garnished with vegetables, its paws in the air and an apple in its mouth. At each corner of the table sits an eager but empty *mouth*, waiting for the **utensils** to arrive so the feast can begin. [15]

口　口口　叩　罘　哭　哭　器

128

臭

stinking

This character is a bit friendlier to the animal world than the last one. Our friend the *St. Bernard* is alive and well, its *nose* in the air sniffing suspiciously after something **stinking** somewhere or other. [9]

自　臭

129

嗅

sniff

You have seen those scratch-'n-**sniff** advertisements for perfumes. This one is for a *mouth*wash that replaces one *stinking* odor with another. [12]

口　嗅

130

妙

exquisite

The primitive for *woman* is on the left (there and at the bottom of another primitive is where you will always find her), and to the right the element for *few*. When we refer to a *woman* as **exquisite**, we mean to praise her as the sort of person we meet but *few* and far between.

If you are interested in etymologies, it might help to recall that the Latin phrase lying at the root of the English word **exquisite**

carries this same sense of "seeking out" the rare from the ordinary. [7]

女　妙

| 131 | focus |

省

When we think of **focusing** on something, we usually take it in a metaphorical sense, though the literal sense is not far behind. It means to block out what is nonessential in order to fix our *eye* on a *few* important matters. The kanji suggests picking up a *few* things and holding them before one's *eye* in order to **focus** on them better. [9]

少　省

| 132 | thick |

厚

When we refer to someone as **thick**-skinned or **thick**-headed, we are usually quick to add—even if only under our breath—something about their upbringing. Perhaps it is because deep down we cherish the belief that by nature people are basically tender and sensitive.

Be that as it may, the Japanese character for **thick** depicts a *child* abandoned out on the wild *cliffs*, exposed to the heat of the *sun*, and thus doomed to develop a head and skin as **thick** as the parent who left it there. [9]

一　厂　厈　厚

| 133 | strange |

奇

The elements we are given to work with here are *St. Bernard dog* and *can*. Lots of phrases pop to mind to attach these words to the key word, but they end up too abstract because of the word *can*.

It is important in such cases (and there will be plenty of them as we go along) to stick closely to the elements, in this case, *mouth* and *nails*. Now all we need do is create a fictitious

"**Strange** But True" column in the Sunday funnies, featuring a *St. Bernard* whose *mouth* has been *nailed* shut because he was hitting the brandy keg around his neck too hard. [8]

Lesson 8

FOUR BASIC ELEMENTS, it was once believed, make up the things of our universe: earth, wind, fire, and water. We have already met the element for *wind*, and now we shall introduce the others, one by one, in a somewhat longer than usual lesson.

Fortunately for our imaginative memories, these suggestive and concrete primitives play a large role in the construction of the kanji, and will help us create some vivid pictures to untangle some of the complex jumbles of strokes that follow.

---

134   stream

川

We have taken the image of a river **stream** over into English to describe things that fall down in straight lines, or ripple along in lines. All of this is more than evident in the kanji given here, a pictograph of a **stream**. [3]

丿   丿丨   川

* As a primitive, this character adds to the meaning of *stream* the more vivid image of a *flood*. Note, however, that there are certain small changes in the writing of the element, depending on where it appears relative to other elements:

       on the left, it is written 川
       on the top, it is written 巛
       on the bottom, it is written 川

135	state

州

Here we see *drops of* land (little islets) rising up out of a *stream*, creating a kind of sandbar or breakwater. Ever wonder how the **state**-line is drawn between **states** separated by a river? If there were little *drops of* land as in the kanji, there'd be nothing to it. [6]

丶 丿 小 州 州 州

136	obey

順

In primitive language, this character would read *stream . . . head*. And that turns out to be convenient for remembering its meaning of **obey**. Either one **obeys** the person who is *head* of an organization or else **obeys** by following the *stream* of opinion ("current" practice, we call it). Both these senses come together in this kanji. [12].

丿 川 川 順

137	water

水

This character, which looks a bit like a snowflake, is actually a pictograph of **water**—not any particular body of water or movement of water, but simply the generic name for **water**. Should you have any difficulty remembering it, simply think of a *walking stick* being dropped vertically into the **water**, sending *droplets* out in all four directions. Then all you need to learn is how to write it in proper order. [4]

亅 刁 水 水

* As a primitive, this character can keep its form, or it can be written with three drops to the left of another primitive, like this: . This latter, as we will see, is far more common.

138	icicle

氺

The appearance of the primitive for *water* in its full form tells us that we have something to do with *water* here. The extra *drop* to the left, added as a second stroke, changes the picture from a

splash caused by a *walking stick* dropped into *water* to form an **icicle**.

If it helps, when you hold an **icicle** up to the light, you can usually see little crystallizations of five-pointed stars inside of it, which is the shape we have in this kanji. [5]

〕 ﹅ 氻 氷 氷

---

139   eternity

永

This kanji also uses the full form of *water*, though its meaning seems to have nothing at all to do with *water*. Remember what William Blake said about seeing "infinity in a grain of sand and **eternity** in an hour"? Well, reading this character from top to bottom, we see "**eternity** in a *drop of water*." [5]

、 刁 刋 氺 永

---

140   spring

泉

Call to mind the image of a fresh, bubbling **spring** of *water*, and you will probably notice how the top of the **spring** you are thinking of, the part where the "bubbling" goes on, is all *white*. Happily, the *white* is just where it should be, at the top, and the *water* is at the bottom. [9]

白 白 身 泉 泉

* We will keep this image of a *spring* when using this kanji as a primitive, but not without first drawing attention to a slight change that distinguishes the primitive from the kanji. The final 4 strokes (the element for *water*) are abbreviated to the three small *drops* that we learned earlier as the kanji for *little*, giving us: 泉.

---

141   gland

腺

Dig into your flesh and pull out a lymph **gland**. Now give it a squeeze and watch a *spring* of lymph spout out of it. [13]

月 腺

| 142 | meadow |

原

Though the kanji is broad enough to embrace both meanings, the **meadow** you should imagine here is not a flatland plain but a mountain **meadow** in the Austrian Alps. (Perhaps the opening scene of "The Sound of Music" will help.) Simply think of little *springs* bubbling up across the **meadow** to form a sort of path that leads you right to the brink of a precipitous *cliff*. Now if you can see Schwester Maria skipping along merrily, dodging in and out of the *springs*, and then falling headlong over the *cliff*, you have a ridiculous story that should help fix this kanji in memory. [10]

厂　戶　原

| 143 | petition |

願

A *meadow* and a *head* are all we are given to work with in the kanji for **petition**. Since the key word already suggests something like a formal request made of some higher power, let us imagine a gigantic Wizard-of-Oz *head* located in the middle of the flowery *meadow* we used in the last frame. Then just picture people kneeling hopefully before it, **petitioning** for whatever it is they want. (The scarecrow wanted brains, the lion, courage, and the tin man a heart. What about you?) [19]

原　願

| 144 | swim |

泳

The primitive to the left, you will recall from FRAME 137, represents *water*. To the right, we see the kanji for *eternity*. Knowing how much children like **swimming**, what could be a better image of *eternal* bliss than an endless expanse of *water* to **swim** in without a care in the world? [8]

 氵　泳

---

145   marsh

沼

Unlike the meadow with its cliffs, the **marsh**lands are low and near a source of *water* that feeds them until they get soggy through and through. Why certain land becomes **marshy** is probably due to the fact that it felt thirsty, and so tried its best to *seduce* the *water* over to its side. But, like most inordinate *seductions*, the last state of the victim is worse than the first. Hence the slushy **marsh**. [8]

氵　沼

---

146   open sea

沖

This kanji could hardly be simpler. The key word **open sea** readily suggests being out *in the middle of* a great body of *water*. Thinking of it in this way should avoid confusion with the kanji for "open," which we will meet later on. [7]

氵　沖

---

147   pan-

汎

The sense of the key word here is the "all-inclusive" we find in terms like "**Pan**-American Games." (It is also the character used in mathematics for "partial" as in partial differentials, in case you are a math major and want to take your story in that direction.) Instead of a *water* sports event that brings together the best talent, think of a meet of the region's most *mediocre* athletes, many of whom cannot even tread *water*. Now try to find a sponsor for the "**Pan**-*Mediocre Water* Sports Competition." [6]

氵　汎

---

148   creek

江

Unlike the river, the ocean, the lake, and the pond, the **creek** is often no more then a dribble of *water* trickling down a small gully. While the geological history of the larger bodies of *water* is hard to surmise sometimes, all of us know from our childhood how **creeks** are made. You probably even dug one or two

in your time. All you need to do is find a mainstream of *water* somewhere and dig a little path into dry land. The **creek** is thus a lesson in *water-craft*, as this kanji would agree. [6]

氵　江

---

149   cleanse

汰

This character can mean both to **cleanse** and to make dirty. We will choose the latter and imagine someone who is displeasingly *plump* going to a skinny spa whose medicinal *waters* promise to **cleanse** him of his unwanted corpulence. Picture him sitting in the spa as the pounds melt away, leaving a greasy scum on top of the *water*. [7]

氵　汰

---

150   soup

汁

To make **soup**, one begins with *water* and then starts adding things to it, often leftovers from the icebox. This is how the thick **soup** or stew called "seven-in-one" is made. This kanji does it three better, giving us a *ten*-ingredient **soup**. [5]

氵　汁

---

151   grains of sand

沙

We have already learned the kanji for *sand* (FRAME 122), so let's use it to remember the character for **grains of sand**. Instead of the "few stones" that make for nice sand, here we have a *few drops of water*, one for each **grain of sand**—a beach in perfect ecological balance. [7]

氵　沙

---

152   tide

潮

Before we get to explaining this character, take a look at it and see if you can figure out the primitive elements on your own.... On the left is the *water*—that much is easy. On the right we have

only one primitive, the kanji for *morning* learned back in FRAME 53. See how an apparently complex kanji falls apart neatly into manageable pieces?

To get the meaning of the key word **tide**, just think of it in connection with the character for *eventide* that we learned back in FRAME 115. Here we have the *morning*-**tide**, its complement.

By the way, if you missed the question about the number of primitives, it is probably because you forgot what we said earlier about kanji becoming primitives, independently of the pieces that make them up. As a rule, look for the largest kanji you can write and proceed from there to primitives stranded on their own. [15]

氵　潮

153　source

源

With the advice of the last frame in mind, it is easy to see *water* and *meadow* in this character for **source**. Both in its etymology (it has a common parent with the word "surge") and in popular usage, **source** suggests the place *water* comes from. In this kanji, it is under the *meadow*, where we just saw it breaking the surface in those bubbly little springs. [13]

氵　源

154　lively

活

When we speak of a **lively** personality or a **lively** party, we immediately think of a lot of chatter. This kanji depicts the idea of **lively** by having *tongues* babble and splash around like flowing *water*. [9]

氵　活

155　extinguish

消

Among the many things *water* is useful for is **extinguishing** fires, and that is just what we have here. First of all, take the *water* at the left as the *drops of water* that are used to depict *water* in general. In the best of all possible worlds, the most effi-

cient way to **extinguish** a fire would be to see that each *drop of water* hits one *spark* of the conflagration. An unthinkable bit of utopian fire fighting, you say to yourself, but helpful for assigning this key word its primitives. [10]

氵 消

| 156 | but of course |

況

This key word is a connector used to link contrasting phrases and sentences together with much the same flavor as the English phrase **but of course**. Just picture yourself ready to go off on your first date as a *teenager*, and having your mother grill you about your manners and ask you embarrassing questions about your hygiene. "Did you have a good shower?" "**But of course**...," you reply, annoyed. So *water* and *teenager* combine to give us **but of course**. [8]

氵 況

| 157 | river |

河

The character in this frame represents a step up from the *stream* we met in FRAME 134; it is a full-sized **river**. The *water* to the left tells us what we are dealing with, and the *can* at the right tells us that our "little engine that *could*" has now become amphibious and is chugging down the Mighty Mississip' like a regular riverboat. [8]

氵 河

| 158 | overnight |

泊

When you stop at an inn for an **overnight** rest, all you expect is a bit of *water* for a wash and a set of clean *white* sheets to wrap your weary bones in. [8]

氵 泊

159	lake

湖

Water . . . old . . . flesh. You have heard of legends of people being abandoned in the mountains when they had become too *old* to work. Well, here is a legend about people being set adrift in the *waters* of a stormy **lake** because their *flesh* had gotten too *old* to bear the burdens of life. [12]

氵　沽　湖

160	fathom

測

Connoting the measurement of the depth of *water*, the key word **fathom** begins with the *water* primitive. To its right, we see the compound-primitive for *rule* (FRAME 92) which we learned in the sense of a "ruler" or "measure." Hence, when we *rule water* we **fathom** it. What could be simpler? But be careful; its simplicity is deceptive. Be sure to picture yourself **fathoming** a body of *water* several hundred feet deep by using a *ruler* of gargantuan proportions. [12]

氵　測

161	soil

土

I don't like it any more than you do, but this kanji is not the pictograph it is trumped up to be: a mound of **soil** piled on the ground. All I can recommend is that you memorize it as it is. Anyway, it will be occurring with such frequency that you have almost no chance of forgetting it, even if you try. [3]

一　十　土

* As a primitive, the sense of *soil* is extended to that of *ground* because of its connection with the kanji for the same (FRAME 554). From there it also takes the added meanings of *dirt* and *land*.

---

162   spit

吐   We have here a rather small *mouth* (it is always compressed
     when set on the left) next to a much larger piece of *dirt*. It is not
     hard to imagine what you might do if you got a *mouth* full of
     dirt. As least I know what I would do: **spit** it out as fast and far
     as I could! [6]

口   吐

---

163   pressure

圧   One of the things that causes the erosion of *soil* is the excessive
     pressure of the top*soil* on the lower *soil*. This can be caused by
     any number of things from heavy rainfall to heavy buildings to
     the absence of sufficient deep-rooted vegetation to hold the lay-
     ers together. Here we see a steep *cliff* without a tree in sight. The
     slightest **pressure** on it will cause a landslide, which, with a little
     help from your imagination, you will be able to see happening
     in this character. [5]

厂   圧

---

164   cape

埼   The **cape** pictured here is a jut of *land* like **Cape** Cod. The *soil*
     on the left tells us we have to do with *land*, and the *strange* on
     the right tells us it is a *cape* where unusual things go on. Put a
     haunted house on it, an eerie sky overhead, and a howling wind
     rustling through the trees, and you have yourself a picture of
     Cape *Strange* (or, if you prefer, **Cape** *Odd*). [11]

扌   埼

---

165   hedge

垣   The **hedge** depicted in this frame is not your ordinary run-of-
     the-suburbs shrubbery, but the miraculous **hedge** of briar roses
     that completely *spanned* the castle *grounds* in which Sleeping
     Beauty lay for a hundred years, so that none but her predestined
     beloved could find his way through it. [9]

扌　垣

166　　　　　　　　　　　　　　　　　　　　　inlay

填

When we hear the word **inlay**, we usually think of setting precious stones in pieces of jewelery, but the primitive elements here suggest *truth* being **inlaid** in the *soil*. You might think instead of the cosmic wisdom that **inlaid** the *truth* of the universe in the stuff of the earth. [13]

扌　填

167　　　　　　　　　　　　　　　　　　　squared jewel

圭

Now I am going to do something unusual. The character in this frame is going to get one meaning and the primitive another, with no relation at all between the two. In time, I hope you will see how helpful this is.

The kanji key word, **squared jewel**, depicts a mammoth precious stone, several feet high, made by piling up large heaps of *soil* on top of one another. Not something you would want to present your betrothed on your wedding day, but a good image for remembering this rare character, used chiefly in personal names nowadays. [6]

一　十　土　士　㚖　圭

* As a primitive, we shall use this character to mean *ivy*, that creepy vegetation that covers the surface of the *ground* to form a sort of "second" *ground* that can get somewhat tricky to walk on without tripping.

168　　　　　　　　　　　　　　　　　　　　　　seal

封

Think of the key word **seal** as referring to a letter you have written and are preparing to close. Instead of using the traditional wax **seal**, you *glue* a sprig of *ivy* on the outside. In this way the elements *ivy* and *glue* give you a curious and memorable way to **seal** your secret letters. [9]

圭 封

169 horizon

涯

After seeing a constant **horizon** of *water, water* everywhere for months at sea, could there be anything more delightful to the eyes than to look astern and see the *ivy*-clad *cliffs* of land on a new **horizon**? Of course, you'd need the eyes of a stellar telescope to recognize that the vegetation was in fact *ivy*, but the phrase "*ivy*-clad *cliffs*" has such a nice ring to it that we won't worry about such details. [11]

氵 氿 涯

170 Buddhist temple

寺

You have heard of people "attaching" themselves to a particular sect? Here is your chance to take that metaphor literally and imagine some fellow walking into a **Buddhist temple** with a fervent resolve to attach himself to the place. Since there is plenty of unused *land* around the precincts, he simply picks out a suitable patch, brushes the soles of his feet with *glue*, steps down firmly, and so joins the **Buddhist temple** as a "permanent member." [6]

土 寺

171 time

時

"What is **time**?" asked St. Augustine in his memoirs. "Ask me not, and I know. Ask me, and I cannot tell you." Here we have the kanji's answer to that perennial riddle. **Time** is a *sun* rising over a *Buddhist temple*. It sounds almost like a Zen kōan whose repetition might yield some deep secret to the initiated. At any rate, imagining a monk seated in meditation pondering it might help us remember the character. [10]

日 時

---

172   level

均

The **level** this key word refers to is not the carpenter's tool but rather the even surface of a thing. It pictures *soil* being scooped up into a *ladle* and then made **level** (apparently because one is measuring *soil*). The excess *drops of soil* are brushed off the top, which accounts for the added *drop* at the *ladle's* edge. [7]

扌 均 均

---

173   fire

火

Just as sitting before a **fire** enlivens the imagination and lets you see almost anything you want to in the flames, this kanji is so simple it lets you see almost any sort of **fire** you want to see. It no longer makes a good pictograph, but I invite you to take a pencil and paper and play with the form—first writing it as shown below and then adding lines here and there—to see what you can come up with. Everything from matchbooks to cigarette lighters to volcanic eruptions to the destruction of Sodom and Gomorrah have been found here. No doubt you, too, will find something interesting to bend your memory around these four simple strokes. [4]

丶 丶ノ ソ 火

* To avoid confusion later on, it is best to keep to the meaning of a *fireplace* (or *hearth*) or a raging *conflagration* like a forest fire for this kanji's primitive meaning. Another primitive element for *fire,* based on this one, is written 灬 and will mean *flames, cauldron, cooking fire,* or an *oven fire.*

---

174   inflammation

炎

A *fire* belongs IN the *hearth,* not OVER it. When the *fire* spreads to the rest of the house, we have an **inflamed** house. And as with any **inflammation**—including those that attack our bodies—the danger is always that it might spread if not checked. This is the sense behind the reduplication of the element for *fire,* one atop the other [8]

丶 丶丶 ソ 火 火 火 歩 炎

175 anxiety

煩

The existential condition of **anxiety** that arises from the inevitable frustration of our worldly passions is contained in this character. The *head* is set *afire*, causing deep torment of spirit (and a whopper of a headache). [13]

丶 丶丶 火 火 煩

176 thin

淡

The primitives in this kanji read: *water . . . inflammation*. Taking *inflammation* in its medical sense, the first *water*-related *inflammation* that pops into mind is dehydration, the principal symptom of which is that it makes one shrivel up and look very, very **thin**. If that is hard to remember, try thinking it backwards: a very **thin** chap passes by and you imagine him suffering from (being *inflamed* with) dehydration (hence the element for *water*). [11]

氵 淡

177 lamp

灯

Since it is very hard to read by the *fireplace* without going blind from the flickering of the flames or burning up from the heat, our ancestors invented a way to *nail* down a bit of that *fire*, just enough to light up the text of their evening newspapers and no more. Voilà! The **lamp**. [6]

火 灯

178 farm

畑

Looking at the primitives, a *fireplace* and a *rice field*, we find the essential ingredients for a **farm**: a warm *hearth* to sit by at night, and a well-plowed *field* to grow one's crops in by day. [9]

火　畑

179

disaster

災

Of all of nature's **disasters**, this kanji picks out two of the worst: *floods* and *fires*. To recall the disposition of the elements, think of nature's solution to nature's own problem: a great *flood* pouring down over a great forest *fire*. [7]

‹　‹‹　‹‹‹　災

180

ashes

灰

The kanji for **ashes** naturally includes the primitive for *fire*, or more specifically, a *fireplace*. Now what do you do with that bucket of **ashes** you have just cleaned out of the *fireplace*? You walk to the edge of a *cliff* and tip it upside down, watching as they are swept away in the wind like a swarm of gray mosquitoes. Thus the *fire*, once it has turned to **ashes**, ends up at the bottom of the *cliff*. [6]

厂　灰

181

spot

点

If you look into the flickering of a *fire* for a long time and then turn aside, you will see **spots** before your eyes. Although nobody ever thought of such a thing before—as least as far as I know, they didn't—imagine using those **spots** as a technique for *fortune-telling*. The old witch sits before her *cauldron* and watches the **spots** that show up when she turns to look at you, and from that *tells your fortune*. Think of it as a kind of **spot**-check on your future. [9]

占　占　点　点　点

182

illuminate

照

Although the range of possible meanings that the kanji for **illuminate** can have is about as rich as the connotations of the

English word, we need to focus on just one of them: to make something *shine*. If you glaze a pot and put it into the *oven* to *fire* it, you in fact *illuminate* it. Hence the kanji for **illuminate** compares the kanji for *shining* with the primitive element for the *oven's fire*. [13]

日　昭　照

---

183   fish

魚

The composition of this kanji shows three elements, which we list in the order of their writing: *bound up . . . rice field . . . cooking fire*. Not much to work with at first sight. But we can join them together by thinking of a three-part story: first a **fish** is caught and *bound up* on a line with its unfortunate school-mates; when the fisherman gets home, he cuts off the head and tosses it, with the entrails, out into the *rice fields* for fertilizer; and the rest he sets in a skillet over a *cooking fire* for his supper. [11]

ク　备　魚

---

184   fishing

漁

To the story we have just made about *fish*, this kanji for the profession of **fishing** adds yet another element BEFORE the others: namely the *water*, where the fish was happily at home before being caught, disemboweled, and eaten. Be sure to get a clear image of the *water* when you put it all together. [14]

氵　漁

Lesson 9

ALTHOUGH THE study of the four basic elements undertaken in the last lesson brought us a lot of new characters—51 in all—we have only scratched the surface as far as *water, earth, wind, and fire* are concerned. Perhaps by now it

is clear why I said at the beginning of this lesson that we are lucky that they appear so frequently. The range of images they suggest is almost endless.

In this chapter our focus will be on a few new "roof" and "enclosure" primitives. But first, a primitive-kanji that we might have included in the last group but omitted so as not to be distracted from the four elements. With just that one element we can pick up no less than 7 new kanji with no trouble at all.

| 185 | | *ri* |

里

That's right—a *ri*. Don't bother looking it up in your English dictionary; it's a Japanese word for measuring distances. One *ri* is about 4 kilometers or 2.5 miles. The kanji depicts how the measure came to be used. Atop we see the *rice field*, and below the element for *land*. Those four sections you see in the *rice field* (and which we made mention of when first we introduced the character in FRAME 14) are actually measurements of *land*, much the same as farm-sections in the United States have given us the notion of a "country mile." The *land* division based on the size of a *rice field* is called a *ri*. [7]

丨 冂 冃 日 甲 甲 里

* To get a more concrete primitive meaning for this kanji, we shall refer to it as a *computer*, a meaning deriving from the kanji for *logic*, which we will meet in LESSON 12.

| 186 | | black |

黒

Like most things electrical, a *computer*, too, can overheat. Just imagine *flames* pouring out of it and charring the keyboard, the monitor, and your desk a sooty **black** color. [11]

丨 冂 冃 日 甲 甲 里 黒 黒

黒 黒

| 187 | | black ink |

墨

Besides meaning **black ink**, this kanji also appears in the word for an inked string that is pulled taut and snapped to mark a

surface, much the same as one might used a chalked string. Here it is used to mark off the *dirt* with *black* lines for a football game (played, I presume, on a white field). [14]

黒 墨

---

188   carp

鯉

These are the same **carp** you see in Japanese "**carp** streamers." Only here we find a small home *computer* or two strung on the line by a father anxious for his son not only to have the courage and determination of a **carp** swimming upstream, but also the efficiency and memory of a *computer*. Ugh. [18]

魚 鯉

---

189   quantity

量

Think of **quantity** as having to do with measuring time and distance, and the rest is simple: you have a quantity of time in the new day that begins with *nightbreak*, and a quantity of distance in the rural *ri*. [12]

日 旦 量

---

190   *rin*

厘

No doubt you will find it in your heart to forgive me for forcing yet another Japanese word on you in this frame. It is not the last time it will happen in this book, but I can assure you they are used only when absolutely necessary.

One *rin* is equal to about 1/1000 of a yen—or rather was worth that much when it still made economic sense to mint them. While inflation took its toll on this kanji as a monetary unit, it survived with the not at all surprising sense of something "very, very tiny."

The kanji shows a *cliff* with a *computer* under it, apparently because it has been pushed over into the abyss by someone fed up with the thing. The total market value of one home *computer* that has fallen over rock and bramble for several hundred feet: about one *rin*! [9]

厂　厴

191　　　　　　　　　　　　　　　　　　　　　　　　　bury

埋　When we speak of **burying** something (or someone, for that matter), we usually mean putting them under *ground*. Only here, we are **burying** our beloved *computer* that has served us so well these past years. Behind us a choir chants the "Dies irae, dies illa" and there is much wailing and grief among the bystanders as they pass by to shovel a little *dirt* into what will be its final resting place. R.I.P. [10]

土　　埋

Before going any further, we might pause a moment to look at precisely WHERE the primitive elements were placed in the kanji of the last frame: the *ground* to the left and the *computer* to the right. Neither of these is an absolutely fixed position. The kanji for *spit* (FRAME 162), for instance, puts *ground* on the right, and that for *plains* (FRAME 1722) will put the *computer* on the left. While there is no reason to bother memorizing any "rules," a quick glance through a few general guidelines may help. Use them if they help; if not, simply adjust the story for a problem character in such a way as to help you remember the position of the elements relative to one another.

In any case, here are the guidelines that follow from the kanji treated up to this point:

1. Many kanji used regularly as primitives have a "strong" position or two from which they are able to give a basic "flavor" to the character. For example, *ground* at the left (or bottom) usually indicates something to do with earth, soil, land, and the like; *fire* at the bottom in the form of the four dots, or at the left in its compressed kanji form, usually tells us we have to do with heat, passion, and the like; a *mouth* at the left commonly signifies something to do with eating, coughing, spitting, snoring, screaming, and so forth. Where these elements appear elsewhere in the kanji, they do not have the same overall impact on its meaning as a rule.

2. Some primitive elements ALWAYS have the same position in a kanji. We saw this earlier in the case of the primitive meaning *head* (FRAME 64) and that for the long *saber* (FRAME 87), as well as in the three drops of *water* (FRAME 137).

3. Enclosures like *cliff* (see FRAME 118) and *bound up* (FRAME 67) are always set above whatever it is they enclose. Others, as we shall see later, "wrap up" a kanji from the bottom.

4. All things being equal, the element with the fewer strokes (usually the more common element) has first rights to the "strong" position at the left or bottom. (Note that the left and bottom cannot BOTH be the dominant position in the same character. Either one or the other of them will dominate, usually the left.) The characters for *nitrate* (FRAME 120) and *chant* (FRAME 21) illustrate the point.

---

*   **hood**

In addition to the basic meaning of **hood**, this shape can be used for a **glass canopy**, such as that used to serve "pheasant under glass." Note its difference from the element for *wind*: the second stroke is hooked INWARDS here. To help remember this detail, think of the wind as blowing "out" and a **glass canopy** as keeping something "in." Among the related images suggested by this primitive are: a monk's **cowl**, a riding **hood**, a **helmet**, and an automobile **hood**. [2]

---

192   **same**

The primitives given are *one* and *mouth* under a *hood*. Take the key word to connote the **sameness** that characterizes the life in a community of monks. They all have the **same** habits, including the "habit" they wear on their backs. Here we see the monk's *cowl*, drawn down over the eyes so that all you can see when you look at him is a *mouth*. But since monks also speak their prayers in common, it is but a short step to think of *one mouth* under a *hood* as the kanji for the **sameness** of monastic life. [6]

* As a primitive, this kanji will mean *monks dressed in a common habit*.

---

193   **den**

洞

The key word **den** refers to an animal lair hollowed out in the side of a mountain. Now if we keep to the image of the monastic life as an image for *same*, we can picture a **den** of wild beasts dressed up in habits and living the common life in a mountain cavern. To bring in the element of *water* we need only give them a sacred "puddle" in the center of their **den**, the focus of all their pious attentions. [9]

氵　洞

---

194   **trunk**

胴

The word **trunk** refers to the *part of the body* that is left when you have "**truncated**" all the limbs. I can hardly think of any reason for doing so, unless one were lumberjacking corpses and needed to have them all properly pruned and made the *same* so they could be floated downstream without causing a *body*-jam. [10]

月　胴

---

195   **yonder**

向

Something referred to as "over **yonder**" is usually far off in the distance and barely within sight—like a wee *drop* in the distance—and is usually an expression used in giving directions or pointing something out. Hence this kanji begins with a *drop*. Then we find a sort of transparent *helmet* with no eyes or nose, but only a prominent *mouth* under it, obviously an extraterrestrial. And what is it jabbering on about with its *mouth* open like that? Why, about his spaceship way over **yonder** with its fuel tank on empty. [6]

′　冂　向

---

196   **esteem**

尚

Above we see the primitive for *little* attached to one of those *glass canopies* you might use to display a family heirloom. The

littleness is important, because what is in fact on display is the shrunken, stuffed, and mounted *mouth* of an **esteemed** ancestor. We may be used to **esteeming** the words our forebears leave behind, but here we also **esteem** the very *mouth* that spoke them. I leave it to you to imagine a suitable place in your room for displaying such an unusual conversation piece. [8]

⺌ 　 肖 　 尚

★

宀

house

This extremely useful primitive element depicts the roof of a **house**. You can see the chimney at the top and the eaves on either side without much trouble. It is a "crown" element, which means that it is invariably set atop other things. Examples follow immediately. [3]

丶　丶丶　宀

197

字

character

Here is the character for **character** itself. Not just kanji, but any written **character** from hieroglyphs to Sanskrit to our own Roman alphabet. It shows us simply a *child* in a *house*. But let us take advantage of the double meaning of the key word to note that just as a *child* born to a Japanese *house* is given **characters** for its name, so it is also stamped with the **character** of those who raise it from infancy on. [6]

丶　丶丶　宀　宀　宁　字

198

守

guard

The notion of **guarding** something easily brings to mind the image of someone standing **guard**, like the royal soldiers in front of Buckingham Palace or the Pope's Swiss **Guard**. The whole idea of hiring **guards** is that they should stick like *glue* to your *house* to protect it from unwanted prowlers. So go ahead and *glue* a **guard** to your *house* in imagination. [6]

宀 守

199   perfect

完   In order not to confuse the key word **perfect** with others nearly synonymous in meaning, pull it apart to have a look at its native Latin roots. *Per-factum* suggests something so "thoroughly made or done" that nothing more needs to be added to it. Now look at the kanji, which does something similar. We see a *house* that has been made **perfectly** from its *beginnings* in the foundation to the roof on the top. Now return to FRAME 101 and make sure not to confuse this key word with the kanji for *complete*. [7]

宀 完

200   proclaim

宣   Under the primitive for *house* we meet the kanji for *span*. Think of the key word in its religious sense of missionary preaching: "**proclaiming** the good news to all nations" and "shouting it from the *housetops*." That should be enough to help you remember this simple kanji, used in fact both for traditional missionary work as well as for one of its contemporary replacements: advertising. [9]

宀 宣

201   wee hours

宵   As the key word hints, the kanji in this frame refers to the late evening or early morning hours, well after one should be in bed asleep. It does this by picturing a *house* with a *candle* in it. The reason is obvious: whoever is living there is "burning the *candle* at both ends," and working night after night into the **wee hours**. [10]

宀 宵

202	relax

安

To be told that the place of the *woman* is in the *house* may not sit well with modern thought, but like all cultural habits the Chinese characters bear the birthmarks of their age. So indulge yourself in a Norman Rockwell image of **relaxing** after a hard day's work: the scruffy and weary *woman* of the *house* slouched asleep in the living room chair, her hair in curlers and a duster lying in her lap. [6]

203	banquet

宴

To carry on from the last frame, we note the entire *day* of work that comes between a *woman* and her *house* in preparing for a dinner **banquet**, pictorially "interrupting" her *relaxation*. [10]

204	draw near

寄

Let the idea of **drawing near** suggest something dangerous or eerie that one approaches with fear and trembling. Here we see a *strange house*—perhaps the haunted *House* of Usher that Edgar Allen Poe immortalized, or the enchanted Gingerbread *House* that lured Hansel and Gretel to **draw near**. [11]

205	wealth

富

Here we have the original character on which the primitive element for **wealth** is based. In keeping with the story introduced back then, note how all the **wealth** is kept under the roof of the same *house*. [12]

---

206 savings

貯 To avoid confusing this frame with the last one, try to think of **savings** as actual money. The only difference is that our currency is not paper bills but *shells*, a not uncommon unit of exchange in older civilizations. The *nail* under the roof of the *house* points to a hiding place in the rafters on which one strings up one's *shells* for safekeeping. [12]

貝　貯　貯

Lesson 10

OF THE SEVERAL primitive elements that have to do with plants and grasses, we introduce two of the most common in this lesson: *trees* and *flowers*. In most cases, as we shall see, their presence in a "strong" position (in this case, to the left and at the top, respectively) helps give a meaning to the kanji. Where this is not the case, we shall do our best to MAKE it so.

---

207 tree

 Here we see a pictograph of a **tree**, showing the main trunk in the long vertical stroke and the boughs in the long horizontal stroke. The final two strokes sweep down in both directions to indicate the roots. Although it may look similar at first sight to the kanji for *water* (FRAME 137), the order in which it is written is completely different and this affects its final appearance. [4]

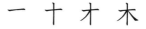

* As a primitive, this kanji can mean *tree* or *wood*. When the last two strokes are detached from the trunk (朩), we shall change its meaning to *pole*, or *wooden pole*.

208	grove
林	Learn this frame in connection with the next one. A **grove** is a small cluster of *trees*. Hence the simple reduplication of the kanji for *tree* gives us the **grove**. [8]

一　十　オ　木　林

209	forest
森	A **forest** is a large expanse of *trees*, or "*trees, trees* everywhere," to adopt the expression we used back in FRAMES 22 and 23. [12]

210	Japanese Judas-tree
桂	Unless you are a botanist, you are not likely to know what a **Japanese Judas-tree** looks like, and probably never even heard of it before, but the name is sufficiently odd to make remembering it easy. Using the primitives as our guide, we define it as a *tree* with *ivy* growing down its branches in the shape of a hangman's rope. [10]

木　桂

211	oak
柏	This kanji calls to mind the famous myth of the "golden bough." As you may recall, what made the sacred **oak** in the forest of Diana the Huntress outside of Rome "golden" were the *white* berries of the mistletoe that grew in the branches of the tree. When the light of the sun shone through them, they turned yellow and the branch to which they clung appeared to be made of gold. (If you don't know the story, take a break today and hunt it down in a dictionary of myth and fable. Even if you forget the kanji—which, of course, you won't—the story of the mistletoe and the fate it brought to Balder the Beautiful is one you are sure to remember.) [9]

木　柏

---

212   **frame**

枠   You might think of the **frame** this character refers to as the sort
of **frame** we have created by drawing a dark line around this
kanji and its explanation. Then think of that line as made of
very thin *wood*; and finally note how each time the line bends it
forms a 90° angle, thus giving us the *nine* and the *ten*. [8]

朮   朳   枠

---

213   **treetops**

梢   As the days grow shorter and shorter, or so the northern
European myth goes, the fear grows that the sun will take its
leave of us altogether, abandoning the world to total darkness. Fixing *candles* to the branches of evergreen *trees*, it was
believed, would lure the sun back (like things attracting like
things), whence the custom of the lighted tree that eventually
found its way into our Christmas customs. The story is a lot
longer and more complex than that, but it should help to fix
the image of climbing high up into the **treetops** to fix *candles*
on the *tree*. [11]

朮   梢

---

214   **shelf**

棚   One often thinks of books as "good *companions*," but here it
is the **shelf** we store them on that is the *companion*. The reasons should be obvious: it is made of the same stuff, *wood*, and
spends a lot more time with them than we do! Here again, be
careful not to let the rationality of the explanation get in the
way before you turn it into a proper story. [12]

朮   棚   ﹅

---

215   **apricot**

杏   Since **apricots** can be eaten just as they fall from the *trees*, picture this *mouth* agape at the bottom of a *tree* (just as the elements have it), waiting for **apricots** to fall into it. [7]

木 杏

216 　　　　　　　　　　　　　　　　　　　paulownia

桐

Since you probably don't know what a **paulownia** *tree* is, we shall let the key word suggest the phrase "the Little Brothers of St. **Paulownia.**" It is a short step to associate the *tree* with the *monks* to its right. (For the curious, the name of this oriental *tree* really comes from a Russian princess, Anna Pavlovna.) [10]

朩　桐

217 　　　　　　　　　　　　　　　　　　　　　plant

植

You have no doubt seen how people practicing the Japanese art of bonsai take those helpless little saplings and twist them into crippled dwarves before they have a chance to grow up as they should. The more proper way to **plant** a young *tree* and give it a fair shake in life is to set it into the earth in such a way that it can grow up *straight*. [12]

朩　植

218 　　　　　　　　　　　　　　　　　　　　　chair

椅

Instead of making a **chair** out of wood from a *tree*, this kanji has us making the whole *tree* into a **chair**, which looks most *strange* sitting in your living room where the sofa used to be. [12]

朩　椅

219 　　　　　　　　　　　　　　　　　　　　　wither

枯

What makes a *tree* begin to **wither** up, and perhaps even die, is a kind of arteriosclerosis that keeps its sap from flowing freely. Usually this is due to simple *old* age, as this character shows us. Be sure to picture a wrinkled *old tree*, **withering** away in a retirement center so that the commonsense explanation does not take over. [9]

木 枯

220
木卜

crude

As all magicians who have passed their apprenticeship know, one makes one's *wand* out of a hazel branch and is careful not to alter the natural form of the *wood*. For the magic of the *wand* derives its power from its association with the hidden laws of nature, and needs therefore to be kept in its **crude**, natural state. [6]

木 朴

221
村

town

The character for *village* was associated with *rice fields* (FRAME 96). That for **town**, a step up on the evolutionary path to cities, shows a circle of *trees glued together* to measure off the confines of a **town**. [7]

木 村

222
相

inter-

The prefix **inter-** stirs up associations of cooperation among people. From there we read off the elements: *tree . . . eye*. With only a slight leap of the imagination, those two words call to mind the scriptural proverb about first taking the block of timber out of one's own *eye* before helping your neighbors remove the splinters in their eyes. What more useful rule for **inter**-human relationships, and what more useful tool for remembering this kanji! [9]

木 相

223
机

desk

We need to fix imagination here on two things to learn the kanji for **desk**: the wonderful rough *wood* of which it has been hewn and the *wind* that blows across it, sending your papers flying all

over the room. These two elements, written in that order, dictate how to write the character. [6]

木　机

224	book

本

Recalling that **books** are made of paper, and paper made of *trees*, one might think of a **book** as a slice of a *tree*. Can you see the "cross-cut" in the trunk of the *tree*? Picture it as a chain-saw cutting you out a few **books** with which to start your own private library. [5]

木　本

225	tag

札

The **tags** you see hanging on *trees* in public places in Japan are helpful to identify what sort of *trees* they are. Next time you see one, imagine the bit of wire that fixes the **tag** to the branch as a large *fishhook*. REALLY imagine it, illogical as it is, and you will never have trouble with this kanji again. [5]

木　札

226	calendar

暦

Look at this character in reverse order, from bottom up. First we see the primitive for *days*, an appropriate enough way to begin a **calendar**. Next we see a *grove of trees* growing under a *cliff*. The laws of nature being what they are, the *trees* would be stunted under such conditions, unless they were strong enough to keep growing upwards until they passed through the layers of rock and soil, right up to the surface. Now imagine that in those little boxes marking off the *days* on your wall **calendar**, you see that very process taking place step by step: 365 or so time-lapse pictures of that *grove of trees* each month, from January under the *cliff* to December on top of the *cliff*. The story is not as complex as it sounds, particularly if you happen to have a **calendar** nearby and can flip through it with this image in mind. [14]

227

案

plan

Without much effort, the elements *relax . . . tree* suggest a hammock strung between two *trees* in your backyard, and you stretched out in it, hands folded behind your head, **planning** something or other. After all, it's something we all do from time to time: kick up our legs on the nearest piece of furniture and daydream about the best **plan** of action to take. Be sure to relate the *relaxation* to the *tree*, so that you don't end up with something else in its place (like "legs" or "desk" or "table"). [10]

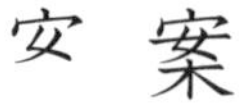

228

燥

parch

Parchment, made from animal skins, was the most common form of writing material used until the beginning of the nineteenth century. When paper took over, a method was devised to make artificial **parch**ment from *wood* pulp. The *fire* at the left and in the "strong" position reminds us of the root word, "**parch**," since nothing dries, puckers, wrinkles, and scorches quite like *fire*. And here is how we put it all together. Take a sheet of paper (a "*wood-good*,"), wet it, and hold it over a *hearth* in your mind's eye. Now watch as it **parches** the paper, leaving it with a strange and bumpy surface resembling **parch**ment. [17]

229

未

not yet

As the key word suggests, this kanji has to do with something not quite over and done with. More concretely, it shows us a *tree* that is **not yet** fully grown. The extra short stroke in the upper branches shows new branches spreading out, leaving one with the feeling that the *tree* has a ways to go yet before it reaches maturity. In other words, the kanji conveys its meaning pictographically, playing on the earlier pictograph of the *tree*. [5]

一　二　キ　才　未

230

末

extremity

This character is best learned in connection with that of the previous frame. The first stroke shows a branch that is longer than the main branch, indicating that the tree has reached the **extremity** of its growth, so that its branches stop spreading and start drooping downwards. Be sure to keep this imagery in mind, to avoid confusing this key word with synonyms that will appear later. [5]

一　二　キ　才　末

231

昧

obscure

The most **obscure** ideas are those that the *sun* of reason has *not yet* dawned on. Be sure to give the *sun* a professorial demeanor, complete with spectacles and a pipe. [9]

日　昧

232

沫

splash

The **splash** this kanji refers to is the dash of *water* against the rocks, with all the foam and spray that this creates. If you think of a **splash** in this sense as a wave that has run its full course and reached its *extremity,* namely the seashore, and if you think of it pictorially in your mind's eye, this somewhat rare (but oh-so-easy-to-learn) kanji is yours for good. [8]

氵　沫

233

味

flavor

When a tree has *not yet* finished growing, it produces fruit with a full **flavor**. When the official taster (the professional *mouth* to the left) determines that full **flavor** has been reached, the tree is pruned back so that it remains permanently *not yet* grown. A neat little agricultural trick and an easy way to see the sense of **flavor** hidden in this character. [8]

口　味

234　younger sister

妹　The **younger sister** in the family is the *woman* in the family who, like the newest branch in a tree, is *not yet* old enough or mature enough to do everything the elder sister can do (see FRAME 442). [8]

女　妹

235　vermilion

朱　That red-orange color we call **vermilion** is found in nature during the fall when the leaves lose their sugar and begin to change color. This kanji depicts the very last leaf on a tree in the fall (the *drop* hung in the first stroke), the leaf that has *not yet* fallen as it one day must. Look at its color—**vermilion**. (Well, not really. The truth is, **vermilion** is made from a mercuric sulfide, but I'm sure you will agree that autumn leaves are a lot easier to work with.) [6]

ノ　 レ　ニ　牛　牛　朱

236　stocks

株　The **stocks** bought and sold on the market by the tens of millions each day get their name from a comparison to a healthy *tree*, in which one takes "**stock**" in the hopes that it will grow and produce more and more *trees* like itself. Usually good **stocks** are referred to as "blue chip," but here we are asked to associate the key word with the color *vermilion*, perhaps because one can assess the value of a tree from the color of its autumn leaves. [10]

木　株

✶	flower

丗

We are not yet equipped with all the pieces necessary to learn the character for **flower**, so shall have to content ourselves here with the first three strokes, which represent the primitive of the same meaning. Concentrate on the actual "bloom" of the **flower**, and keep a particular flower in mind. Try a rose, a tulip, or a daisy, since none of them will have their own kanji. Think about it well, since once you have decided on your **flower** of choice, you will be using it in a rather large number of stories later on. [3]

一　十　丗

237　　　　　　　　　　　　　　　　young

若

Here we see a *flower* held in the *right* hand. You can imagine yourself in a magic garden where *flowers* picked with the *right* hand grant eternal **youth**; and those picked with the left, premature senility. Go ahead, pick one with each hand and watch what happens. [8]

一　十　丗　ザ　芋　若

238　　　　　　　　　　　　　　　　grass

草

Perhaps you know the custom of seeding **grass** randomly or in some particular pattern with the *flower* called the crocus, which blooms for a few days each year in *early* spring. As the **grass** begins to turn green again after winter has passed, these tiny *flowers* dot up here and there. Now just look out your window at a patch of **grass** somewhere and think what a nice idea it would be to have your name spelled out in *flowers* once as a sort of *early* harbinger of spring. [9]

丗　草

239　　　　　　　　　　　　　　　　suffering

苦

The picture of **suffering** we are given here is that of a *flower* that has grown *old*. When a flower ages, it pales and dries up, and

probably even **suffers**. If you think that plants are incapable of such feelings, then ask yourself why so many people believe that talking to their flowers helps them bloom better. [8]

艹　苦

240

苛 **bullying**

A nosegay of *flowers* make a nice gift, but if those flowers are poison oak, they *can* amount to **bullying**. Be sure to emphasize the word *can* when you repeat this little phrase to yourself. [8]

艹　苛

241

寛 **tolerant**

The *house* of *flowers* or "hothouse" has become a metaphor for a narrow-minded, biased, and intolerant attitude distrustful of change. **Tolerance**, in contrast, is open-minded and welcomes novelty. The way to encourage **tolerance** in those who lack it is first to have them *see* through their own hothouse attitudes, which is the very counsel we are given in this kanji. [13]

宀　宎　寛

242

薄 **dilute**

Take a good look at this kanji: the "strong" element here is really the *flower*, not the *water* as you might have thought on first glance. To the right is the *acupuncturist* from FRAME 48. Taking the key word to connote **diluting** the vital humors of the body, we can imagine our *acupuncturist* performing his task with *flowers* in place of needles, and using their hollow stems to pipe *water* into the body of the patient. [16]

艹　汁　薄

243

葉 **leaf**

Three elements are given here: *flower . . . generation . . . tree*. The first and last seem logical enough, since it is the **leaf** that feeds

the *flowers* on a *tree*. The element for *generation* interposed between the two suggests that the movement of a *tree* from one *generation* to the next is like its "turning over a new **leaf**." [12]

艹　莊　葉

★

莫

graveyard

The element shown here should be taken to represent a modern **graveyard**. Gone are the cobwebs and gnarled trees, the tilted headstones and dark, moonless nights that used to scare the wits out of our childhood imaginations. Instead, we see brightly colored *flowers* placed before the tombstones, the *sun* shining gloriously overhead, and a cuddly *St. Bernard* sitting at the gate keeping watch. [10]

艹　苩　莫

244

模

imitation

Ah, but haven't modern *graveyards* become a parody of their ancestors! The flowers are plastic, the writing on the stones is unimaginative and cold, and the whole thing looks more like a marble orchard than a right and proper graveyard. This kanji continues with the modernization trend by picturing **imitation** *trees* in the *graveyard*. But of course, how convenient! They don't need pruning or fertilizing, their leaves don't fall, and they remain the same color all year long. [14]

木　模

245

漠

vague

Think of the key word as having to do with something viewed through a haze, or in the twilight and from a distance, so that only its outlines are **vaguely** discernible. Now we are back again to the essence of the true *graveyard*. The *water* may be taken as the sound of waves dashing up against the rocks or the dripping of moisture on cold rock—anything that helps you associate **vagueness** with the *graveyard* and keep it distinct from the imitation we met in the last frame. [13]

氵 漠

246 grave

墓

The mounds of *soil* with crude wooden crosses set at their head suggests those boot-hill **graves** we all know from cowboy lore. The only odd thing about this kanji is that the *soil* comes UNDER the *graveyard*, rather than to its left, where we might expect. Just think of the bodies as "lying under boot-hill" if you have any trouble.

By the way, this is not the first time, nor will it be the last, that we learn a kanji whose key word is the same, or almost the same, as a primitive element based on it, but whose shape differs somewhat. There is no cause to worry. By using the primitive in a variety of other characters, as we have done here, the confusion will be averted as a matter of course. In most cases, as here, the primitive element is taken from a part of the fuller kanji. [13]

莫 墓

247 livelihood

暮

Imagine that you have chosen the occupation of the keeper of a *graveyard* and spend your *days* tending to other's deadhood in order to make your means of **livelihood**. [14]

莫 暮

248 membrane

膜

The *part of the body* first affected by a stroll through a haunted *graveyard* is the skin, which gets goose bumps. But we save the word "skin" for another kanji, and use the odd word "**membrane**" here. Think of being so scared through and through that the goose flesh moves from the outside in, giving you goose **membranes**. [14]

月 膜

249	seedling

苗　To avoid confusion with the image of rice seedlings to appear later, we shall take these **seedlings** out of their agricultural setting in the *rice fields* and into the frame of Brave New World surgery, where "ideas" or "values" are being implanted into *brains* like **seedlings** to insure a harmonious society. Then you need only imagine them taking root and breaking out into *flower* right through the tops of the skulls of people walking around on the streets. [8]

艹　苗

Lesson 11

NOW THAT WE have made our way through well over 200 characters, it is time to pause and consider how you are getting on with the method introduced in this book. While this lesson will be a short one (only 15 new kanji) you might want to spend some time reviewing your progress in the light of the remarks that follow. In them I have tried to draw out the main principles that have been woven into the fabric of the text from frame to frame and lesson to lesson. Perhaps the easiest way to do this is to single out some of the typical problems that can arise:

If you can remember the key word when you see the kanji, but have trouble remembering the kanji when you have only the key word to go on…

Probably you did not take seriously the advice about studying these stories with a pad and pencil. If you try to shortcut the process by merely learning to recognize the characters for their meaning without worrying about their writing, you will find that you have missed one bird with two stones, when you could have bagged two with one. Let me repeat: study only from key word to kanji; the reverse will take care of itself.

If you find yourself having to go back to a kanji, once you have written it, to make corrections or additions…

My guess is that you are asking your visual memory to do the work that belongs to imaginative memory. After LESSON 12, you will be given more leeway to create your own images and stories, so it is important that you nip this problem in the bud before going any further. A small step in the wrong direction on a journey of 2,200 kanji will land you in deep trouble in no time. Here are the steps you should be following each time you come to a new frame:

1. Read the key word and take note of the particular connotation that has been given it. There is only one such meaning, sometimes associated with a colloquial phrase, sometimes with one of the several meanings of the word, sometimes with a well-known cultural phenomenon. Think of that connotation and repeat it to yourself. When you're sure you've got the right one, carry on.

2. Read through the particular little story that goes with the key word and let the whole picture establish itself clearly.

3. Now close your eyes, focus on those images in the story that belong to the key word and primitive elements, and let go of the controls. It may take a few seconds, sometimes as long as a minute, but the picture will start to change on its own. The exaggerated focal points will start to take on a life of their own and enhance the image with your own particular experiences and memories. You will know your work is done when you have succeeded in creating a memorable image that is both succinct and complete, both faithful to the original story and yet your very own.

4. Open your eyes and repeat the key word and primitive elements, keeping that image in mind. This will clear away any of the fog, and at the same time make sure that when you let go you didn't let go of the original story, too.

5. In your mind, juxtapose the elements relative to one another in line with your image or the way they normally appear in the characters.

6. Take pencil and paper and write the character once, retelling the story as you go.

These are basically the same steps you were led through in reading the stories, even though they were not laid out so clearly before. If you think back to the kanji that "worked" best for you, you will find that each of these steps was accomplished perfectly. And if you look back at the ones you are forgetting, you should also be able to locate which step you skipped over. In reviewing, these same steps should be followed, with the only clue to set the imagination in motion being the key word.

If you find you are forgetting the relative position of the elements in a kanji…

Before all else, go back and reread the frame for that character to see if there were any helpful hints or explanatory notes. If not, return to the frame where the particular primitives were first introduced to see if there is any clue there. And if this is not the problem, then, taking care not to add any new words or focal points to your story (since they might end up being elements later on), rethink the story in such a way that the image for each element actually takes the position it has in the kanji itself. This should not happen often, but when it does, it is worth spending a few minutes to get things sorted out.

If you are confusing one kanji with another...

Take a careful look at the two stories. Perhaps you have made one or the other of them so vivid that it has attracted extraneous elements to itself that make the two kanji images fuse into one. Or again, it may be that you did not pay sufficient attention to the advice about clarifying a single connotation for the key word.

Whether or not you have had all or only a few of these problems, now is the time to review the first 10 lessons keeping an eye out for them. Put aside any schedule you may have set yourself until you have those lessons down perfectly, that is, until you can run through all 6 steps outlined above for every character, without a hitch. The most important thing in this review is not really to see whether you are remembering the characters, but to learn how to locate problems and deal with them.

One final note before you close the book and begin running your review. Everyone's imagination works differently. Each has its own gifts and its own defects. The more you pay attention to how you imagine things, the more likely you are to find out what works best for you—and more importantly, *why*. The one thing you must distrust, if the system outlined in this book is to work for you, is your ability to remember kanji just as they are, without doing any work on them. Once you start making exceptions for characters you "know" or "have no trouble with" or "don't need to run through all the steps with," you are headed for a frustration that will take you a great deal of trouble to dig yourself out of. In other words, if you start using the method only as a "crutch" to help you only with the kanji you have trouble with, you will quickly be limping along worse than ever. What we are offering here is not a crutch, but a different way to walk.

That said, let us pick up where we left off. In this lesson we turn from primitive elements having to do with plants to those having to do with animals, 4 of them in all.

---

250 portent

兆

Here we have a pictograph of the back of a turtle, the two sloping vertical strokes representing the central ridge and the four short strokes the pattern. Think of reading turtle shells as a way to foretell the future, and in particular things that **portend** coming evils. [6]

丿 丿 ㇉ 北 兆 兆

* When this character is used as a primitive in its full form, we keep the key-word sense of a *portent*. When it appears to the left in its abbreviated form (namely, the left half only, ㇉), we shall give it the pictographic sense of a *turtle*.

---

251 peach tree

桃

To associate the **peach tree** with the primitive for a *portent*, recall the famous Japanese legend of Momotarō, the **Peach** Boy. It begins once upon a time with a fisherman and his wife who wanted badly to have a child, but none was born to them. Then one day the old man caught a giant **peach**, out of which jumped a healthy young lad whom they named **Peach** Boy. Though the boy was destined to perform heroic deeds, his birth also *portended* great misfortune (how else could he become a hero?). Thus the *tree* that is associated with a *portent* of coming evil comes to be the **peach tree**. [10]

木 桃

---

252 stare

眺

To give someone the "evil *eye*" is to **stare** at them, wishing them evil. The roots of the superstition are old and almost universal throughout the cultures of the world. In this kanji, too, being stared at is depicted as an *eye* that *portends* evil. [11]

目 眺

| 253 | dog |

犬

We know that the kanji for *large* takes on the meaning of the *St. Bernard* **dog** when used as a primitive. In this frame we finally see why. The *drop* added as a fourth and final stroke means that we have to do with a normal-sized **dog**, which, compared to the *St. Bernard,* is no more than a *drop* in the kennel. [4]

一　ナ　大　犬

* As a primitive this character can take two meanings. In the form given here it will mean a very small dog (which we shall refer to as a *chihuahua* for convenience sake). When it takes the form 犭 to the left of a character, we shall give it the meaning of *a pack of wild dogs.*

| 254 | status quo |

状

Did you ever hear the legend of the *turtle* who fell madly in love with a *chihuahua* but could not have her because their two families did not like the idea of their children intermarrying? Like all classic stories of ill-fated love, this one shows how the young upset the **status quo** with an emotion older and more powerful than anything their elders have devised to counter it: blind love. [7]

｜　丬　丬　状

| 255 | silence |

黙

Oddly enough, the character for **silence** shows us a *black chihuahua.* Actually, the cute little critter's name is Darkness, as I am sure you remember from the famous song about **silence** that begins, "Hello, Darkness, my old friend...."

Note how the four dots reach all the way across the bottom of the character. [15]

里　默　黙

256 · sort of thing

然

The key word in this frame refers to a suffix that gives the word before it an adjectival quality; hence we refer to it as "**sort of thing.**" Reverting to the time when dog was more widely eaten than it is today (see FRAME 127), we see here a large cauldron boiling over an *oven flame* with the *flesh* of a *chihuahua* being thrown into the whole concoction to make it into a "hot-diggity, dog-diggity" **sort of thing.** [12]

丿　勹　夕　夕　夕　狄　然　然

257 · reed

荻

You've no doubt seen cattails, those swamp **reeds** with a furry *flower* to them like the tail of a cat. This might just turn out to be a good way to get rid of a troublesome *pack of wild dogs*: lure them into a swamp of these **reeds** with the cattail *flowers* and then set *fire* to the swamp. Take care to focus on the *flower* rather than the "cattail" to avoid confusion with FRAME 259 below. [10]

艹　艹　芍　芍　荻

258 · hunt

狩

One of the worst problems you have to face when you go **hunting** is to *guard* your take from the *wild dogs*. If you imagine yourself failing at the task, you will probably have a stronger image than if you try to picture yourself succeeding. [9]

丿　犭　犭　狩

259 · cat

猫

Knowing how much dogs love to chase **cats**, picture a *pack of wild dogs* planting "**cat**-*seedlings*," watering them, and fertilizing them until they can be harvested as a crop of **cats** for them to chase and torment. If you begin from the key word and think of a "crop of **cats**," you will not confuse this story with the apparently similar story of two frames ago. [11]

犭 猫

260

COW

牛

Can you see the "doodle" of a **cow** that has just been run over by a steamroller? The small dot in the first stroke shows its head turned to one side, and the next two strokes, the four legs. [4]

ノ ⺧ ⺦ 牛

* As a primitive, the same sense of *cow* is kept. Note only that when it is placed OVER another element, its tail is cut off, giving us ⺧. In this case, and when the element appears on the left, the stroke order is changed.

261

special

特

Despite the strong phonetic similarity, there will be no problem keeping the key word **special** distinct from the character we met earlier for *specialty* (FRAME 47), since the latter has immediate connotations lacking in this kanji.

Anyway, we shall let the key word of this frame refer to something in a **special** class all its own—like the sacred *cows* of India that wander freely without fear of being butchered and ground into hamburger. Even though the practice is originally a Hindu one, and in any case no longer followed among the majority of Japanese Buddhist monks, the Buddha's refusal to take the life of any sentient being makes it only fitting that the *cows* should be placed on the sacred grounds of a *Buddhist temple* in this kanji. [10]

ノ ⺧ ⺦ 牛 特

262

revelation

告

Folklore throughout the world tells us of talking animals who show a wisdom superior to that of human beings, and that same tradition has found its way into television shows and cartoons right into our own century. This character depicts **revelation** through the *mouth* of a *cow*, suggesting oracular utterances about truths hidden to human intelligence. [7]

ノ ⺊ ⺧ 牛 生 告

263   **before**

先 Take this key word in its physical, not its temporal, sense (even though it refers to both). If you have a *cow* with *human legs,* as the elements show us here, it can only be because you have two people in a *cow*-suit. I always thought I'd prefer to be the one standing **before,** rather than the one that holds up the rear and becomes the "butt" of everyone's laughter. [6]

ノ ⺊ ⺧ 生 牛 先

264   **wash**

洗 This character is so logical that one is tempted to let the elements speak for themselves: *water . . . before.* But we have already decided we will not allow such rationalism to creep into our stories. Not even this once.

Instead, let us change the character from the Peanuts comic strip called "Pigpen," who is always preceded by a little cloud of dust and grime, and rename him "**Wash**-Out." Everywhere he walks, a spray of *water* goes *before* him to sanitize everything he touches. [9]

氵 洗

Lesson 12

IN THIS THE final lesson of PART ONE we introduce the useful compound primitive for metals and the elements needed to form it, in addition to picking up a number of stray characters that have fallen by the wayside.

★

umbrella

The actual kanji on which this primitive meaning **umbrella** is based will not show up until FRAME 1103. Think of it as a large and brightly-colored beach **umbrella**. If you compare this with FRAME 8, you will notice how the two strokes touch here, while the kanji for *eight* would leave a gaping leak in the top. [2]

265

jammed in

The idea of something getting **jammed into** something else is depicted here by having a *walking stick* get **jammed into** an *umbrella* frame by someone shoving it into an already occupied slot in the *umbrella* stand at the door. First notice the vertical strokes: on the left is the curved umbrella handle, and on the right the straight *walking stick*. Now try to imagine the two parties tugging at their respective properties like two kids on a wishbone, creating a scene at the entrance of an elegant restaurant. [4]

266

界

world

As the **world** gets *jammed* with more and more people, there is less and less space. Imagine yourself taking an air flight over a **world** so densely populated that every bit of it is sectioned off like a gigantic checkerboard (the *rice fields*). If you look closely at the character, you should be able to see a kind of movement taking place as still more is being **jammed into** that already narrow space. [9]

田　界

267

茶

tea

As everyone knows, **tea** is made from **tea** leaves. But the **tea** plant itself has its own *flowers,* which can be quite beautiful and add a special flavor to the **tea**, as the Chinese found out already

over 4,598 years ago. With the image of a terrace of *flowering* **tea** bushes in mind, picture a number of brightly painted and very l-o-n-g *wooden poles* (FRAME 207) placed here and there in their midst, with a tiny *umbrella* at the top to shade the delicate-tasting **tea** *flowers*. [9]

艹　芡　芡　苯　荼　茶

---

268   spinal column

脊

The **spinal column** has sprouted out of the *flesh* of your back into an *umbrella* that you always have with you, rain or shine. The pair of 2s on each side are the "ribs" of the *umbrella*. Take care to keep your image of the key word distinct from that for spine (FRAME 24). [10]

 ＝　＝＝　夫　脊

---

*   meeting

仐

This compound primitive depicts a **meeting** as a massive gathering of people under *one umbrella*. The full kanji from which this derives will be introduced later in FRAME 814. The important thing here is to picture the scene just described and associate it with the word **meeting**. [3]

ノ　人　仐

---

269   fit

合

The kanji for **fit** reads literally, top to bottom, as a *meeting* of *mouths*—which is a rather descriptive way of speaking of a romantic kiss. We all know what happens when there is no meeting of minds and when people's ideas don't **fit** with one another. But this kanji invites us to imagine what happened to the romance of a certain unfortunate couple whose *mouths* didn't **fit**. [6]

 仐　合

| 270 | pagoda |

塔

On the left we see a mound of *dirt,* and to the right *flowers* made to *fit* together. The two sides combine to create a great **pagoda** made of *dirt,* with *flowers* by the tens of thousands *fitted* together for the roofing of each of the layers. Be sure to put yourself in the scene and *fit* a few of the *flowers* in place yourself so that the image works its way into memory with full force. [12]

扌 扩 塔

| 271 | king |

王

See what you can do to come up with a pictograph of a **king's** scepter here that suits your own idea of what it should look like. You might even begin with the basic element for *I beam* and then try to fit the remaining third stroke in. [4]

一 丁 千 王

* As a primitive, this can mean either *king* or *scepter,* but it will usually be taken to mean *ball,* as an abbreviation of the character in the next frame.

| 272 | jewel |

玉

Note the *drop* here in the king's *scepter,* which is exactly what you would expect it to be: a precious **jewel** handed down from of old as a symbol of his wealth and power. [5]

王 玉

* As a primitive, we can use this to mean either *jewel* or *ball.* When it appears anywhere other than on the left side of a kanji, it generally takes the same shape as here. On the left, it will be lacking the final stroke, making it the same as the character in the previous frame, 王.

---

273   treasure

宝

Every *house* has its **treasure**, as every thief knows only too well. While the things we **treasure** most are usually of sentimental value, we take the original sense of the term **treasure** here and make it refer to *jewels* kept in one's *house*. [8]

宀　宝

---

274   pearl

珠

Take care to keep the meaning of this kanji distinct from that for *jewel*. Think of the most enormous **pearl** you have ever seen, a great *vermilion*-colored *ball* sitting on your ring—and making it extremely difficult to move without falling over from the weight of the thing. [10]

王　珠

---

275   present

現

Do not think of a "gift" here, but of the **present** moment, as distinct from the future and the past. The kanji gives us a *ball* in which we see the **present**—obviously a crystal *ball* that enables us to *see* things going on at the **present** in faraway places. [11]

王　現

---

276   toy

玩

If, at some aboriginal level, **Toys Я Us**, then the archetypal *ball* must have been there at the *beginning*, before evolving into beach balls, ping-pong balls, rugby balls, and marbles. [8]

王　玩

---

277   lunatic

狂

A **lunatic** is literally one driven mad by the light of the moon, and the most famous of the "**looneys**" are the legendary lycanthropes or "wolfmen." Sometimes the transformation is only

a temporary phenomenon, sometimes it is permanent. In the latter case, the poor chap takes off on all fours to live with the beasts. To remember this kanji, imagine one of these lycanthropes going **looney** and setting himself up as *king* of a *pack of wild dogs* that roams about and terrorizes innocent suburban communities. [7]

犭　狂

---

278   effulgent

旺

The radiant, **effulgent** splendor of the *sun* makes it *king* of all the planets and other stars. Just to be sure you don't take this too abstractly, picture the *sun* seated on a throne, flourishing its *scepter* this way and that. [8]

日　旺

---

279   emperor

皇

An **emperor**, as we all know, is a ruler—something like a *king* but higher in status. The *white bird* perched above the *king*, elevating him to **imperial** heights, is the messenger he sends back and forth to the gods to request advice and special favors, something that *white birds* have long done in folklore throughout the world. [9]

白　皇

---

280   display

呈

The trick to remembering this character lies in associating the key word with the line from the nursery rhyme about 4 and 20 blackbirds baked in a pie: "Wasn't this a dainty dish to set before the *king*?" If we think of **display** in terms of that famous line, and the *king* with his head thrown back and his *mouth* wide open as 4 and 20 blackbirds fly in one after the other, we shall have satisfied both the elements and their position. [7]

281 全 whole

Wholeness suggests physical and spiritual health, "having your act together." The kanji-image for **wholeness** depicts being "*king under your own umbrella,*" that is, giving order to your own life. I know it sounds terribly abstract, but what could be more abstract than the word **whole**? [6]

人 全

282 栓 plug

Here we think of **plug** in the sense of a cork or stopper used to seal the mouth of a bottle, water faucet, or something with liquid running out of it. Forgetting the abstract picture of the former frame, let us work with all the primitive units: *tree . . . umbrella . . . ball.* Imagine a *tree* with a faucet in the side out of which tennis *balls* are flowing, bouncing all over the ground by the hundreds. You fight your way up to it and shove your giant beach *umbrella* into the *tree* to **plug** it up. [10]

木 栓

283 理 logic

We first referred to this character back in FRAME 185, to which you might want to return to have a peek. The image of **logic** we are given is something like a central *jewel* in a *computer,* like the *jewels* in old clocks that keep them running smoothly. Try to picture yourself making your way through all the RAMS and ROMS and approaching this shining *jewel,* a chorus of voices and a blast of trumpets in the background heralding the great seat of all-knowing **logic**. [11]

王 理

284 主 lord

"A man's home is his castle," goes the proverb from an age where it was the male who was **lord** of the household. Fundamentally, it means only that every one of us is a bit (or *drop*) of a *king* in

our own environment. As for the positioning of the elements, if you take care to "read off" the primitives in this way, you won't end up putting the *drop* down below, where it turns the kanji into a jewel. [5]

`　主

* As a primitive element, we set the key word aside entirely and take it as a pictograph of a solid brass *candlestick* (with the drop representing the flame at the top).

285

注

pour

Picture **pouring** *water* from a lighted *candlestick*. What could be more ridiculous, or simpler, as a way to recall this kanji? [8]

氵　注

286

柱

pillar

The **pillar** referred to here is the *wooden* beam that stands at the entrance to a traditional Japanese house. Carve it in imagination into the shape of a gigantic *candlestick* and your work is done. [9]

木　柱

287

金

gold

If this were not one of the most common characters you will ever have to write, I would apologize for having to give the explanation that follows. Anyway, we want to depict bars of **gold** bullion with an *umbrella* overhead to shade them from the heat (and perhaps to hide them as well). The bullion is made by melting down all the *scepters* of the kingdom, *drop* by *drop*, and shaping them into bars. [8]

丿　入　스　슷　全　全　金　金

* As a primitive, it means not only *gold* but any *metal* at all.

---

288   **pig iron**

銑

Pig iron refers to iron in the crude form in which it emerges from the smelting furnaces. Of all the various forms *metal* can take, this one shows us metal *before* it has been refined. Imagine two photographs labeled *"before"* and *"after"* to show the process. [14]

金   銑

---

289   **bowl**

鉢

Let **bowl** suggest a large and heavy *golden* **bowl** into which you are throwing all the *books* you own to mash them into pulp, for some outrageous reason you will have to think up yourself. [13]

金   鉢

---

290   **copper**

銅

Picture an order of *monks* serving as chaplains for the police force. Their special habit, made of protective *metal,* is distinguished by a row of **copper** buttons just like the "**cops**" they serve. [14]

金   銅

---

291   **angling**

釣

The character we learned for *fishing* (FRAME 184) refers to the professional, net-casting industry, while the **angling** of this character refers to the sport. The odd thing is that your **angling** rod is a *golden ladle* which you are using to scoop *gold*fish out of a river. [11]

金   釣

292	needle

針

In FRAME 10 we referred ahead to this full character from which the primitive for *needle* (on the right) derives. Since we already expect that **needles** are made of *metal,* let us picture a set of solid *gold* darning *needles* to complete the kanji. [10]

金　針

293	inscription

銘

Take **inscription** in the sense of the *name* you ask the jeweler to carve on a *gold* bracelet or inside a *gold* ring to identify its owner or communicate some sentimental message. It will help if you can recall the first time you had this done and the feelings you had at the time. [14]

金　銘

294	tranquilize

鎮

The first lie-detector machines of the twentieth century worked by wiring pieces of *metal* to the body to measure the amount of sweat produced when questions were asked. It was discovered that nervousness produced more sweat, indicating subconscious reactions when the *truth* was getting too close for comfort. Nowadays, people can take drugs that **tranquilize** them in such a way as to neutralize the effect of the device, which is why other means have had to be developed. [18]

金　鎮

With that, we come to the end of Part One. Before going on to Part Two, it would be a good idea to return now to the Introduction and read it once again. The explanation of the method we are following here and the rationale behind it should make more sense now.

By this time, too, you should be familiar with the use of all four of the

Indexes. If not, take a few minutes to go through them one by one, reading the introduction to each and taking note of how they are arranged. As the number of characters you have learned increases, you will find them useful in navigating your way back to kanji or primitive elements that need reviewing in their original context.

Plots

Lesson 13

BY THIS TIME, if you have been following along methodically frame by frame, you may find yourself growing impatient at the thought of having to read through more than 2,000 of these little stories. You probably want to move at a quicker pace and in your own way. Take heart, for that is precisely what we are going to start doing in Part Two. But if you happen to be one of those people who are perfectly content to have someone else do all the work for them, then brace yourself for the task that lies ahead.

We begin the weaning process by abbreviating the stories into simple plots, leaving it up to you to patch together the necessary details in a manner similar to what we did in Part One. As mentioned in the Introduction, the purpose of the longer stories was to impress on you the importance of recreating a complete picture in imagination, and to insure that you did not merely try to associate words with *other words* but with *images*. The same holds true for the kanji that remain.

Before setting out on our way again, a word of caution is in order. Left to its own, your imagination will automatically tend to add elements and see connections that could prove counterproductive in the long run. For example, you might think it perfectly innocent and admissible to alter the primitive for *old* to *old man*, or that for *cliff* to *cave*. In fact, these changes would be confusing when you meet the kanji and primitives with those meanings later on. You would return to the earlier kanji and find that everything had become one great confusion.

You may have experienced this problem already when you decided to alter a story to suit your own associations. That should help you appreciate how hard it is to wipe out a story once you have learned it, particularly a vivid one. To protect yourself against this, stick faithfully to the key words as they are given, and try not to move beyond the range of primitive meanings listed. Where such confusion can be anticipated, a longer story will be presented as a protective measure, but you will have to take care of the rest.

We start out Part Two with a group of 26 characters having to do with travel, and the primitives that accompany them: a *road*, a pair of *walking legs*, and a *car*.

⋆

辶

road

The **road** envisioned here is a road for traffic, or a path or walk-way. The natural sweep of these three simple strokes should be easy to remember, as it appears so often. [3]

丶　　氵　　辶

295

道

road-way

The key word carries both the sense of a **road** for transit and a **way** or method of doing something, but the former is better for forming an image. The primitives read: the *neck* of a *road*. Think of a crowded **road-way** where traffic has come to a standstill—what we commonly refer to as a "bottle*neck*." [12]

首　　首　　道　　道

296

導

guidance

When we accept someone's **guidance**, we permit ourselves to be *glued* to a certain *road* or *way* of doing something, and try to "stick" to it. [15]

道　　導

297

辻

crossing

Take the first two strokes in the sense we gave them back in FRAME 10, as the pictograph of a *cross*, and set it on a *road* to create a "**crossing**." [5]

十　　辻

298

迅

swift

Here we see a *crossing* in the form of a barbed *fishhook*, sug-gesting a **swifter** alternate not only to the roundabouts used in Europe but also to the "cloverleaf" design used on superhigh-ways in the United States. [6]

乁 乁 凡 迅

299

造

create

Think of **creating** as making something out of nothing. Then recall how the *way* of *revelation* laid out in the Bible begins with the story of how God **created** the world out of a dark and chaotic nothingness. [10]

告 造

300

迫

urge

To **urge** someone to do something, you make the *way* as appealing as possible, perhaps even *white*washing it a bit. [8]

白 迫

301

逃

escape

When **escaping** from something or someone, one always feels as if one is not going fast enough, like a *turtle* on an expressway. (Since the *turtle* is on the *road* and not on the left, it can keep its full kanji shape as given in FRAME 250.) [9]

兆 逃

302

辺

environs

To keep the **environs** clean and safe, you could cement *daggers* in the *road*, blades pointed upwards, so that no polluting traffic could pass by. You could, if you were an ecologically minded terrorist. [5]

刀 辺

303

巡

patrol

A virtual *flood* of motorcycle police washing down a *road* is this kanji's image for a **patrol**. [6]

〈　　《　　巛　　巡

304　　　　　　　　　　　　　　　　　　　　　　　　**car**

車　You may keep the whole range of connotations for this key
word, **car**, provided it does not interfere with the pictograph.
Look for the front and back wheels (the first and last horizontal
strokes) and the seat in the carriage in the middle. As an exercise, try to isolate the primitives on your own and make a story
out of them. [7]

一　厂　冂　冃　冐　亘　車

* *Car, cart, wagon,* and *vehicle* may all be used as primitive
meanings.

305　　　　　　　　　　　　　　　　　　　　　　　**take along**

連　What you are meant to **take along** in this kanji are not things
but people. The image of the *car* on the *road* should ground
your image for picking up your friends to *take* them *along* to
wherever you are going. [10]

車　連

306　　　　　　　　　　　　　　　　　　　　　　　　**rut**

軌　Combine the primary and secondary meanings of this key word
to form your story. Begin with the *car* whose tires get caught in
a **rut** and spin without going anywhere. Then go on to the *baseball team* who can't win a game because it has fallen into a **rut**
of losing. [9]

車　軌

307　　　　　　　　　　　　　　　　　　　　　　　**transport**

輸　On the left we see a *vehicle* used for **transport**. On the right,
we see a new tangle of elements that need sorting out. The first
three strokes, you will remember, are the primitive for *meeting.*
Below it we see the elements for *flesh* and *saber,* which com-

bine to create a compound element for a *butcher* and his trade. Together they give us the image of a "truckers' convoy." [16]

車　軯　軨　輸

308　　　　　　　　　　　　　　　　　　　　metaphor

喻

People who try to sound literary often end up sounding like so much noisy racket. They open their *mouth* and out rolls a whole *trucker's convoy* of **metaphors**. [12]

口　喻

309　　　　　　　　　　　　　　　　　　　　in front

前

We waited to introduce this character until now, even though we had all the elements, because it helps to reinforce the odd kanji of the last frame. Picture the *butcher* hacking away with his knife at a slab of meat on his table with a pair of ram's *horns* placed **in front** of him (or on his head, if you prefer).

There is no need to worry about confusing this kanji with that for *before* (FRAME 263), since it will not appear as a primitive in any other character used in this book. [9]

丶　䒑　䒑　苜　前

310　　　　　　　　　　　　　　　　　　　　roast

煎

Think of **roasting** the guest of honor at a party—literally, in *front* of an *oven-fire*. [13]

前　煎

---

*　　　　　　　　　　　　　　　　　　　　walking legs

夂

We call this element **walking legs** because it indicates "legs in motion," whether you want to think of them as jogging or walking in long strides, as the shape seems to suggest. Be careful how you write it, with the first two strokes like a stylized "7." [3]

丿　勹　夂

311 — each

各

"Suum cuique" goes the popular Latin proverb. A certain disease of the English language makes it almost impossible to translate the phrase without gender bias. In any event, here we see someone walking with his/her *mouth* between his/her *walking legs*, giving us an image of "To **each** his/her own." [6]

ノ ク 夂 冬 各 各

* The sense of the proverb should help when using this kanji as a primitive; otherwise, reduce it to its original elements. But do not associate it in any way with the word "every," which we shall meet later in another context.

312 — status

格

If you see *trees* as **status** symbols (as they might be for those living in Japan's congested cities, where greenery has become something of a luxury item), then *each* might be aiming to have his/her own *tree*, just to keep up with the Suzukis. [10]

木 格

313 — graft

賂

To those who believe in the inevitability of **graft** in government, everything has a price—or as this character has it, to *each* office its outlay of *shells*. [13]

貝 賂

314 — abbreviation

略

Each field has its own **abbreviations** (chemistry, philosophy, sports, etc.). Needless to say, the "stronger" primitive—that is to say, the simpler and more often used one—takes the dominant position on the left, even though the story would read them off the other way around. [11]

田 略

315

guest

客

When you are a **guest** in a courteous town, *each house*hold has its own way of welcoming you, and *each house* becomes your home. [9]

宀 客

316

forehead

額

As Miss Manners will be the first to tell you, out of respect, one does not look straight into the eyes of one's *guests*, but focus on the top button of their collar. Here, however, you are told to look above the eyes to the **forehead** of your *guest*. [18]

客 額

317

summer

夏

In the **summer**, fatigued by the heat, your *head* hangs down nearly as far as your *walking legs*, or rather, your "dragging legs." Note how the *walking legs* (instead of "animal legs") are the only thing that distinguishes this character from that for *page* (FRAME 64). [10]

一 丆 百 夏

318

dispose

処

Both the stretching out of the *walking legs* and the little bit of *wind* tucked in on the right suggest using one's legs to kick something out of the way, or **dispose** of it. [5]

丿 夕 夂 処 処

319

twig

条

Geppetto made *walking legs* for his little Pinocchio from two **twigs** of a *tree*, giving him a set of "**twiggy**" shanks. [7]

丿 夕 夂 冬 条 条 条

---

320   **fall**

落   When *water* **falls**, it splishes and splashes; when *flower* petals fall, they float gently in the breeze. To *each* thing its own way of **falling**. [12]

艹　氵　落

Lesson 14

WE MAY NOW GO a step further in our streamlining, this time in the stroke order of the kanji. From here on in, only the order in which the composite primitive elements are written will be indicated; if you are not sure of the writing of any of the particulars in a given character, you will have to hunt it down yourself. Index II should help. New primitives and unusual writings will be spelled out as before, however. At any rate, you should ALWAYS count the strokes of the character when you learn it, and check your results against the number given in square brackets in each frame.

The next group of primitives, around which this lesson is designed, have to do with lids and headgear.

---

*   **crown**

⌐   This pictograph of a simple **crown** is distinguished from the *roof* only by the absence of the chimney (the first *drop* at the top). It can be used for all the principal connotations of the word **crown**. We will meet the full character from which this element is derived later on, in FRAME 326. [2]

／　⌐

---

321   **superfluous**

冗   Picture a *weather vane* beneath a regal *crown*, spinning round and round. It is not only **superfluous** but makes a perfect ass out of the one who wears it. [4]

冖 冗

---

322   Hades

冥

The key word in this frame refers to the underworld, the world of the dead. By way of the classic Greek association, it is also used for the "dwarf planet" Pluto. Since no one knows precisely when this part of the cosmos was finished, we may imagine it as the *crowning* deed of *day six* of the creation. [10]

冖 冝 冥

---

323   army

軍

The *crowned vehicle* depicted here is a "chariot," symbol of an **army**. [9]

冖 軍

* Used as a primitive this kanji means only *chariot*.

---

324   radiance

輝

Take advantage of the first syllable of the key word to think of the *ray* of light to the left. Now add the glittering *chariot* that is emitting those *rays* and you have **radiance**. [15]

光 輝

---

325   carry

運

A row of "sweet" *chariots* "swinging low" to our *roads* is a sure sign that the Lord is "comin' for to **carry**" someone home. [12]

軍 運

---

326   crown

冠

By having the **crown** pass from one age to the next, a people keeps itself *glued* to its *beginnings*. [9]

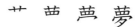

327   dream

夢

To have a **dream** after going to bed is really the *crown* to a perfect *evening*. The *flower* petals over the *eyes* (instead of the "sand" that Westerners are used to finding there when they awake in the morning) only confirms the image of a pleasant **dream** suggested by the rest of this rather complex kanji. [13]

艹　茈　萝　夢

＊   top hat

⊥

The broad rim and tall top of the **top hat** is pictured graphically here in these two simple strokes.

At this point, by the way, you can revert back to FRAME 6. If you have had any trouble with that character, you now have the requisite elements to make a story: **Six** suggests the number of an ant's *legs*; just set a tall silk *top hat* on the crawling creature and you have your character. [2]

ノ　⊥

＊   whirlwind

兀

A formal high silk *top hat* resting atop a *weather vane* represents a **whirlwind**. To keep it distinct from the primitive for *wind*, try to picture the vortex, or tornado-like spinning movement, of a **whirlwind**. The next frame should help. [4]

ノ　ニ　兀

---

328   pit

坑

A *whirlwind* begins to dig its way into the *soil* like a drill until it makes a deep **pit**. [7]

扌　坑

| 329 | tall |

高

Recalling an image from FRAME 195, first see the *mouth* under the extraterrestrial's glass *hood*, and then the *mouth* under the *top hat* of one of his mates who has tried on the strange earthling's headgear only to find that it makes him look much, much **taller** than everyone else. [10]

亠　高　高

* As a primitive, this character keeps its sense of *tall* and its position at the top of other primitives, but its writing is abbreviated to the first 5 strokes: 亠.

| 330 | receive |

享

Tall children **receive** more attention. *Tall children* grow up to make better wide **receivers**. Take your pick, depending on whether you prefer child psychology or American football. At any rate, be sure you have some particular *tall child* in mind, someone who really was outstanding and always attracting attention, because he or she will come in handy in the next two frames. [8]

亠　享

| 331 | cram school |

塾

Cram schools are after-hours educational institutions where kids can do concentrated preparing for their coming entrance examinations or drill what they missed during regular class hours. The exceptions are the *tall children* who are out on the school *grounds* practicing sports, and the *fat* ones who are out there burning off calories. So this character depicts those who do NOT go to the **cram schools**, rather than those who do. [14]

享　孰　塾

332

熟

mellow

The *tall* and *fat children* from the last frame are here cast into a cauldron over an *oven flame* until they have sufficiently **mellowed** that they can return to the normal life of a student. [15]

享 孰 熟

333

亭

pavilion

Think of all the **pavilions** at County Fairs or World Expos you have wandered into or seen advertised in the media, and you will no doubt see rising up among them the towering *tall crowned nail* (the *crown* being a revolving restaurant)—that architectural monstrosity that has become a symbol of science and technology at such events. [9]

古 亭 亭

334

京

capital

When we think of a **capital** city today we think of *tall* skyscrapers dwarfing the endless swarms of *little* folk scurrying here and there about their business. [8]

古 京

335

涼

refreshing

Since few things are as **refreshing** on a warm day as a cool shower (the *water*), here we picture an entire *capital* city treating itself to one, and in full view of everyone. [11]

氵 涼

336

景

scenery

Scenery is depicted as a *sun* rising over a *capital* city, which is a bit of natural **scenery** the city dwellers themselves rarely get to see! [12]

曰　景

337 鯨 — whale

The **whale** swallows a whole school of fish, who turn their new abode into a proper little *fish-capital*. [19]

魚　鯨

* 吉 — lidded crock

Soil over the *mouth* of a container gives us a piece of clay pottery with its lid. Behold the **lidded crock**. [6]

土　吉

338 舍 — cottage

A *lidded crock* with an *umbrella* overhead gives us a mixture of the modern and the nostalgic in this design for a **cottage**. [8]

ハ　舍

339 周 — circumference

Look more closely at your *lidded crock* and you will see little ruler marks along its bottom edge. This is so you can use it to calculate the **circumference** of your *motorcycle helmet*: just begin at a fixed point and turn the *lidded crock* around and around, keeping it flush against the side of the *helmet*, until you come back to your starting point. If you kept track of how many turns and part-turns your *lidded crock* made, you now know the **circumference**. [8]

丿　冂　冃　周

* As a primitive, this character can take the added significance of a *lap*.

340　　　　　　　　　　　　　　　　　　　　　　　　**week**

週

Picture a circular *road* with 7 markers on it, one for each day of the **week**. When you have walked one complete *lap* on this *road*, you shall have completed one **week**. [11]

周　週

341　　　　　　　　　　　　　　　　　　　　　　**gentleman**

士

The shape of this kanji, slightly differing from that for *soil* by virtue of its shorter final stroke, hints at a broad-shouldered, slender-waisted warrior standing at attention. When feudalism collapsed, these warriors became Japan's **gentlemen**. [3]

一　十　士

* The primitive meaning reverts to the more colorful image of the *samurai*, Japan's warrior class.

342　　　　　　　　　　　　　　　　　　　　　　**good luck**

吉

Here we see a *samurai* standing on a street with an open *mouth*, which people walk up to and look down deep inside of for **good luck**. [6]

士　吉

* As a primitive, we shall take this shape to mean an *aerosol can*, from the *mouth* and the very tightly-fitting *lid* (note how it differs here from the *lidded crock*).

343　　　　　　　　　　　　　　　　　　　　　　　**robust**

壮

Robust is seen as a *turtle* turned *samurai*. [6]

丬　壮

344	villa

荘

The **villa** pictured here is filled with exotic *flowers* at every turn, and has a pair of *turtle-samurai* standing before its gates. [9]

艹　犷　荘

345	sell

売

A *samurai*, out of a job, is going door-to-door **selling** little windup *crowns* with *human legs* that run around on the floor looking like headless monarchs. [7]

士　声　売

Lesson 15

IN THIS LESSON WE consider a group of primitives associated one way or another with schooling. Be sure to give your stories enough time to come to life in imagination, because your images will need a lot more vividness than these brief "plots" allow for. You know that you are NOT giving enough time when you find yourself memorizing definitions rather than playing with images.

★	schoolhouse

丷丷

Here we see a little red **schoolhouse** with the 3 dots on the roof. As you write it in the following frames, you should acquire a "feel" for the way the first two short strokes move left to right, and the third one right to left. Write it twice now, saying to yourself the first time as you write the first 3 strokes, "In the **schoolhouse** we learn our A-B-Cs," and the second time, "In the **schoolhouse** we learn our 1-2-3s." [5]

丶　丷　丷　丷　丷丷

346   study

学

The *child* in the little red *schoolhouse* is there for one reason only: to **study**. Anyone who has gone through the schooling system knows well enough that **study** is one thing and *learning* quite another again. In the kanji, too, the character for *learning* (FRAME 616) has nothing to do with the *schoolhouse*. [8]

⺌ 学

347   memorize

覚

The idea of **memorizing** things is easily related to the *schoolhouse;* and since we have been at it for more than a hundred pages in this book, the idea that **memorizing** involves *seeing* things that are not really there should make it easy to put the two elements together. [12]

⺌ 覚

348   flourish

栄

The botanical connotations of the word **flourish** (to bud and burst into bloom, much as a *tree* does) are part of the ideal of the *schoolhouse* as well. [9]

⺌ 栄

*   brush

聿

This primitive element, not itself a kanji, is a pictograph of a writing **brush**. Let the first 3 strokes represent the hairs at the tip of the **brush**, and the following two strokes the thumb and forefinger that guide it when you write. Note how the long vertical stroke, cutting through everything, is drawn last. This is standard procedure when you have such a stroke running the length of a character. However, as we saw in the case of *cow*, when this primitive appears on top of another primitive, its "tail" is cut off, giving us ⺻. [6]

フ ヲ ヨ ヨ 亖 聿

349	write
書	The sage talks rapidly with his *tongue wagging in his mouth*, while the *brush* of the scribe runs apace to **write** down the master's words. [10]

ㄱ ㄱ ㅋ ㅋ ㅋ ㅌ 聿 書

350	haven
津	Seeing the tiny boats of poor mortals tossed about in a stormy sea like so many corks, the All-Merciful took its *brush* and drew little inlets of *water* where the hapless creatures might seek shelter. And so it is that we have **havens**. [9]

氵 津

*	taskmaster
夂	First find the long rod (the first stroke), held in the hand of someone seated (the next 3 strokes, not unlike the pictograph for *woman*, but quite different from that for *walking legs* introduced in LESSON 13). The only thing left to do is conjure up the memory of some **taskmaster** (or taskmistress) from your past whom you will "never forget." [4]

丿 ㇏ ㇇ 夂

351	breed
牧	When it is time to **breed** new cattle, the bull is usually willing but the *cow* is often not. Thus the *taskmaster* to the right forces the *cow* into a compromising position, so to speak, so that she and her mate can **breed**. [8]

牛 牧

352	aggression
攻	The special *craft* of successful *taskmasters* is their ability to remain constantly on the **aggressive**, never allowing their underlings a moment to ponder a counter-**aggression**. [7]

工　攻

353　　　　　　　　　　　　　　　　　　　　　　**failure**

敗　The *taskmaster* is acknowledging the **failure** of a *clam* to make the grade in some marine school or other. [11]

貝　敗

354　　　　　　　　　　　　　　　　　　　　　**a sheet of**

枚　English counts thin, flat objects, like bed linen and paper, in **sheets**. The kanji does this with a *taskmaster* whipping a *tree* into producing **sheets** against its will. [8]

木　枚

355　　　　　　　　　　　　　　　　　　　**happenstance**

故　Call it fate or providence or plain old Lady Luck, **happenstance** is the *oldest taskmaster* we know. It nearly always has its way. [9]

古　故

356　　　　　　　　　　　　　　　　　　　　　　　**awe**

敬　Standing in **awe** of someone, you get self-conscious and may try to speak in *flowery phrases* out of veneration or fear. The *taskmaster* at the right is drilling you in the practice of your "honorifics." [12]

艹　苟　敬

357　　　　　　　　　　　　　　　　　　　　　　　**say**

言　Of all the things we can do with our *mouth*, speech requires the greatest distinctness and clarity. Hence the kanji for **say** has four little sound-waves, to show the complexity of the task. [7]

丶　亠　≛　言　言　言　言

* This kanji, which appears often as a primitive, can mean *saying*, *speech*, or *words*, depending on which is most useful.

358

admonish

警

Here you have a perfect example of how an apparently impossible snarl of strokes becomes a snap to learn once you know its elements. The idea of being **admonished** for something already sets up a superior-inferior relationship between you and the person you are supposed to stand in *awe* of. While you are restricted to answering in honorifics, the superior can use straightforward and ordinary *words*. [19]

敬 警

359

plot

計

Words and a meter's *needle* combine to form the sense of **plot**: to talk over plans and to calculate a course of action. [9]

言 計

360

elucidate

詮

Think of **elucidating** as presenting something in *whole words*, as distinct from broken, fragmented sentences. [13]

言 詮

361

prison

獄

Although we did not make note of it at the time, the kanji for *dog* is also a low-grade term for a spy. And later (FRAME 1517) we will meet another association of criminals with *dogs*. The **prison** here depicts a *pack of wild dogs* (the long-timers and hardened criminals) into which the poor little *chihuahua* (first-offender) has been cast. The only thing he has to protect himself against the pack are his shrill and frightened *words*. [14]

犭 犸 獄

362	revise

訂
After completing the first draft, you **revise** it by *nailing* down your *words* and "hammering" them into shape. [9]

言　訂

363	obituary

訃
The *words* of this **obituary** work like a *magic wand*, conjuring up the deceased. [9]

言　訃

364	chastise

討
Words spoken to **chastise** us stick to us like *glue* in a way no other *words* can. [10]

言　討

365	instruction

訓
The personalism connoted by the word **instruction**, as opposed to "teaching" or "discipline," suits the picture here of *words* guiding one's progress like the gentle flowing of a *stream*. Even the etymology of the word **instruction** suggests the sense of "pouring into". [10]

言　訓

366	imperial edict

詔
The **imperial edict**, spoken with the force of unquestionable law, is made up of *words* intended to *seduce* the masses—be it through fear or respect—to follow obediently. [12]

言　詔

---

367   packed

詰

A piece of writing that is pregnant with meaning and needs to be reread several times to be understood we refer to colloquially as "**packed**." The character sees the *words* as sealed tightly inside an *aerosol can*. [13]

言　詰

---

368   tale

話

That the *words* of the *tongue* should come to mean a **tale** is clear from the etymology: a *tale* is something "talked," not something read from a book. [13]

言　話

---

369   recitation

詠

Listening to the *words* of poets **reciting** their poetry is like being transported for a moment into *eternity* where the rules of everyday life have been suspended. [12]

言　詠

---

370   poem

詩

Since silence is treasured so highly at a *Buddhist temple* the *words* spoken there must be well chosen. Perhaps this is why the records of the monks often read to us like **poems**. Before going on, back up a frame and make sure you have kept **poem** and *recitation* distinct in your mind. [13]

言　詩

---

371   word

語

Whereas the character for *say* focused on the actual talking, the kanji for **words** stresses the fact that although it is *I* who *say* them, the **words** of a language are not my own. You can see the clear distinction between *I* and **words** just by looking at the kanji. [14]

言 語

372

読

read

In the age of advertising, most *words* we **read** are out to *sell* some product or point of view. [14]

言 読

373

調

tune

A complete **tune** is composed not only of a succession of notes but also of one *lap* of the *words* that go with it. [15]

言 調

374

談

discuss

In almost every attempt to **discuss** an issue, the fervor of one's convictions comes to the surface and creates an *inflammation* of *words* (if you will, the "cuss" in **discuss**). [15]

言 談

375

諾

consent

The *words* of the *young* do not have legal validity unless backed up by "parental **consent**." [15]

言 諾

376

諭

rebuke

The stern tone of a **rebuke** is seen here in the image of *words* spoken at a *meeting* of *butchers* (see FRAME 307) waving their choppers at one another and "cutting one another down" as only *butchers* can. [16]

言 諭

Lesson 16

IN THIS SHORT lesson of 19 characters we come to an interesting cluster of primitive elements—unique among all those we have met or will meet throughout this book—built up step by step from one element. Be sure to study this lesson as a unit in order to appreciate the similarities and differences of the various elements, which will appear frequently later on.

---

* **arrow**

Here we see a pictograph of a long and slightly warped **arrow**. By extending the short final stroke in both directions, you should see the **arrow**head without any difficulty. The hook at the bottom represents the feathers at the butt end. When it serves as a semi-enclosure for other primitives, the first stroke is drawn longer, as we shall see in the following frames. [3]

---

377 **style**

式

Take **style** in its sense of some fashion design or model. Then let the element *arrow* and *craft* stand for the well-known **style** of shirts known as "*Arrow* shirts" because of the little *arrow* sewn on each one. [6]

一　工　式

---

378 **test**

試

When a manufacturer produces a new *style* for the market, the first thing that is done is to run a **test** on consumers, asking them to *speak* their opinions frankly about the product. Never mind the anachronism (the kanji was there well before our capitalistic market system) if it helps you remember. [13]

---

quiver

*

弐

This primitive is easy to remember as depicting something used to bring all one's *arrows* together into *one* handy place: the **quiver**. [4]

一 二 弌 弋

379

II (two)

弐

We use the Roman numeral II here to stress that this kanji is an older form of the kanji for *two*. Think of *two* arrows in a *quiver*, standing up like the numeral II. [6]

一 二 三 弎 弐 弐

---

fiesta

*

戈

The picture in this primitive is what we may call a "tassled *arrow*." A decorative tassle is strung on the shaft of an *arrow* to indicate that it is no longer a weapon but a symbol of a **fiesta**. As before, the first stroke is extended when it serves as a semi-enclosure. [4]

一 弌 戈 戈

380

range

域

From its original meaning of a defined area or zone, a **range** has also come to mean a grazing *land* where cowboys roam and do whatever it is they do with cows. When the herds have all been driven to market, there is a great homecoming *fiesta* like that pictured here. As soon as the cowboys come home, home on the **range**, the first thing they do is kiss the ground (the *mouth* on the *floor*), and then get on with the *fiesta*. [11]

扌 圹 垃 垳 域

| 381 | burglar |

賊

From a **burglar's** point of view, a *fiesta* is an occasion to take out the old lockpicking *needle* and break into the unattended safe filled with the family *shells* (the old form of money, as we saw in FRAMES 84 and 206). [13]

貝　貯　貯　賊

| ✷ | Thanksgiving |

戈

I choose the word **Thanksgiving** as only one possible way of making this primitive more concrete. The sense, as its composite primitives make clear, is of a "*land fiesta*," or a harvest feast. If you choose a word of your own, make sure it does not conflict with *fiesta*. [6]

一　十　土　圡　圥　戈

| 382 | plantation |

栽

On a fruit **plantation** it is the *trees* that one is particularly grateful for at the time of *Thanksgiving*. Imagine yourself inviting a few representative *trees* from the fields and orchards to join you around the table to give thanks. [10]

土　未　栽

| 383 | load |

載

One **loads** bales on a wagon or *cart* in preparation for the great Hay Ride that follows the *Thanksgiving* dinner each year. [13]

土　車　載

| ✷ | parade |

戌

Note first the order of the writing. The first stroke, added to *fiesta*, gives us a full-fledged enclosure, because of which we should always think of this as a **parade of** something or other, namely whatever is inside the enclosure. [5]

丿 厂 厈 戊 戊

384

overgrown

茂

The sense of the key word **overgrown** is of something grow-ing luxuriously, though not necessarily in excess—in this case a whole *parade* of weeds (outcast *flowers*). By way of exception, the *flowers* take their normal place over the enclosure. [8]

艹 茂

385

relatives

戚

If you think of a *parade* of particularly disagreeable **relatives**, it should not be hard to imagine them as large bodies with *little pea-brains above*. [11]

丿 厂 戶 戶 戚

386

turn into

成

Let the phrase "**turn into**" suggest some sort of a magical change. What happens here is that the *parade* marching down main street **turns into** a *dagger*-throwing bout between competing bands. Note how only one stroke has to be added to make the change. [6]

丿 厂 厉 成 成 成

387

castle

城

In this frame, we see a mound of *dirt* that is being *turned into* a **castle** (the way you may have done as a child playing on the beach). [9]

土 城

388   sincerity

誠

The sure sign of **sincerity** is that one's mere *words* are *turned into* deeds. [13]

言　誠

*   march

戌

As distinct from the *parade*, the **march** points to a formal demonstration, whose emotions are generally a far cry from the happy spirit of the *parade*. The inclusion of the *one* gives the sense of the singlemindedness and unity of the group joined in the **march**. As was the case with *parade*, the primitive inside the enclosure indicates who or what is **marching**. [6]

丿　厂　厂　兂　戌　戌

389   intimidate

威

Here we see a *march* of *women* demonstrating on behalf of equal rights, something extremely **intimidating** to the male chauvinist population. [9]

厂　反　威

390   destroy

滅

Picture a *march* of *flames* demonstrating against the Fire Department for their right to **destroy**, but being doused with *water* by the police riot squads. [13]

氵　氵　沪　泝　滅

391   dwindle

滅

A group of unquenchable *mouths* sets out on a *march* across the country, drinking *water* wherever they can find it until the *water* supply has **dwindled** to a trickle, triggering a national disaster. [12]

氵 氵 沪 减

---

392   revile

蔑

The verbal abuse involved in **reviling** those who do not deserve it can be compared to a *march of flowers* in full boom having an *eyeball* of nastiness cast over them (literally, of course).[14]

艹 苩 蔑

---

*   float

戋

The **floats** that are such an important part of a *fiesta* are shown here by the addition of the two extra horizontal strokes, which you may take as a quasi-pictographic representation of the platform structure of a **float**. [6]

一 二 三 𡶡 戋 戋

---

393   scaffold

桟

Prior to the use of metal, *trees* were once cut down and bound together for use as **scaffolding** material. In the case of the kanji shown here, what is being constructed is not a skyscraper but a simple *float*. [10]

木 桟

---

394   coin

銭

Those special *gold*-colored tokens minted each year for the Mardi Gras and thrown into the crowds from people on the *floats* give us the kanji for **coins**. [14]

金 銭

---

395   shallow

浅

An entourage of *floats* going from one town to the next must always seek a **shallow** place to cross the *water*. Try to picture what happens if they don't. [9]

氵 浅

Lesson 17

BECAUSE OF THE rather special character of that last group of primitives (7 in all), it might be a good idea not to rush too quickly into this lesson until you are sure you have them all learned and fitted out with good images. Now we will take up another set of primitives built up from a common base, though fewer in number and lacking the similarity of meaning we saw in the last lesson.

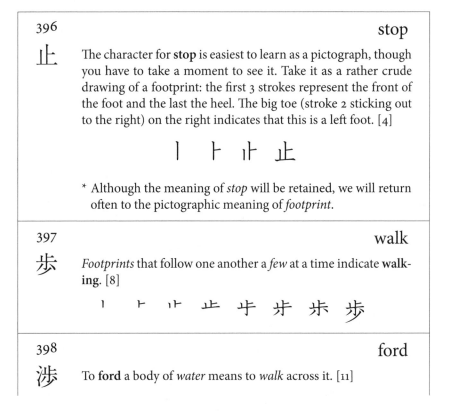

| 396 | stop |

止

The character for **stop** is easiest to learn as a pictograph, though you have to take a moment to see it. Take it as a rather crude drawing of a footprint: the first 3 strokes represent the front of the foot and the last the heel. The big toe (stroke 2 sticking out to the right) on the right indicates that this is a left foot. [4]

丨　卜　止　止

* Although the meaning of *stop* will be retained, we will return often to the pictographic meaning of *footprint*.

| 397 | walk |

步

Footprints that follow one another a *few* at a time indicate **walk-ing**. [8]

丿　卜　止　止　牛　步　步　步

| 398 | ford |

涉

To **ford** a body of *water* means to *walk* across it. [11]

氵 氵 涉

399

repeatedly

頻

The image of something occurring **repeatedly**, over and over again, is of having one's *head walked* on. [17]

步 頻

400

agreement

肯

Seeing *footprints* on someone's *flesh* indicates a rather brutal way of having secured that person's **agreement**. [8]

止 肯

401

undertake

企

To **undertake** a project is to take some idea floating in the air and *stop* it so that it can be brought down to earth and become a reality. Here we see some **undertaking** made to *stop* under a beach *umbrella*. [6]

丿 𠆢 个 个 企 企

402

curriculum

歴

That same *grove of trees* from FRAME 226 shows up in the character for **curriculum** (as in a record of one's life or academic achievements, the **curriculum** vitae). Instead of the *grove* making its way slowly through the surface of the *cliff* as before, here we see it *stopped*, much the same as a **curriculum** vitae calls a halt to the calendar and talks only about the past. [14]

厂 厤 歴

403

warrior

武

With a *quiver* of *arrows* set on one's back, the goal of the **warrior** depicted here is not to attack but merely to *stop* the attack of others: the oldest excuse in history! [8]

一 二 丁 干 于 正 武 武

---

404   **levy**

賦

A certain portion of *shells* (money) is collected by the *warrior* from the local villages as he passes through to defray the costs of keeping the land safe, and this is called a **levy**. [15]

貝 賦

---

405   **correct**

正

"A journey of a thousand miles begins with a single step," says the Chinese proverb. Here we see *one footprint*, complementing that proverb with the sound advice that if the first step is not made **correctly**, the whole point of the journey will be forfeited. This is the ideal that teachers are supposed to have in **correcting** their students, and parents in **correcting** their children. [5]

一 丁 下 īF 正

---

406   **evidence**

証

Words that testify to the *correctness* of some fact are classified as **evidence**. (Here we see a good example of how the more common primitive element takes the "strong" position to the left, even though it has more strokes.) [12]

言 証

---

407   **politics**

政

To the many definitions for **politics** that already exist, this character offers yet another: *correct taskmastering*. Think about what the primitives tell us. On the one hand, we see the pessimistic wisdom that **politics** has to do with *taskmastering*, maneuvering people with or without their will. And on the other, we see the campaign assurances that this duty can be performed *correctly* if only the right candidate is given a chance. [9]

正 政

---

*

正

mending

This primitive differs from the kanji for *correct* only by the movement added to the last two strokes, the "-ing" of **mending** if you will. But take a more concrete sense, like **mending** holes in socks. [5]

一　丁　下　芷　正

408

定

determine

Determination, in the sense of settling on a certain course of action, is likened here to *mending* one's *house*. [8]

宀　定

409

錠

lock

Metal of itself doesn't **lock**. It needs to be so *determined* by a **lock**smith. Now make a concrete image of that. [16]

釒　錠

410

走

run

Running, we are told here, *mends* the *soil*. Observe in the following frames how this kanji can embrace other elements from below, much the same way as the element for *road* does. Note, too, that in order to do this, the final stroke needs to be lengthened. [7]

土　走

411

超

transcend

When one is *running* after something, the goal that *seduces* one is said to **transcend** the seeker. [12]

走 超

412

赴

proceed

In **proceeding** to a new city or a new job, something in you *runs* ahead with excitement, and something else holds you back, like a *divining rod* built into your psyche warning you to check things out carefully before rushing in too wildly. [9]

走 赴

413

越

surpass

Here we see two *parades* in competition, each trying to **surpass** the other by *running* at high speed from one town to the next. Note the little "hook" at the end of the first stroke of the element for *parade*. This is the ONLY time it appears like this in the kanji treated in this book. [12]

走 越

414

是

just so

In this kanji we are shown someone spending an entire *day* at *mending* one stocking, because they want the job done "**just so.**" Be sure to make a clear image of a finicky old fusspot to make the abstract idea as concrete as possible. [9]

日 是

415

題

topic

In many kinds of research, one can find information on a given **topic** only if the *headings* are prepared *just so*. [18]

是 題

416

堤

dike

A **dike** is a successful bit of engineering only if the amount of *earth* piled up is measured *just so* for the height and pressure of the water it is meant to contain. [12]

土　堤

---

*

廴

stretch

The primitive meaning to **stretch** might at first seem similar to that for *road*. Take a moment to study it more carefully and you will see the difference. Like *road*, this character holds other primitives above its sweeping final stroke. [3]

フ　了　廴

417

建

build

To construct a **building**, you first draw a set of plans (the writing *brush*) and then *s-t-r-e-t-c-h* your drawing out to scale in reality. [9]

聿　建

418

鍵

key

The *golden* **key** you have been presented by the mayor gives you access to all the *buildings* in the city. [17]

釒　鍵

419

延

prolong

This character is a kind of pictographic image of how **prolonging** is a clever way of *stopping* things by trying to *stretch* them out a little bit at a time (the extra *drop* at the top of *stop*). Be sure to get a concrete image of this process, by imagining yourself **prolonging** something you can really, physically, *stretch*. [8]

正　延

420 — nativity

誕

The key word of course calls to mind the feast of Christmas. As the famous poem at the start of St. John's gospel tells us, the **nativity** we celebrate at Christmas had its origins at the very start of time and governs all of human history: it represents the *prolongation* of the eternal *Word* in time and space. [15]

言　誕

* — ZOO

疋

To avoid confusion with the other animals that will be showing up, this primitive will signify a **zoo**. Except for the downward hook at the end of the first stroke, this element is indistinguishable from *mending*. Perhaps by now you have developed a quick eye for such details. If not now, you will before long. [5]

一　丁　下　疋　疋

421 — cornerstone

礎

This character depicts a **cornerstone** as a *stone* set at the end of a wildlife preserve (the "*zoo* in the *grove*"). [18]

石　砕　礎

422 — bridegroom

婿

What makes a man a **bridegroom** is obviously a *woman* and her dowry, here presented as a small *zoo* (animals were often used for this purpose in earlier societies) and a *month* away from it all (the "honey*moon*"). [12]

女　婿　婿

Lesson 18

THE THREE GROUPS of characters brought together in this rather long lesson are clustered around three sets of primitives dealing respectively with cloth and garments, weather, and postures.

423

衣

garment

At the top we see the *top hat*, and at the bottom a pictographic representation of the folds of a **garment**. If you break the "4-fold" fold into 2 sets of 2 strokes, you will find it easier to remember. [6]

* Used as a primitive, the additional meanings of *cloak* or *scarf* will come in handy. What has to be noted particularly are the changes in shape the kanji can undergo when it becomes an element in other kanji. In fact, it is the most volatile of all the kanji we shall treat, and for that reason deserves special attention here.

When it appears to the left, it looks like this: 衤, and we shall take it to mean *cloak*. At the bottom, when attached to the stroke immediately above it, the first two strokes (the *top hat*) are omitted, giving us: 𧘇, which we shall take to mean a *scarf*.

On rare occasions, the element can be torn right across the middle, with the first 2 strokes appearing at the top and the last 4 at the bottom of another primitive or cluster of primitives: 亠𧘇, in which cases we shall speak of a *top hat and scarf.*

And finally, of course, it can keep its original kanji shape, along with its original meaning of *garment* in general.

Note that when any of the above forms have something beneath them (as in FRAME 429), the third from final stroke is "unhooked," like this: 𧘇.

424　　　　　　　　　　　　　　　　　　　　**tailor**

裁

You might think here of *garments* that have been specially **tailored** for *Thanksgiving* celebrations to look like traditional Pilgrim garb. [12]

土　表　哉　裁　裁

425　　　　　　　　　　　　　　　　　　　　**attire**

装

The character for **attire** can be remembered as a picture of what we may call a "*turtle-samurai*" sweater. At the top we see the *turtle-samurai* and at the bottom the element for *garment*. [12]

爿　爿土　装

426　　　　　　　　　　　　　　　　　　　　**back**

裏

An innocent looking *top hat and scarf* lying there in front of you, turned over, reveal a hidden *computer* sewn into the **back** of each—obviously the tools of a master spy. Such experiences teach one always to have a look at the **back** side of things. [13]

亠　亩　裏

427　　　　　　　　　　　　　　　　　　　**demolition**

壊

The right half of this character shows a *garment* woven so fine that it can pass through the *eye* of a *needle*, fittingly draped around the slithering, ethereal form of a poltergeist. In this frame, our eerie visitor brushes its robes against a nearby block of apartments and completely **demolishes** them, razing them to the *ground*. [16]

土　坤　壊

428　　　　　　　　　　　　　　　　　　　**pathetic**

哀

A drunken sod in a tattered *top hat* and soiled silk *scarf* with a giant *mouth* guzzling something or other gives us a **pathetic**

character role in which W. C. Fields might find himself right at home. [9]

哀

---

429   distant

遠

A **distant** figure on the *road* is such a blur it looks like a *lidded crock* wearing a silk *scarf*. [13]

袁 遠

---

430   monkey

猿

This clever little **monkey** has captured an entire pack of *wild dogs*, locked them inside a *lidded crock*, and wrapped the whole thing up in a silk *scarf* to present to the dogcatcher. [13]

犭 猎 猿

---

431   first time

初

The primitives here take care of themselves: *cloak* and *dagger*. What I leave to you is to decide on an appropriate connotation for "**first time**" to take advantage of them. [7]

初

---

432   towel

巾

This character depicts a bolt of cloth wrapped around a pole. From there it gets its meaning of a **towel** [3].

巾

---

433   linen

布

The maid, *towels by her side,* distributes the **linen**. [5]

布

434	sail

帆

A **sail** made of a *towel* makes a *mediocre* vessel. [6]

巾　帆

435	hanging scroll

幅

A *towel* owned by the *wealthiest* tycoon in the world is made into a **hanging scroll** after his death and auctioned off to the highest bidder. [12]

巾　幅

436	cap

帽

Because of the *risk* involved (of getting the *sun* in one's *eyes*), one puts together a makeshift **cap** out of a dirty old *towel*. [12]

巾　帽　帽

437	curtain

幕

A dirty *towel* draped over the entrance to the old *graveyard* is painted to look like the **curtain** of death that leads to the other world. [13]

莫　幕

438	canopy

幌

A large *towel* stretched overhead with only a few of the *sun's* rays breaking through represents a **canopy** over one's bed. [13]

巾　帽　幌

439	brocade

錦

A strip of *white towel* and some scraps of *metal* have the makings of a primitive kind of **brocade**. [16]

釒 釒 錦

440

市

market

Dressed in nothing but a bath *towel* and *top hat*, one sets off to the **market**place in search of a bargain or two. [5]

╮ ㇐ 广 方 市

441

柿

persimmon

Imagine a village *market* with stalls set up around an immense **persimmon** *tree* with watermelon-sized fruit. If it weren't for the fact that the *tree* is sacred to the village, people would get impatient as the **persimmons** fall from the *tree* and wreak havoc on buyers and sellers alike. [9]

木 柿

442

姉

elder sister

Of all the *women* of the family, it is the **elder sister** who has the duty to go to *market* to do the shopping. [8]

女 姉

443

肺

lungs

One is surprised, strolling through the *market*, to find among the *meats* hung out for sale a slab marked: **lungs**. [9]

月 肺

*

帀

apron

The *towel* that has edges jagged like little *crowns* is the cook's **apron**. [5]

冖 帀

444   **sash**

帯

The part of the *apron* where one finds the *buckle* (represented pictorially by the first 5 strokes) is on the **sash**. [10]

一　十　卅　卅　卅　芾　帯

---

445   **stagnate**

滞

People that have been "*sashed*" to something (whether their mother's apron strings or a particular job) for too long become like *water* that has stopped moving: they start to **stagnate**. [13]

氵　滞

---

*   **belt**

冂

This primitive, clearly derived from that for *towel*, is always hung on another vertical stroke, and takes the meaning of a **belt**. [2]

丨　冂

---

446   **thorn**

刺

Thorns grow on a bush here that has wrapped itself around a *tree* like a *belt*, cutting into the poor *tree* like little *sabers*. [8]

一　厂　冂　肀　束　束　束　刺

---

447   **system**

制

This kanji show a unique **system** for leading *cows* to the slaughterer's *saber*: one ties a *belt* about their waist and fixes that *belt* to an overhead cable, pulling the *cow* up into the air where it hangs suspended, helpless against the fate that awaits it. [8]

丿　ト　匕　乍　与　朱　制　制

448　made in...

製

A label indicating that a *garment* was **made in** U.S.A. or Taiwan or Japan is itself a symbol for the *systematization* of the *garment* industry. [14]

制リ　製

*　rising cloud

云

This primitive is meant to depict in graphic fashion a **cloud** of something **rising** upwards, like vapor or smoke or dust. [4]

一　二　云　云

449　revolve

転

As the wheels of the *car* **revolve**, they kick up small *rising clouds* of dust and debris behind them. [11]

車　転

450　technique

芸

The secret **technique** of making a *rising cloud* of smoke turn into a bouquet of *flowers* is shown here. [7]

艹　芸

451　rain

雨

This kanji, also a primitive, is one of the clearest instances we have of a complex pictograph. The top line is the sky, the next 3 strokes a pair of clouds, and the final 4 dots the **rain** collected there and waiting to fall. [8]

一　厂　冂　帀　雨　雨　雨　雨

* As a primitive it can mean either *rain* or *weather* in general. Because it takes so much space, it usually has to be contracted into a crown by shortening the second and third strokes into a *crown* like this: 帚.

452

雲

cloud

Here is the full character for **cloud** from which the primitive for a *rising cloud* derives. *Clouds* begin with vapors *rising* up in small *clouds* from the surface of the earth, and then gathering to make **clouds** that eventually dump their *rain* back on the earth. [12]

帚　雲

453

曇

cloudy weather

We refer to days when the *sun* is covered by the *clouds* as **cloudy weather**. [16]

日　曇

454

雷

thunder

The full rumble and roar and terror of **thunder** is best felt not with your head tucked under your pillow safe in bed, but out in an open *rice field* where you can get the real feel of the *weather*. [13]

帚　雷

455

霜

frost

Think of **frost** as a cooperative venture, an *inter*-action of the malevolent forces of *weather* that sit around a conference table and finally decide to allow a very light amount of moisture to fall just before a short and sudden freeze. [17]

帚　霜

---

*

氵

ice

The condensation of the three drops we have been using to mean *water* into two drops signals the solidifying of *water* into **ice**. Note that when this primitive appears to the left, it is written like the last two strokes of the element for *water*, 氵, whereas under another primitive, it is written like the first two strokes of the *water* primitive: 冫. [2]

丶　冫

456

冬

winter

Walking legs slipping on the *ice* are a sure sign of **winter**. [5]

夂　冬

457

天

heavens

This character is meant to be a pictograph of a great man, said to represent the Lord of the **Heavens**. (You may, of course, use the elements *ceiling* and *St. Bernard* instead.) [4]

一　二　デ　天

* The primitive can mean either the *heaven* of eternal bliss or the general term for sky, the *heavens*. Pay special attention to the fact that in its primitive form the first stroke is written right to left, rather like the first stroke of *thousand* (FRAME 40), rather than left to right, giving us: 天. From the next character, we shall give it the primitive meaning of a *witch*.

458

妖

bewitched

You are **bewitched** by a *woman* who is, of course, a *witch* [7].

女　妖

459 沃	**irrigate**

Suffering from a drought, the farmers call on a *witch* who conjures up *water* to **irrigate** their crops. [7]

氵 沃

* 喬	**angel**

The sense of the primitive, **angel**, derives from the primitive for *witch* replacing the *top hat* in the character for *tall*. [12]

夭 喬

460 橋	**bridge**

The **bridge** shown here is made of *trees* in their natural form, except that the trunks have been carved into the forms of *angels*, a sort of "Ponte degli Angeli." [16]

木 橋

461 嬌	**attractive**

Associating a particularly **attractive** *woman* you know with an *angel* should be no problem. [15]

女 嬌

462 立	**stand up**

This picture of a vase **standing up** has its meaning extended to represent the general posture of anything **standing up**. [5]

丶 亠 六 立 立

* Used as a primitive, it can also mean *vase*. Using its kanji meaning, think of something *standing up* that is normally lying down, or something standing up in an unusual way.

463	cry

泣

One **cries** and **cries** until one is *standing up* knee-deep in *water* (or until one has a *vase*-full of *water*). [8]

氵　泣

464	badge

章

Try to imagine a club **badge** pinned to your lapel in the form of a mammoth *sunflower* protruding from a wee little *vase*. [11]

立　章

465	vie

競

Two *teenagers* are seen here *standing up* to one another, **vying** for the attention of their peers. [20]

立　竞　競

466	sovereign

帝

An uncommon, but not altogether unlikely picture of a reigning **sovereign** has him *standing up* in his *apron*, presumably at the behest of HIS **sovereign** (she who is to be obeyed), who needs help with washing the dishes. [9]

宀　产　帝

467	renunciation

諦

The key word **renunciation** has to do with the wisdom and clarity of mind in knowing when to "let go." This is what makes the *words* of acquiescence *sovereign*. [16]

言　諦

468 juvenile

童

This frame shows up the image of a **juvenile** hacker *standing* on top of a *computer*, or rather jumping up and down on it, because it refused to come up with the right answer. [12]

立 童

469 pupil

瞳

Begin with the double meaning of the key word **pupil**: "student" and the "apple of one's *eye*." Now all you have to do is dwell on the phrase "*juvenile* of one's *eye*" (the meaning here) until it provides you with an image. [17]

目 瞳

470 bell

鐘

This **bell** is made of cheap *metal*, and so badly made that when you ring it, it lets out a noise like the "**bell**owing" of *juveniles* who aren't getting their own way. [20]

金 鐘

471 make a deal

商

See the peddler *standing* atop his *motorcycle helmet* as if it were a soapbox, hawking his wares to passersby. The *legs* and *mouth* represent the tools of the trade of **making a deal** any way you can. [11]

立 产 产 商

* antique

商

The primitive meaning **antique**, not itself a kanji, depicts a *vase* kept under a *glass hood* because it is very, very old. [11]

ᅩ 产 商

472

legitimate wife

嫡

The phrase **legitimate wife** would have no meaning if there were not such a thing as an "illegitimate wife," taken because one's legal *woman* has turned into an *antique*. The very offense of the idea should help you remember the kanji. [14]

女 嫡

473

suitable

適

Can you imagine anything less **suitable** to do with one's precious *antiques* than to display them in the middle of a crowded *road-way*? [14]

商 適

474

drip

滴

Picture *water* **dripping** on what you thought were precious *antiques,* only to find that the artificial aging painted on them is running! [14]

氵 滴

475

enemy

敵

Picture your most precious *antique* (it doesn't matter how old it really is, so long as it is the oldest thing YOU own) being knocked over by your most unlikable *taskmaster*, and you have a good picture of how people make themselves **enemies** for life. [15]

商 敵

476

spoon

比

This character, a pictograph of a **spoon**, is easy enough to remember, provided you keep it distinct from that for *seven*, where the first stroke is written left to right (the opposite of here) and cuts noticeably across the second. [2]

丿　匕

* As a primitive, this kanji can take on the additional meaning of someone *sitting on the ground*, of which it can also be considered a pictograph. In general, the second stroke does not cut through the first—or if it does in some fonts, only slightly.

477

scold

叱

Recall some particularly harsh **scolding** you got as a child in school. This character has you *sitting on the ground* in the corner as your teacher stands over you, her *mouth* wide open as she reprimands you in front of the entire class. [5]

口　叱

478

aroma

匂

You will have to imagine "capturing" a favorite **aroma** by having it gagged and *bound up* in a *spoon*. [4]

勹　匂

479

about that time

頃

When Uncle Bob starts his comic routine of sticking *spoons* on his *head*, you know it is **about that time** to come up with a reason to excuse yourself. [11]

匕　頃

480 北 north

The cold air from the **north** is so strong that we see *two people sitting on the ground* back to back, their arms interlocked so they don't blow away. (Pay special attention to the drawing of the first 3 strokes.) [5]

一　丬　丬　北ˊ　北

481 背 stature

One's **stature** is measured according to the "*northern*-most" *part of the body.* [9]

北　背

482 比 compare

With *two spoons*, one in each hand, you are **comparing** your mother's cooking with your mother-in-law's. [4]

一　ヒ　比

483 昆 descendants

By *comparing* apes with anthropoids, we not only discover the latter have **descended** from those progenitors educated in the higher branches, but that the very idea of seeing everything **descended** from everything else, one way or another, means that there is "nothing new UNDER the *sun*." [8]

日　昆

484 皆 all

Think of the housewives in TV commercials "*comparing the whiteness*" of their laundry across the fence, a typical advertisement for the popular detergent known as **All**. (If you don't know the brand, surely you've heard the phrases "**all**-purpose detergent" or "**all**-temperature detergent.") [9]

比 皆

485 block letters

楷

The key word refers to kanji that are written in full, squared form, as opposed to cursive writing which is more flowing and abbreviates some of the strokes. Here **block letters** are pictured as tidy rows of *trees* that are *all* the same size and can be read easily by *all*, whatever calligraphic skills they possess. [13]

木　楷

486 orderliness

諧

The harmony of "a place for everything and everything in its place" is applied here to the **orderliness of** *all* the *words* one speaks. [16]

言　諧

487 mix

混

Mixed marriages, this character suggests, *water* down the quality of one's *descendants*—the oldest racial nonsense in the world! [11]

氵　混

★ siesta

曷

Conjure up the classic portrait of the Latin *siesta*: a muchacho *sitting on the ground*, propped up against some building, *bound up* from neck to ankles in a serape, one of those great, broad-rimmed mariachi hats pulled down over his face, and the noonday *sun* beating down overhead. Always use the complete image, never simply the general sense of **siesta**. [8]

日　号　曷

488   **thirst**

渇

As you pass by the muchacho taking the *siesta*, he cries out that he is **thirsty** and asks for something to drink. So you turn the *water* hose on him. [11]

氵   渇

---

489   **audience**

謁

Imagine an **audience** with the emperor or the pope in which all those in attendance are sitting down, leaning against the wall, sleeping like our muchacho on *siesta*, as the honorable host delivers his *speech*. [15]

言   謁

---

490   **brown**

褐

The color of the serape or *cloak* of our muchacho on *siesta* is a dull **brown**, the color this kanji indicates. [13]

衤   褐

---

491   **hoarse**

喝

When the muchacho on *siesta* looks up and opens his *mouth* to talk, his voice is so **hoarse** you cannot understand him. [11]

口   喝

---

492   **kudzu**

葛

Kudzu is a word taken over from the Japanese to name the crawling vines that creep up and completely take over trees. Seeing it at its worst in the Georgia countryside makes it easy to understand why it has a reputation as the "plague of the South." From there it should not be hard to arrange the primitives, *flowers* and *siesta* into a memorable image. [11]

艹   葛

493 旨	**delicious**

Something is so downright **delicious** that one spends the entire *day* with a *spoon* in hand gobbling it up. [6]

匕　旨

494 脂	**fat**

This kanji tells us that if you feed the *flesh* with too many *delicious* things, it soon picks up a thick layer of **fat**. [10]

月　脂

495 詣	**visit a shrine**

Here you "savor your *words*" as something *delicious* when you describe your recent **visit to a shrine** or pilgrimage site. [13]

言　詣

496 壱	**I (one)**

The Roman numeral I—like that for II we met earlier in FRAME 379—is only rarely used now. In the midst of all the *samurai*, we notice one in particular *sitting on the ground* with a *crown* on his head, indicating that he is "number I" in the current rankings. [7]

士　声　壱

* 宀	**reclining**

The picture is obvious: the first stroke represents the head, and the second the body of someone **reclining**. You may also use the synonyms *lying* or *lying down*. [2]

丿　宀

497	every

毎

"Behind **every** successful person *lies* a woman…," who usually turns out to be one's *mama*! [6]

ノ 毎

498	cleverness

敏

Behind *every* successful *taskmaster*, the **cleverness** of a fox to outwit his charges. [10]

毎 敏

499	plum

梅

Behind *every* Jack Horner's pie maker, a *tree* full of **plums**. [10]

木 梅

500	sea

海

Behind *every drop of water*, a **sea** from which it originated. [9]

氵 海

501	beg

乞

See someone *lying down* in a public place with a *hook* in place of a hand, **begging** a morsel of rice or a few pence. [3]

ノ 乞

502	drought

乾

In times of **drought** anything at all will do. Here we see the victims *begging* for just a little *mist* for relief. [11]

卓 乾

*

复 double back

Either the idea of turning around and heading back during one's travels, or of folding an object in half will do. The kanji depicts someone **doubling back** to the nearest inn to *lie down* and rest a weary pair of *walking legs* after a full *day's* voyage. [9]

亠　白　复

503

腹 abdomen

If you *double back* (fold over) most animals—or people, for that matter—in the middle, the *part of the body* where the crease comes is the **abdomen**. [13]

月　腹

504

複 duplicate

In its original and etymologically transparent sense, to **duplicate** something means to *double* it *back* with a fold, like the fold of a *cloak*. [14]

ネ　複

505

欠 lack

The pictograph hidden in this character is of someone yawning. The first stroke shows the head thrown back; the second, the arm bent at the elbow as the hand reaches up to cover the mouth; and the last two, the legs. Since yawning shows a **lack** of something (psychologically, interest; physiologically, sleep), the connection is plain to see. [4]

丿　𠂉　ク　欠

* When used as a primitive element, this kanji can mean either *yawn* or *lack*.

506

blow

吹

To **blow** is really no more than a deliberate effort to make one's *mouth lack* all the air that is in it. [7]

口　吹

507

cook

炊

Better to picture what happens when you do not pay attention to your work in the kitchen. Here we see a blazing *fire* and an inattentive, *yawning* **cook** who let things get out of control. [8]

火　炊

508

song

歌

The **song** in this kanji is being sung by a chorus line of *can-can* girls. Why it should be eliciting nothing but *yawning* from the audience, I leave to you to decide. [14]

哥　歌

509

soft

軟

If the cushions of one's *car* are too **soft**, one may begin *yawning* at the wheel. [11]

車　軟

510

next

次

This key word connotes the "**next** in line" of a succession of people or things. Let there be a *lack* of *ice* on the hottest day of summer, and you stand impatiently in line waiting for the distributor to call out "**Next!**" [6]

冫　次

* As a primitive, this character can either retain its key word meaning of *next* or the related meaning of *second*.

511	briar

茨

Earlier we made mention of the story of **Briar** Rose (or "Sleeping Beauty," as we called her in FRAME 165) and drew attention to the **briar** hedge that grew up all about her castle. But in the *second* part of the story, these **briars** blossomed into *flowers*. Hence her name, **Briar** Rose. Be careful not to confuse this character with that for *thorn* (FRAME 446). [9]

艹　茨

512	assets

資

The first *shells* (money) you earn, you use to pay your debts. From then on, the *next shells* you accumulate become your **assets**. [13]

次　資

513	figure

姿

This kanji depicts a *woman's* **figure** as a sort of *second* self. [9]

次　姿

514	consult with

諮

To seek the *words* of a *second mouth* is to **consult with** someone about something. [16]

言　訟　諮

Lesson 19

WE CONCLUDE Part Two by picking up most of the remaining primitives that can be built up from elements already at our disposal, and learning the kanji that are based on them. When you have completed this section, run through all

the frames from LESSON 13 on, jotting down notes at any point you think helpful. That way, even if you have not made any notations on your review cards, you will at least have some record of the images you used.

∗ 音	muzzle

The element for **muzzle** shows a *vase* fixed over a *mouth*, perhaps with a rubber band running around the back of the head to keep it in place. [8]

立 音

---

515 賠	compensation

Picture a *clam* used as a *muzzle* to quiet the complaints of a fisherman's widow asking **compensation** for her husband lost at sea. [15]

貝 賠

---

516 培	cultivate

The barrel hoops used by many Japanese farmers to stretch clear plastic over row of vegetables in a garden patch in the hopes of **cultivating** bigger and bigger vegetables is a way of *muzzling* the *soil*. [11]

土 培

---

517 剖	divide

To "**divide** and conquer" you use a *saber* and a *muzzle*. [10]

音 剖

---

518 音	sound

The kanji for **sound** depicts something *standing* in the air over a *tongue wagging in a mouth*, much the same as a **sound** does for the briefest of moments before disappearing. [9]

立 音

* The primitive from this kanji also means simply a sound.

519

暗

darkness

When "**darkness** covered the earth" at the beginning of time, there was neither *sun* nor *sound*. [13]

日　暗

520

韻

rhyme

Poetry restricted to verses that **rhyme** often finds it has to abandon clarity of thought in order to make the **rhyme** of the words work. In this kanji's picture, one becomes a kind of "*sound-employee*." [19]

音　韻

---

*

戠

kazoo

This primitive's special usefulness lies not in its frequency but in its simplification of a few otherwise difficult kanji. It pictures the *sound* of a *fiesta*, namely a **kazoo**. Note how the element for *sound* is written first, the fifth stroke extended so that it can be used in the element for *fiesta*. [12]

亠　立　音　戠

521

識

discriminating

A person of **discriminating** intellect can tell the difference between mere *kazoo*-buzzing and *words* spoken wisely. [19]

言　識

---

*

竟   **mirror**

This primitive gets its meaning from the following frame. It shows a pair of *human legs* and a *tongue-wagging mouth* looking at a **mirror** *standing* on the wall, asking perhaps who might be the fairest of them all. [11]

立   音   竟

---

522   **mirror**

鏡

After lakes but before glass, polished *metal* was used for **mirrors**. These *metal mirrors* are recalled in this character for a **mirror**. [19]

釒   鏡

---

523   **boundary**

境

Imagine the **boundary** of a plot of *land* marked with gigantic *mirrors* enabling the landowner to keep trespassers in sight at all times. [14]

土   境

---

524   **deceased**

亡

A *top hat* hanging on a *hook* in the front hall, right where the **deceased** left it the day he died, reminds us of him and his kanji. [3]

亠   亡

* In addition to *deceased*, the primitive meaning of *to perish* will also be used for this character.

---

525   **blind**

盲

If one's *eyes perish* before death, one remains **blind** for the rest of life. [8]

亡 盲

---

526   **delusion**

妄

The "ideal *woman*" one daydreams about is no more than a **delusion**. Hence, *perish* the thought of her. [6]

亡　妄

---

527   **laid waste**

荒

The *flowers* that *perish* in the *flood* are taken here as symbols of an area that has been **laid waste**. [9]

艹　芒　荒

---

528   **ambition**

望

The story of **ambition** talks of a *king* walking under the *perishing* (or "waning") *moon* dreaming great dreams about his kingdom. (The roots of **ambition** are from the same word as "ambulate," meaning to walk about.) [11]

亡　亡月　望

---

529   **direction**

方

Spinning a *dagger* about on its hilt on the top of a *top hat*—waiting to see in which **direction** it points when it comes to rest—one leaves to fate where one is going next. Take care in writing this character. [4]

亠　亍　方

* As a primitive, this character will take the sense of a *compass*, the instrument used to determine *direction*.

| 530 | disturb |

妨

Imagine a *compass* that is **disturbed** every time a *woman* passes by, sending the needle spinning madly round and round. [7]

女　妨

| 531 | boy |

坊

The character for a **boy** shows us a **Boy** Scout cleaning the *dirt* out of his *compass*—the more *dirt*, the better. [7]

土　坊

| 532 | perfumed |

芳

Here we see a special *compass* used to pick out those *flowers* most suited for making good **perfumes**. [7]

艹　芳

| 533 | obese |

肪

If you eat too much, you may need a *compass* to find your way around the **obese** mass of *flesh* that piles up in your midsection. Compare this with the stories for *round* (FRAME 44) and *fat* (FRAME 494), similar in meaning but distinct in imagery. [8]

月　肪

| 534 | call on |

訪

When making a courtesy **call on** a dignitary, one has to gauge one's *words* with great care. Hence the need for a *compass*. [11]

言　訪

| 535 | set free |

放

The *taskmaster* **sets** an unruly servant **free**, giving him no more than a quick glance at the *compass* and a boot from behind. [8]

方　放

536　　　　　　　　　　　　　　　　　　　　　　　**violent**

激

Some cosmic *taskmaster* hovering overhead whips up the waves to make them dash **violently** against the shore. In the *white* foam that covers the *water* we see a broken *compass* floating, all that remains of a shipwreck. [16]

氵　沪　澇　激

＊　　　　　　　　　　　　　　　　　　　　　　　　　**devil**

兊

The two *horns* on the head of the *teenager* are enough to suggest to most parents of adolescents a good image of a **devil**. [7]

丷　兊

537　　　　　　　　　　　　　　　　　　　　　　　**undress**

脱

To **undress** is to expose the *flesh* and tempt the *devil* in the eyes of one's onlookers. Ignore the moral if you want, but not the *devil*. [11]

月　脱

538　　　　　　　　　　　　　　　　　　　　　　**explanation**

説

Not inappropriately, this character likens an **explanation** to the *devil's* own *words*. [14]

言　説

539　　　　　　　　　　　　　　　　　　　　　　　**pointed**

鋭

Metal that has been **pointed** (as an awl, a pick, a nail, or a knife) tends to serve the *devil's* purposes as well as civilization's: our tools are also our weapons. [15]

金　鋭

540   **formerly**

曽

This primitive (named for its associations with the kanji of the following frame) is composed of a pair of *horns* growing out of a *brain* with a *tongue wagging in the mouth* beneath. Think of "**former**" in connection with administrators or heads of state who have just left office but continue to make a nuisance of themselves by advertising their opinions on public policy. [11]

丷 曽 曽

* The primitive meaning, *increase,* comes from the next frame. Always think of something multiplying wildly as you watch.

---

541   **increase**

増

This kanji depicts an **increase** of *soil*, multiplying so fast that it literally buries everything in its path. [14]

扌 増

---

542   **presents**

贈

The **presents** offered here are *money* that *increases* each time you give it away. Do not confuse with the temporal word "present" (FRAME 275). [18]

貝 贈

---

543   **east**

東

As a "Western" language, English identifies the **east** with the rising *sun*. In more fanciful terms, we see the *sun* piercing through a *tree* as it rises in the **east**. [8]

一 厂 冂 冃 目 車 東 東

* Both the direction *east* and the part of the world called "the *East*" are primitive meanings of this character.

544   ridgepole

棟

If the piece of *wood* in the roof known as the **ridgepole** points *east*, the sunrise will be visible from the front door. [12]

木 棟

---

545   frozen

凍

The whole secret to breaking the *ice* with the *East* is to peek behind those mysteriously "**frozen** smiles." [10]

冫 凍

---

*   porter

壬

Let the extended dot at the top represent the load that the *samurai* is carrying in his role as the master's **porter**. [4]

一 壬

---

546   pregnancy

妊

A *woman* who is in her **pregnancy** is a bit like a *porter*, bearing her new companion wherever she goes. [7]

女 妊

---

547   courts

廷

Those who rule the **courts**, the *porters* of justice and order, are often found to *stretch* the law to suit their own purposes. Recall the kanji for *prolong* from FRAME 419 and keep it distinct. [7]

壬 廷

PART THREE

Elements

WE COME NOW to the third major step in our study of the kanji: the invention of plots from primitive elements. From now on, the ordering of the remaining characters according to their primitives will be taken care of, but the reader will be required to do most of the work. As before, particularly difficult kanji will be supplied with supplementary hints, plots, or even whole stories.

You should now have a feel for the way details can be worked into a kanji story so as to create a more vivid ambience for the primitive elements to interact. What may be more difficult is experimenting with plots and discarding them until the simplest one is fixed on, and then embellished and nuanced. You may find it helpful occasionally to study some of the earlier stories that you found especially impressive, in order to discover precisely why they struck you, and then to imitate their vitality in the stories you will now be inventing. Equally helpful will be any attention you give to those characters whose stories you have found it difficult to remember, or have easily confused with those of other characters. As you progress through this final section, you may wish even to return and amend some of those earlier stories. But do it with the knowledge that once a story has been learned, it is generally better to review it and perhaps repair it slightly than to discard it entirely and start over.

Lesson 20

To BEGIN OUR work with the primitives alone, let us take six kanji of varying difficulty that use primitives we have already learned, and that have been kept apart deliberately for the sake of this initial sally into independent learning.

548		dye

 Water . . . nine . . . tree. From those elements you must compose a plot for the key word, **dye**. Here, as elsewhere, any of the alternate meanings of the primitives may be used, provided they do not require a position other than that of the kanji in question. [9]

氵　氿　染

549　burn

燃

Hearth . . . sort of thing. Beware of letting the simple reading off of the primitive elements do your work for you. Unless you make a vivid image of something **burning** and relate it just as vividly to those primitive meanings, you can count on forgetting this character very quickly. [16]

火　燃

550　V.I.P.

賓

The **v.i.p.** indicated here is an important guest making a visit. The elements are: *house . . . ceiling . . . few . . . shells.* [15]

宀　宇　穼　賓

551　year-end

歳

Stop . . . march . . . little. Be sure not to forget that final dot in the element for *march.* [13]

止　庐　岸　歳

552　prefecture

県

Above, an *eye* and a *fishhook,* and below the primitive for *little.* Although apparently the simplest of these first six kanji, when you begin to work on its plot and story you will soon find out that the number of strokes and visual complexity of a kanji does not make it easier or harder to remember. It is the primitives you have to work that are the critical factor, as in this case where the meaning of the key word is so seemingly distant from the elements. Remember, you can always break larger elements down (*eye of a needle* into *eye* and *fishhook*) if you think it helps. [9]

旦　県

553	horse chestnut

栃   *A tree . . . cliff . . . ten thousand.* [9]

木   朽   栃

Lesson 21

IF YOU FOUND some of the characters in the last brief lesson difficult to work with, I assure you that it will get easier with time, indeed already with this long lesson. More important is to take heed that as it *does* get easier you don't skip over the stories too quickly, trusting only in the most superficial of images. If you spend up to five minutes on each character focusing on the composition of the primitives into a tidy plot, and then filling out the details of a little story, you will not be wasting time, but saving yourself the time it takes to relearn it later.

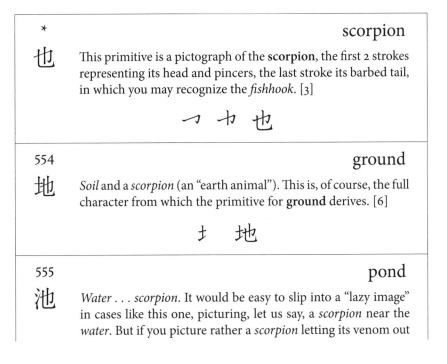

*	scorpion

也   This primitive is a pictograph of the **scorpion**, the first 2 strokes representing its head and pincers, the last stroke its barbed tail, in which you may recognize the *fishhook*. [3]

ㄱ   卅   也

554	ground

地   *Soil* and a *scorpion* (an "earth animal"). This is, of course, the full character from which the primitive for **ground** derives. [6]

土   地

555	pond

池   *Water . . . scorpion.* It would be easy to slip into a "lazy image" in cases like this one, picturing, let us say, a *scorpion* near the *water*. But if you picture rather a *scorpion* letting its venom out

drop by drop until it has made a whole **pond** of the stuff, the image is more likely to remain fixed. [6]

氵　池

556　　　　　　　　　　　　　　　　　　　　　　　　　insect

虫　Work with the pictograph as you wish. [6]

口　中　虫　虫

* As a primitive, this insect will refer to the whole *insect* kingdom;, it can be specified for each kanji that contains it.

557　　　　　　　　　　　　　　　　　　　　　　lightning bug

蛍　*Schoolhouse . . . insect.* [11]

⺌　蛍

558　　　　　　　　　　　　　　　　　　　　　　　　　snake

蛇　*Insect . . . house . . . spoon.* [11]

虫　虴　蛇

559　　　　　　　　　　　　　　　　　　　　　　　　rainbow

虹　*Insect . . . craft.* [9]

虫　虹

560　　　　　　　　　　　　　　　　　　　　　　　butterfly

蝶　*Insect . . . generation . . . tree.* [15]

虫　蝬　蝶

561　　　　　　　　　　　　　　　　　　　　　　　　　single

独　Think of this key word in connection with bachelorhood. The elements: *wild dogs . . . insect.* [9]

犭 独

---

562   silkworm

蚕

Heavens . . . insect. Be sure to do something about the position of the two elements. [10]

天 蚕

---

563   wind

風

Windy . . . drops of . . . insects. Hint: think of the last two primitives as representing a swarm of *gnats,* those tiny *drops of* pesky *insects.* [9]

几 凡 風

---

564   self

己

The kanji carries the abstract sense of the **self,** the deep-down inner structure of the human person that mythology has often depicted as a *snake*—which is what the kanji shows pictographically. Be sure to keep it distinct from the similar key words, *oneself* (FRAME 36) and *I* (FRAME 17). [3]

コ ユ 己

* As a primitive element, this kanji can be used for the *snake*—of which it is a pictograph—or any of the various concrete symbolic meanings the *snake* has in myth and fable. [3]

---

565   rouse

起   *Run . . . snake.* [10]

走 起

---

566   queen

妃   *Woman . . . snake.* [6]

女　妃

567　　　　　　　　　　　　　　　　　　　　reformation

改

Pluralizing the *snake* and focusing on a single *taskmaster* may help recommend the image of Ireland's most famous **reformer**, St. Patrick, who, legend has it, drove away the *snakes* from the land. [7]

己　改

568　　　　　　　　　　　　　　　　　　　　scribe

記　　*Words . . . snake.* [10]

言　記

569　　　　　　　　　　　　　　　　　　　　wrap

包　　*Bind up . . . snake.* [5]

勹　包

* The primitive meaning of *wrap* should always be used with the *snake* in mind to avoid confusion with similar terms. Just let "*wrap*" mean "with a snake coiled about it."

570　　　　　　　　　　　　　　　　　　　　placenta

胞　　*Part of the body . . . wrap.* [9]

月　胞

571　　　　　　　　　　　　　　　　　　　　cannon

砲　　*Stones . . . wrap.* [10]

石　砲

| 572 | bubble |

泡 *Water . . . wrap.* [8]

ミ　泡

| 573 | tortoise |

亀 This is not a *turtle* (see FRAME 250) but a **tortoise**, however you wish to picture the difference. Let the "*bound up*" at the top refer to the head, and the two *suns*, with a long tail running through it, to the shell. [11]

负　鲁　亀

* As a primitive, this kanji is abbreviated to its bottom half, 电, and comes to mean *eel*. (If it is any help, this kanji in its full form can also be remembered through its abbreviation's primitive meaning.)

| 574 | electricity |

電 *Rain/weather . . . eel.* [13]

雨　電

| 575 | dragon |

竜 *Vase . . . eel.* In order not to confuse this kanji with the zodiacal *sign of the dragon*, which we will meet later (FRAME 2164) and use as a primitive, you might think here of a paper parade **dragon**. [10]

立　竜

| 576 | waterfall |

滝 *Water . . . vase . . . eels.* To avoid the confusion mentioned in the previous frame, the character learned there for *dragon* should not be used as a primitive. [13]

氵 浐 滝

---

*

SOW

豕

Let this primitive represent a fat **sow**. Easier than pulling it apart into smaller elements is remembering its shape as a highly stylized pictograph. Practice its 7 strokes a few times before going on to examples of its use in the next six frames. [7]

一 ⼂ 丁 豸 豸 豸 豕

577

pork

豚

Flesh . . . sow. [11]

月 豚

578

pursue

逐

Sows . . . road. [10]

豕 逐

579

consummate

遂

The *horns* atop the *sow* suggest a boar at work in the background. Add the element for a *road*. Now create a story whose meaning is: **consummate**. [12]

 豕 遂

580

house

家

This is the full character whose primitive form we learned already. To help a little, this kanji recalls the times when the "domestic" animals were, as the word itself suggests, really kept in the **house**. Hence: *house . . . sow.* [10]

宀 家

581	marry into

嫁

The kanji in this frame demonstrates the traditional Japanese approach to marriage: it is the *woman* who leaves her family for another *house*hold, thus **marrying into** a man's family. [13]

女　嫁

582	overpowering

豪

Tall . . . crowned . . . sow. [14]

亠　亠　豪

★	piglets

豕

This abbreviation of the full primitive for a *sow*, quite naturally, means **piglets**. [5]

一　厂　歹　歹　豕

★	piggy bank

昜

This very helpful primitive element is worth the few moments it takes to learn it. Just remember that each *day* you put a few pennies into the back of the little *piglet* on your bureau that you call a **piggy bank**. [9]

日　昜

583	intestines

腸

Flesh . . . piggy bank. [13]

月　腸

584	location

場

Soil . . . piggy bank. [12]

土　場

---

585   hot water

湯   *Water . . . piggy bank.* [12]

氵   湯

---

586   sheep

羊   This pictograph shows the animal *horns* at the top attached to the head (3rd stroke), the front and back legs (strokes 4 and 5) and body (final stroke). [6]

丷   兰   羊

* The primitive meaning of *sheep* can add the further connotations given in the following frame. As we saw with the *cow*, the "tail" is cut off when it is set immediately over another element: ⺶. Note the change in stroke order, as exemplified in the following frame.

---

587   beauty

美   Try to think of what the Chinese were on to when they associated the idea of **beauty** with a *large sheep*. [9]

⺶   丷   ⺷   羊   美

---

588   ocean

洋   *Water . . . sheep.* Be sure to keep the stories and key word of this kanji distinct from those for *sea.* (FRAME 500). [9]

氵   洋

---

589   detailed

詳   *Words/speaking . . . sheep.* [13]

言   詳

590

鮮

fresh

Fish . . . sheep. [17]

魚　鮮

591

達

accomplished

The key word is meant to connote someone "skilled" at something. On the *road* we find *soil* OVER *a sheep*. You may have to work with this one a while longer. [12]

土　幸　達

592

羨

envious

Sheep . . . water . . . yawn/lack. Although this character looks rather simple, special care should be taken in learning it because of the proximity of the final two elements to the character for *next*, which we learned in FRAME 510. Note, too, that the *water* comes UNDER the *sheep*, rather than on its own to the left. [13]

羊　羊　羨

---

*

关

wool

This rather uncommon primitive is made by pulling the tail of the *sheep* to one side to create a semi-enclosure. The meaning of **wool** is derived from the fact that the shearer is holding the *sheep* by the tail in order to trim its **wool**. [7]

羊　关

593

差

distinction

Wool . . . craft. [10]

关　差

594 着	don
	I cannot resist doing this one for you, since it clearly describes **donning** (putting on) one's clothes as "pulling the *wool* over one's *eyes*." [12]

羊 着

★ 隹	turkey
	This primitive is best remembered as an old **turkey**, complete with pipe and monocle. Its writing is somewhat peculiar, so take note of the order of the strokes. Let the first four strokes stand for the *turkey's* head, neck, and drooping chin. The remainder can then be pictographic of the plumage. [8]

ノ 亻 亻 亻 什 仹 隹 隹

595 唯	solely
	Mouth . . . turkey. [11]

口 唯

596 堆	piled high
	Soil . . . turkey. [11]

597 椎	sweet oak
	Tree . . . turkey. [12]

598 誰	who
	Words . . . turkey. [15]

599 焦	char
	Turkey . . . oven fire. [12]

隹 焦

600		reef
礁	*Rocks . . . char.* [17]	

石　礁

601		gather
集	*Turkeys . . .* atop a *tree.* [12]	

隹　集

602		quasi-
准	*Ice . . . turkey.* [10]	

冫　准

603		advance
進	*Turkey . . . road.* [11]	

隹　進

604		miscellaneous
雑	*Baseball . . . trees . . . turkey.* [14]	

九　朵　雑

605		female
雌	This character for **female** forms a pair with that for *male,* which we will learn later (FRAME 804). The elements: *footprint . . . spoon . . . turkey.* [14]	

止　此　雌

---

606 **semi-**

準

Think of this in terms of the **semifinals** of some sports competition. *Water . . . turkeys . . . needle.* [13]

氵　淮　準

---

607 **stirred up**

奮

St. Bernard dog . . . turkey . . . rice field/brains. [16]

大　奞　奮

---

608 **rob**

奪

Whereas *burglary* (FRAME 381) implies clandestine appropriation of another's property, **robbery** refers to taking by force. The primitive elements: *St. Bernard dog . . . turkey . . . glue.* [14]

大　奞　奪

---

609 **assurance**

確

On the left you see the *rock*, which is familiar enough. But pay attention to the right. Taking careful note of the unusual stroke order that has the "chimney" on the *house* doubled up with the first stroke of the *turkey*, we may see the right side as a *turkey house* (or "*coop*").

We shall see this pattern only on one other occasion (FRAME 2093), but even for these two characters it is well worth the trouble to single it out as a primitive. [15]

石　矿　矿　確

---

610 **noon**

午

With a bit of stretching, you might see a horse's head pointing leftward in this character. That gives the primary meaning of the Chinese zodiacal sign of the horse, which corresponds to the hour of **noon**. Note how this kanji primitive differs from that for *cow* (FRAME 260). [4]

ノ ← ⊢ 午

* As a primitive, this character gets the meaning of a *horse*. Any *horse* image will do, except that of a *team of horses*, which will come later (FRAME 2132) and get its own primitive.

---

611   **permit**

許   Words . . . horse. [11]

言   許

---

*   **Pegasus**

雈   By combining the *horse* (giving a twist to its final stroke a bit to the left to keep the strokes from overlapping) with the *turkey*, we get a *flying horse* or **Pegasus**. Be sure not to confuse with the rarer element for *turkey house* (隹) that was introduced in FRAME 609. [11]

牛   雈

---

612   **delight**

歡   Again I cannot resist sharing my own associations. If you've ever seen Disney's animated interpretation of classical music, "Fantasia," you will recall what was done there with Beethoven's "Pastoral Symphony" (the 6th), and the *flying horses* that figured in it. The mares are bathing in the stream and the stallions begin to gather. As dusk sets in, the *flying horses* all start *yawning* and pair off for the night: a perfectly **delightful** portrait of **delight**. [15]

雈   歡

---

613   **authority**

権   Tree . . . Pegasus. [15]

木   権

614		outlook
観	*Pegasus . . . see.* [18]	

隹　観

615		feathers
羽	From the pictograph of two bird-wings, we get **feathers**. [6]	

丁　刁　刁　羽

> * The related image of *wings* can be added as a primitive meaning. It can also take the form ⋿ when used as a primitive, as we shall see in FRAMES 618 and 619.

616		learn
習	*Feathers . . . white bird.* [11]	

刁刁　習

617		the following
翌	*Feathers . . . vase.* Be sure to contrast the connotation of this key word with that for *next* (FRAME 510). [11]	

刁刁　翌

618		weekday
曜	*Day . . . feathers . . . turkey.* [18]	

日　日ⴲ　曜

619		laundry
濯	*Water . . . feathers . . . turkey* [17]	

氵　氵ⴲ　濯

Lesson 22

THIS IS A GOOD time TO stop for a moment and have a look at how primitive elements get contracted and distorted by reason of their position within a kanji. Reference has been made to the fact here and there in passing, but now that you have attained greater fluency in writing, we may address the phenomenon more systematically.

1. At the left, a primitive will generally be squeezed in from the sides and slanted upwards. For instance, *gold* 金 comes to be written 金 when it functions as the primitive for *metal*. Or again, *tree* has its kanji form 木 flattened into 木 when it comes to the left.

2. Long strokes ending in a hook, which would normally flow out gracefully, are squeezed into angular form when made part of a primitive at the left. We see this in the way the kanji for *ray* 光 gets altered to 光 in the kanji for *radiance* 輝. In like manner, the *spoon* that is spread out on the right side of *compare* 比 is turned in on itself on the left. Certain characters are pressed down and widened when weighted down by other elements from above. Such is the case, for example, with *woman*, which is flattened into 女 when it appears in the lowest position of *banquet* 宴.

3. A long vertical stroke cutting through a series of horizontal lines is often cut off below the lowest horizontal line. We saw this in changing the *cow* 牛 to fit it in *revelation* 告, the *sheep* 羊 to fit in *beauty* 美, and the *brush* 聿 that appeared in the kanji for *write* 書.

4. The long downward swooping stroke that we see in *fire* is an example of another group of distortions. Crowded in by something to its right, it is turned into a short stroke that bends downwards: 火. Hence *fire* 火 and *lamp* 灯.

5. Again, we have seen how horizontal lines can double up as the bottom of the upper primitive and the top of the lower primitive. For instance, when *stand* 立 comes in the primitive for *make a deal* 商.

6. Finally, there are situations in which an entire kanji is changed to assume a considerably altered primitive form. *Water* 水, *fire* 火, and *portent* 兆 thus become 氵, 灬, and 冫 in other characters. Because the full forms are ALSO used as primitives, we have altered the meaning or given distinctions in meaning in order to be sure that the story in each case dictates precisely how the character is to be written.

From this chapter on, the stroke order will not be given unless it is entirely new, departs from the procedures we have learned so far, or might otherwise cause confusion. Should you have any trouble with the writing of a particular primitive, you can refer to Index II which will direct you to the page where that primitive was first introduced.

With that, we carry on.

---

*

pent in

This primitive depicts a corral or pen surrounding something, which is thus **pent in**. [3]

| ⊓ □

620

sayeth

Pent in . . . one. The key word refers to famous sayings of famous people, and is the origin for the primitive meaning of a *tongue wagging in the mouth* that we learned in FRAME 12. The size of this kanji, a relatively rare one, is what distinguishes it from *day*. [4]

⊓ 𠮛 曰

621

quandary

Pent in . . . trees. [7]

| ⊓ 冂 困 困 困 困

622

harden

Old . . . pent in. Leave the people out of your story to avoid complications later when we add the element for person to form a new kanji (FRAME 1047). [8]

623

weld

Metal . . . harden. [16]

624	country
国	Jewels . . . pent in. [8]

625	group
団	Glued . . . pent in. [6]

626	cause
囚	St. Bernard dog . . . pent in. [6]

627	matrimony
姻	Woman . . . cause. Think here of the "state of **matrimony**" and you will not confuse it with other characters involving marriage, one of which we have already met (FRAME 581). [9]

628	windpipe
咽	Mouth . . . cause. [9]

629	park
園	Pent in . . . lidded crock . . . scarf. [13]

630	-times
回	The suffix "-**times**" refers to a number of repetitions. Its elements: a mouth . . . pent in. Hint: you may find it more helpful to forget the primitives and think of one circle revolving inside of another. [6]

冂 冋 回

631	podium
壇	Soil/ground . . . top hat . . . -times . . . nightbreak. With kanji as difficult as this one, it generally pays to toy with the various connotations of its primitives before settling on one image. Aim for as much simplicity as you can. [16]

---

*

cave

广

This primitive combines the *cliff* (the last 2 strokes) with the first dot we use on the roof of the *house*. Together they make a "cliff house" or **cave**. It "encloses" its relative primitives beneath it and to the right. [3]

丶　亠　广

632

store

店

Cave . . . fortune-telling. [8]

广　店

633

warehouse

庫

Cave . . . car. [10]

634

courtyard

庭

Cave . . . courts. [10]

635

government office

庁

Cave . . . a spike. [5]

636

bed

床

Cave . . . tree. [7]

637

hemp

麻

Cave . . . grove. If it helps, this is the **hemp** marijuana comes from. [11]

638

grind

磨

Hemp . . . stone. [16]

麻　磨

639	heart

心

This character, a pictographic representation of the **heart**, is among the most widely used primitives we shall meet. [4]

丶　　心　心　心

* As a primitive, it can take three forms, to which we shall assign three distinct meanings.

In its kanji-form, it appears BENEATH or to the RIGHT of its relative primitive and means the physical organ of the *heart*.

To the LEFT, it is abbreviated to three strokes, 忄, and means a wildly emotional *state of mind*.

And finally, at the very BOTTOM, it can take the form 灬, in which case we give it the meaning of a *valentine*.

640	forget

忘

Perish . . . heart. [7]

641	selfish

恣

Second . . . heart. [10]

642	endure

忍

Blade . . . heart. **Endure** here means long-suffering patience. [7]

643	acknowledge

認

Words . . . endure. [14]

644	mourning

忌

Snake . . . heart. [7]

645	intention

志

Samurai . . . heart. [7]

646 誌	document *Words . . . intention.* [14]
647 芯	wick *Flowers . . . heart.* [7]
648 忠	loyalty *In the middle of a . . . heart.* [8]
649 串	shish kebab This pictograph of two pieces of meat on a skewer, a **shish kebab**, will help us in the next frame. [7] <center>冂　吕　串</center>
650 患	afflicted *Shish kebab . . . heart.* [11]
651 思	think *Brains . . . heart.* [9]
652 恩	grace Take **grace** in its sense of a favor freely bestowed, not in its meaning of charming manners or fluid movement. The primitives: *cause . . . heart.* [10]
653 応	apply *Cave . . . heart.* The sense of the key word here is of something appropriate that fills a particular need, and hence "**applies**." [7]
654 意	idea *Sound . . . heart.* [13]

655 臆	cowardice
	Flesh . . . idea. [17]

656 想	concept
	To distinguish this kanji from that of the previous frame, focus on the sense of the "con-" in the word "**concept**." Its elements are: *inter- . . . heart.* [13]

657 息	breath
	Nose . . . heart. [10]

658 憩	recess
	Tongue . . . nose . . . heart. The sense of *breath* from the last frame should not be used; it could lead you to put only the *nose* over the *heart* and leave the *tongue* off to one side. [16]

659 恵	favor
	Ten . . . fields (or: *needle . . . brains*) *. . . heart.* [10]

660 恐	fear
	Craft . . . mediocre . . . heart. [10]

661 惑	beguile
	The first three elements, *fiesta . . . mouth . . . floor*, appeared together once already in FRAME 380. Beneath them, once again, the *heart*. [12]

662 感	emotion
	Mouths . . . marching . . . heart. [13]

663 憂	melancholy
	Head . . . crown . . . heart . . . walking legs. Two things merit mention here. First, the doubling-up of the last stroke of *head*

with the top of the *crown* serves to make the whole more aesthetically beautiful. It happens so rarely that the exceptions are easily learned. Second, try to make a single image out of the four elements. (Religious statuary of **melancholy** figures should offer plenty of suggestions.) [15]

百　亘　惪　憂

664　　　　　　　　　　　　　　　　　　　　　　　　widow

寡　*House . . . head . . . dagger.* Immediately we get another instance of a very odd exception. Notice how the final stroke of the *head* is lengthened, giving the final two strokes a chance to stretch out and make room for the *dagger* that fits in beneath. [14]

宀　宀　宣　寅　寡

665　　　　　　　　　　　　　　　　　　　　　　　　busy

忙　*State of mind . . . perish.* [6]

丶　忄　忄　忄　忙　忙

666　　　　　　　　　　　　　　　　　　　　　　　　ecstasy

悦　*State of mind . . . devil.* [10]

667　　　　　　　　　　　　　　　　　　　　　　　　constancy

恒　*State of mind . . . span.* [9]

668　　　　　　　　　　　　　　　　　　　　　　　　lament

悼　To keep this character distinct from others of similar connotation, one need only think of the Prophet Jeremiah whose poetry gave an *eminence* to *the state of mind* we call **lamentation**. [11]

669　　　　　　　　　　　　　　　　　　　　　　　enlightenment

悟　I know of an Indian religious sect which teaches that **enlightenment** is to be had by covering the eyes with one's index fingers, the ears with the thumbs, and the mouth with the little fingers.

While these differ a bit from the *five holes* that we used to represent the "*I*" (FRAME 17), the idea of achieving a special *state of mind* by covering those five places can help you learn this kanji. You might try the position out while you are learning this character. [10]

670 怖	**dreadful** *State of mind . . . linen.* [8]
671 慌	**disconcerted** *State of mind . . . laid waste.* [12]
672 悔	**repent** *State of mind . . . every (see* FRAME 497*).* [9]
673 憎	**hate** *State of mind . . . increase.* [14]
674 慣	**accustomed** *State of mind . . . pierce.* [14]
675 愉	**pleasure** *State of mind . . . butchers (see* FRAME 307*).* [12]
676 惰	**lazy** *State of mind . . . left (i.e. "sinister") . . . flesh.* [12]
677 慎	**humility** *State of mind . . . truth.* [13]
678 憾	**remorse** *State of mind . . . emotion.* Hint: the etymology of "**remorse**" indicates a memory that returns again and again to "bite at" one's conscience and disturb one's peace of mind. [16]

679	recollection
憶	*State of mind . . . idea.* [16]

680	disquieting
惧	*State of mind . . . tool.* [11]

681	yearn
憧	Think of the *state of mind* you were in as a child with a particularly *juvenile* **yearning**. [15]

682	hanker
憬	*State of mind . . . scenery.* [15]

683	pining
慕	*Graveyard . . . valentine.* Note carefully the stroke order of the *valentine* primitive. [14]

莫　募　慕　慕　慕

684	annexed
添	*Water . . . heavens . . . valentine.* [11]

685	invariably
必	First note the stroke order of this character, which did not really evolve from the *heart,* even though we take it that way. If one takes it as a pictograph "dividing" *the heart* in half, then one has one of those **invariably** true bits of human anatomy: the fact that each *heart* is divided into two halves. [5]

丶　ソ　义　必　必

686	ooze
泌	*Water . . .* the *invariably* divided heart. [8]

Lesson 23

WHEN YOU FINISH this lengthy lesson you shall have passed well beyond one-third of our way through this book. Here we focus on elements having to do with hands and arms. As always, the one protection you have against confusing the elements is to form clear and distinct images the first time you meet them. If you make it through this chapter smoothly, the worst will be behind you and you should have nothing more to fear the rest of the way.

687		hand
手	Any way you count them, there are either too many or too few fingers to see a good pictograph of a **hand** in this character. But that it is, and so you must. [4]	

ノ 二 三 手

* Keep to the etymology when using this kanji as a primitive: a single *hand* all by itself.

688		watch over
看	*Hand . . . eyes.* [9]	

手 看

689		chafe
摩	*Hemp . . . hand.* [15]	

690		ego
我	*Hand . . . fiesta.* Note how the second stroke of the *hand* is stretched across to double up as the first stroke of the tasseled arrow we use for *fiesta*. Compare to FRAMES 17, 36, and 564. [7]	

ノ 二 千 手 扑 我 我

691	righteousness
義	*Sheep . . . ego.* [13]

692	deliberation
議	*Words . . . righteousness.* [20]

693	sacrifice
犠	*Cow . . . righteousness.* Do NOT use the image of an animal **sacrifice** here, as that will have its own character later on. [17]

*	fingers
扌	This alternate form of the primitive for *hand* we shall use to represent *finger* or *fingers*. It always appears at the left. [3]

$$ ー \quad 十 \quad 扌 $$

694	rub
抹	*Fingers . . . extremity.* [8]

695	wipe
拭	*Fingers . . . style.* [9]

696	yank
拉	The sense of this key word is to pull or jerk, as in opening a door or making "ramen" noodles. Its elements: *fingers . . . vase.* [8]

697	embrace
抱	*Fingers . . . wrap.* [8]

698	board
搭	The key word refers to **boarding** vessels for travel. Its elements are: *finger . . . flowers . . . fit together* (see FRAME 270). [12]

699 抄	extract
Fingers . . . a few. [7]	

700 抗	confront
Fingers . . . a whirlwind. [7]	

701 批	criticism
Finger . . . compare. [7]	

702 招	beckon
Finger . . . seduce. [8]	

703 拓	clear the land
Fingers . . . rocks. [8]	

704 拍	clap
Fingers . . . white. [8]	

705 打	strike
Finger . . . spike. [5]	

706 拘	arrest
Fingers . . . phrase. [8]	

707 捨	discard
Fingers . . . cottage. [11]	

708 拐	kidnap
Finger . . . mouth . . . dagger. [8]	

709 摘	pinch
Finger . . . antique. [14]	

710 挑	*Fingers . . . portent.* [9]	challenge
711 指	*Finger . . . delicious.* [9]	finger
712 持	*Fingers . . . Buddhist temple.* [9]	hold
713 拶	*Fingers . . . flood . . . evening.* [9]	imminent
714 括	*Finger . . . tongue.* [9]	fasten
715 揮	*Finger . . . chariot.* [12]	brandish
716 推	*Fingers . . . turkey.* [11]	conjecture
717 揚	*Fingers . . . piggy bank.* [12]	hoist
718 提	*Fingers . . . just so.* [12]	propose
719 損	*Finger . . . employee.* [13]	damage
720 拾	*Fingers . . . fit together.* Compare FRAME 698. [9]	pick up

721 担	shouldering
	The key word of this frame refers to **shouldering** a burden of some sort. Its elements are: *fingers . . . nightbreak*. [8]

722 拠	foothold
	Fingers . . . dispose. [8]

723 描	sketch
	Fingers . . . seedling. [11]

724 操	maneuver
	Fingers . . . goods . . . tree. [16]

725 接	touch
	Fingers . . . vase . . . woman. [11]

726 掲	put up a notice
	Fingers . . . siesta. [11]

727 掛	hang
	Fingers . . . ivy . . . magic wand. [11]

728 捗	make headway
	Let your *fingers* do the *walking* as you **make headway** through the Yellow Pages in search of something hard to find. [11]

* 开	two hands
	Let this primitive represent a union of **two hands**, both of which are used at the same time. Whenever this element appears at the bottom of its relative primitive, the top line is omitted, whether or not there is a horizontal line to replace it. [4]

一 二 于 开

729 研	polish
	Stone . . . two hands. [9]

730 戒	commandment
	Two hands . . . fiesta. [7]

一　开　戒

731 弄	tinker with
	Jewel . . . two hands. [7]

732 械	contraption
	Tree . . . commandment. [11]

733 鼻	nose
	Let me share a rather grotesque image to help with this kanji. Imagine taking your *two hands* and reaching up into someone's *nostrils*. Once inside you grab hold of the *brain* and yank it out. At the end, you would have a picture something like that of this character, the full kanji for **nose**. [14]

734 刑	punish
	Two hands . . . saber. [6]

735 型	mould
	Punish . . . soil. In cases like this, you might find it easier to break the character up into its more basic elements, like this: *two hands . . . saber . . . soil.* [9]

736 才	genius
	Whatever one is particularly adept at—one's special "**genius**"—one can do very easily, "with one finger" as the phrase goes. This kanji is a pictograph of that one finger. Note how its distinctive form is created by writing the final stroke of the element for *fingers* backwards. [3]

一　十　才

* The primitive meaning, *genie*, derives from the roots of the word *genius*. Use the *genie* out in the open when the primitive appears to the right of or below its relative primitive; in that case it also keeps its same form. At the left, the form is altered to 才, and the meaning becomes a *genie in the bottle*.

737		**property**
財	Clam . . . genie. [10]	

738		**lumber**
材	Tree . . . genie. [7]	

739		**suppose**
存	Genie in the bottle . . . a child. Hint: focus on the key word's connotation of "make believe". [6]	

一　ナ　才　存

740		**exist**
在	Genie in the bottle . . . soil. [6]	

741		**from**
乃	This pictograph of a clenched fist is another of the "hand-primitives." Take note of its rather peculiar drawing. Try to think of drawing a *fist* (the primitive meaning) "**from**" this character to give yourself a connotation for the otherwise abstract key word. [2]	

丿　乃

* The primitive meaning is taken from the pictograph: a *fist*.

742	portable

携

Fingers . . . turkey . . . fist. [13]

743	reach out

及

The addition of a final stroke transforms this character from the primitive for a clenched *fist* into the kanji for **reaching out**, much as a stroke of kindness can often turn anger into acceptance. [3]

ノ　乃　及

* As a primitive, this shall stand for *outstretched hands*. Only take care not to confuse it with that for *beg* (FRAME 501)

744	suck

吸

Mouth . . . outstretched hands. Hint: use the image of a nursing baby. [6]

745	handle

扱

Finger . . . outstretched hands. [6]

*	arm

人

The picture of an **arm** dangling from the trunk of the body gives us the element for **arm**, or **tucked under the arm** (relative to the element below it). Examples of both usages follow. Unlike most primitives, the kanji that bears the same meaning (FRAME 1522) has absolutely no connection with it. [2]

ノ　人

746	length

丈

The **length** whose measure this kanji depicts extends from the tip of one hand to the tip of the other with *arms* at full length. Notice the final stroke, which cuts across the vertical second stroke to distinguish it from *large* (FRAME 112). [3]

一 ナ 丈

747

史

history

A mouth . . . tucked under the arm. [5]

ロ 史 史

748

吏

officer

One . . . mouth . . . tucked under the arm. [6]

749

更

grow late

The implication behind the meaning of **grow late** is that things are changing in the same way that the day turns into night. The elements: *ceiling . . . sun . . . tucked under the arm.* [7]

日 亊 更

750

硬

stiff

Rocks . . . grow late. [12]

751

梗

spiny

This character refers originally to a deciduous, rough tree that grows on mountain plains. From this it gets the secondary sense of rugged or **spiny**. Its primitive elements: *tree . . . grow late.* [11]

752

又

or again

Like the several abbreviations in Roman script to indicate "and" (+, &, etc.), this short two-stroke kanji is used for the similar meaning of **or again**. [2]

フ 又

* As a primitive, it will mean *crotch*, as in the *crotch* of the arm. Or whatever.

753		pair
双	The *crotch* reduplicated gives us a **pair**. [4]	

754		mulberry
桑	*Crotches, crotches* everywhere . . . *tree*. Hint: think of a group of children playing an original version of "Here We Go 'Round the **Mulberry** Bush." [10]	

755		vessels
隻	The key word indicates the Japanese generic term for counting ships. Its elements: *turkey . . . crotch*. [10]	

756		safeguard
護	*Words . . . flowers . . . vessels*. [20]	

757		seize
獲	A pack of *wild dogs . . . flowers . . . vessels*. Do not confuse this with the character for *arrest* (FRAME 706). [16]	

758		guy
奴	*Woman . . . crotch*. [5]	

759		angry
怒	*Guy . . . heart*. [9]	

760		friend
友	*By one's side . . . crotch*. [4]	

一 ナ 方 友

761		slip out
抜	*Fingers . . . friend*. [7]	

* 殳	**missile**
	Although modern connotations are more suggestive, this primitive simply refers to something thrown as a weapon. Its elements: *wind . . . crotch.* [4]

几　殳

762 投	**throw**
	Fingers . . . missile. [7]

763 没	**drown**
	Water . . . missile. [7]

764 股	**thigh**
	Flesh . . . missile. [8]

765 設	**establishment**
	Words . . . missile. [11]

766 擊	**beat**
	Car . . . missile . . . hand. [15]

車　軐　擊

767 殼	**husk**
	Samurai . . . superfluous . . . missile. [11]

士　壳　殼

768 支	**branch**
	Needle . . . crotch. [4]

十　支

769 技	skill
	Fingers . . . branch. [7]

770 枝	bough
	Tree . . . branch. Take a moment to focus on the differences between a **bough**, a *branch*, and a *twig* (FRAME 319). [8]

771 肢	limb
	Part of the body . . . branch. [8]

★ 圣	spool
	Here we see a simplified drawing of a **spool** (the element for *earth* at the bottom) with threads being wound about it tightly (the *crotch* at the top). You may remember it either pictographically or by way of the primitives. [5]

又 圣

772 茎	stalk
	Flower . . . spool. [8]

773 怪	suspicious
	State of mind . . . spool. [8]

774 軽	lightly
	Car . . . spool. [12]

775 叔	uncle
	Above . . . little . . . crotch. [8]

上 卡 叔

776 督	coach
	Uncle . . . eye. [13]

777 寂	loneliness
House . . . uncle. [11]	

778 淑	graceful
Water . . . uncle. [11]	

779 反	anti-
Cliff . . . crotch. [4]	

780 坂	slope
Ground . . . anti-. [7]	

781 板	plank
Tree . . . anti-. [8]	

782 返	return
Anti- . . . road. [7]	

783 販	marketing
Shells/money . . . anti-. [11]	

784 爪	claw
This character is a pictograph of a bird's **claw**, and from there comes to mean animal **claws** in general (including human fingernails). [4]	

$$\qquad ´\qquad 厂\qquad 爪\qquad 爪$$

* As a primitive, we shall use the graphic image of a *vulture*, a bird known for its powerful *claws*. It generally appears above another primitive, in which case it gets squeezed into the form 爫.

785 妥	gentle
	Vulture . . . woman. [7]

* 孚	fledgling
	The *vulture* and *child* combine to create the image of an aerie full of **fledglings**. [7]

ㄅ　孚

786 乳	milk
	Fledglings . . . hook. [8]

787 浮	floating
	Water . . . fledglings. [10]

788 淫	lewd
	Water . . . vulture . . . porter. [11]

789 将	leader
	Turtle . . . vulture . . . glue. [10]

790 奨	exhort
	Leader . . . St. Bernard dog. Do not confuse with *urge* (FRAME 300). [13]

791 采	grab
	Vulture . . . tree. [8]

792 採	pick
	Unlike *pick up* (FRAME 720), this character is used for **picking** fruits from trees. Its elements: *finger . . . grab.* [11]

793	vegetable
菜	Flower . . . grab. [11]

*	birdhouse
㢆	The *claw* and crown of the roof of a *house* (whose chimney is displaced by the *claw*) combine to give us a **birdhouse**. [6]

㢆 㢆

794	accept
受	Birdhouse . . . crotch. [8]

795	impart
授	Fingers . . . accept. [11]

796	love
愛	Birdhouse . . . heart . . . walking legs. [13]

㢆 惢 愛

797	unclear
曖	Sun . . . love. [17]

*	elbow
ム	This pictograph of an arm bent at the **elbow** is obvious. [2]

ㄥ ム

798	pay
払	Finger . . . elbow. [5]

799	wide
広	Cave . . . elbow. [5]

800 勾	hooked
	Bound up . . . elbow. Think of this key word in the sense of something that has been nabbed or caught. [4]

801 拡	broaden
	Fingers . . . wide. The connection with the previous character is very close. Beware. [8]

802 鉱	mineral
	Metal . . . wide. [13]

803 弁	valve
	Elbow . . . two hands. [5]

804 雄	male
	By one's side . . . elbow . . . turkey. Its match can be found in FRAME 605. [12]

805 台	pedestal
	Elbow . . . mouth. [5]

806 怠	neglect
	Pedestal . . . heart. [9]

807 治	reign
	Water . . . pedestal. [8]

808 冶	metallurgy
	Ice . . . pedestal. [7]

809 始	commence
	Woman . . . pedestal. [8]

810	womb
胎	*Part of the body . . . pedestal.* [9]

811	window
窓	*House . . . human legs . . . elbow . . . heart.* [11]

宀　穴　窓　窓

812	gone
去	*Soil . . . elbow.* [5]

土　去

813	method
法	*Water . . . gone.* [8]

*	wall
乙	The *elbow* hanging under a *ceiling* will become our element for a **wall**. [3]

一　乙　乙

814	meeting
会	*Meeting . . . wall.* This is the full character for **meeting**, from which the abbreviated primitive that we met back in Lesson 12 gets its name. [6]

个　会

815	climax
至	*Wall . . . soil.* The key word allows for the full variety of connotations: to peak, to arrive at the end, and the like. [6]

乙　至

816 室	room

House . . . climax. [9]

817 到	arrival

Climax . . . saber. [8]

818 致	doth

The archaic English form for "does" indicates a humble form of the verb "to do." It is made up of *climax* and *taskmaster*. [10]

819 互	mutually

When you draw this character think of linking two *walls* together, one right side up and the other upside down. [4]

一 ⼕ 瓦 互

★ 去	infant

This primitive can be seen as an abbreviation of the full primitive for *child*, the second stroke dividing the head from the body much as it does in 子 and the other strokes condensing the long form so that it can be used atop its relative primitive. We change the meaning to **infant** to facilitate keeping the full form and its abbreviation distinct. [4]

亠 去

820 棄	abandon

Infant . . . buckle (see FRAME 444*) . . . tree.* [13]

去 奋 棄

821 育	bring up

Since the key word has to do with raising children to be strong both in mind and body, it is easy to coordinate the primitive elements: *infant . . . meat.* [8]

| 822 撤 | *Fingers . . . bring up . . . taskmaster.* [15] | remove |

扌　捛　撤

| 823 充 | *Infant . . . human legs.* [6] | allot |

| 824 銃 | *Metal . . . allot.* [14] | gun |

| 825 硫 | *Rock . . . infant . . . flood.* [12] | sulfur |

| 826 流 | *Water . . . infant . . . flood.* Be sure to distinguish the two water-primitives from one another in making your story. [10] | current |

| 827 允 | *Elbow . . . human legs.* [4] | license |

| 828 唆 | *Mouth . . . license . . . walking legs.* [10] | tempt |

口　唉　唆

Lesson 24

AFTER THAT LONG excursus into arm and hand primitives, we will take a breather in this lesson with a much easier group built up from the kanji for *exit* and *enter*.

234 234 REMEMBERING THE KANJI 1

829 出	**exit**
	The kanji for **exit** pictures a series of mountain peaks coming out of the *earth*. Learn it together with the following frame. [5]

丨　屮　屮　出　出

830 山	**mountain**
	Note the clearer outline of a triangular **mountain** here. [3]

丨　山　山

831 拙	**bungling**
	Fingers . . . exit. [8]

832 岩	**boulder**
	Mountain . . . rock. [8]

833 炭	**charcoal**
	Mountain . . . ashes. [9]

834 岐	**branch off**
	Mountains . . . branch. [7]

835 峠	**mountain pass**
	Mountain . . . above . . . below. [9]

山　山⊢　峠

836 崩	**crumble**
	Mountain . . . companion. [11]

837 密	**secrecy**
	House . . . invariably . . . mountain. [11]

宀 宓 密

838 蜜	honey *House . . . invariably . . . insect.* [14]
839 嵐	storm *Mountain . . . winds.* [12]
840 崎	promontory *Mountain . . . strange.* Hint: you might save yourself the trouble of a story here simply by recalling the kanji for *cape* (FRAME 164) and toying around with the differing images suggested by the key words **promontory** and *cape*. [11]
841 崖	bluffs *Mountain . . . cliff . . . ivy.* [11]

842

入

enter

This character is meant to be a picture of someone walking leftward, putting one leg forward in order to **enter** someplace. Since the "in" side of a character is the left, it should be easy to remember the writing of this character. [2]

ノ 入

* As a primitive, the meaning of the key word is expanded to include: *to go in, to put in, to come in,* and the like. It generally appears atop its relative primitive, where, unlike the element for *umbrella* 𠆢, the two strokes do not touch each other, making it virtually the same as the kanji for *eight*. When it appears in any other position, however, it retains its original form.

843

込

crowded

Enter . . . road. [5]

844	part
分	Go in . . . dagger. [4]

八 分

845	poverty
貧	Part . . . shells/money. [11]

846	partition
頒	Part . . . head. [13]

847	public
公	Come in . . . elbows. Use the key word in its adjectival sense, not as a noun. [4]

848	pine tree
松	Tree . . . public. [8]

849	venerable old man
翁	Public . . . feathers. [10]

850	sue
訟	Words . . . public. [11]

851	valley
谷	Go in . . . an umbrella . . . a mouth. Because of space restrictions, the element for *go in* is shortened in this character. If you stand on your head and look at this kanji, the image of a **valley** stands out more clearly: the *mouth* of the river whose water flows down at the intersection of the two mountains, with the final two strokes adding the element of perspective. Now get back on your feet again and see if the image still remains clear. If not, then return to the primitives and make a story in the usual way. [7]

八 父 谷

852	bathe
浴	*Water . . . valley.* [10]

853	contain
容	This character depicts a *house* so large that it can **contain** an entire *valley*. [10]

854	melt
溶	*Water . . . contain.* [13]

855	longing
欲	*Valley . . . yawn.* Be sure to keep the key word distinct from *pining* (FRAME 683). [11]

856	abundant
裕	This character shows the typical *cloak* of *valley* folk, which, unlike the tailor-made, high-fashion overcoats of city folk, is loose-fitting and free-form. Hence the key word's meaning of **abundant**. [12]

*	gully
谷	As an abbreviation of the kanji for a *valley*, this primitive gets its meaning as a small valley or **gully**. [5]

八 谷

857	lead (metal)
鉛	*Metal . . . gully.* [13]

858	run alongside
沿	*Water . . . gully.* The key word is meant to refer to things like rivers and railway tracks that **run alongside** something else. [8]

Lesson 25

THE FOLLOWING GROUP of kanji revolve about primitive elements having to do with human beings. We shall have more to add to this set of primitives before we are through, but even the few we bring in here will enable us to learn quite a few new characters. We begin with another "roof" primitive.

★ 尚		outhouse

The combination of the element for *little*, the basic "roof" structure here (in which the chimney was overwritten, as it was in the element for *birdhouse*), combined with the "window" (*mouth*) below, gives this element its meaning of **outhouse**. Although the window is not an essential part of an **outhouse**, I think you will agree that its inclusion is a boon to the imagination, greatly simplifying the learning of the characters in which it appears. [8]

ッ   ㄓ   尚

859

賞   **prize**

Outhouse . . . shellfish. [15]

860

党   **party**

Think of this key word as referring to a political **party**, not a gala affair. Its elements: *human legs . . .* sticking out of an *outhouse* window. [10]

861

堂   **hall**

Outhouse . . . land. [11]

862

常   **usual**

Outhouse . . . towel. [11]

863 裳	skirt
	The key word refers to an ancient **skirt** once used as part of a woman's costume. The primitives you have to work with are: *outhouse . . . garment.* [14]

864 掌	manipulate
	Outhouse . . . hand. [12]

865 皮	pelt
	The simplest way to remember this character is to see it as built up from that for *branch*. The first stroke can then stand for something "hanging" down from the *branch*, namely its bark or **pelt**. The barb at the end of the second stroke is the only other change. Merely by concentrating on this as you write the following small cluster of characters should be enough to fix the form in your mind. By way of exception, you might doodle around with the kanji's form to see what you can come up with. [5]

丿　厂　广　广　皮

866 波	waves
	Water's . . . pelt. [8]

867 婆	old woman
	Waves . . . woman. [11]

868 披	expose
	Fingers . . . pelt. [8]

869 破	rend
	Rock . . . pelt. [10]

870 被	incur
	Cloak . . . pelt. [10]

礻 被

	bone
歹	This character is meant to be a pictograph of a **bone** attached to a piece of flesh (or vice versa.) The first stroke serves to keep it distinct from the character for *evening* (FRAME 114). [4]

一 丆 歹 歹

871 残	remainder
	Bones . . . (parade) *float.* [10]

872 殉	martyrdom
	Bones . . . decameron. [10]

873 殊	particularly
	Bones . . . vermilion. [10]

874 殖	augment
	Bones . . . straightaway. [12]

875 列	file
	Bones . . . saber. The sense of the key word is of people or things lined up in a row. [6]

876 裂	split
	File . . . garment. [12]

877 烈	ardent
	File . . . oven fire. [10]

878	death
死	*Bones . . . spoon.* Note how the first stroke is extended to the right, forming a sort of "roof" overhead. [6]

879	interment
葬	*Flowers . . . death . . . two hands.* Do not confuse with *bury* (FRAME 191).[12]

*	sunglasses
舛	These two elements are actually the full form whose abbreviation we learned as the character for *measuring box* in FRAME 42. To the left, we see the familiar shape of *evening*, and to the right a completely new shape. The meaning we have assigned, **sunglasses**, is entirely arbitrary. [7]

ノ　ク　タ　タ　夗　夗　舛

880	wink
瞬	*Eye . . . birdhouse . . . sunglasses.* [18]

881	ear
耳	The pictograph for the **ear** looks much like that for *eye*, but note how the stroke order gives it a different look. [6]

一　丁　下　下　耳　耳

882	take
取	*Ear . . . crotch.* [8]

883	gist
趣	*Run . . . take.* [15]

884	utmost
最	*Sun . . . take.* [12]

885 撮	snapshot
	Finger ... utmost. This character *is* used for taking photographs. Note how, conveniently, the element for "*take*" is included in it. [15]

886 恥	shame
	Ear ... heart. It is most rare to have the *heart* at the right, rather than at the bottom. Take advantage of this fact when you compose your story. [10]

887 職	post
	The key word refers to one's occupation, or position of employment. Its elements: *ear ... kazoo.* [18]

888 聖	holy
	Ear ... mouth ... king. [13]

889 敢	daring
	Spike ... ear ... taskmaster. [12]

890 聴	listen
	Ear ... needle ... eye ... heart. Compare FRAME 427 for this and the following kanji, and then once again when you get to FRAME 950. [17]

891 懐	pocket
	State of mind ... needle ... eyes ... garment. [16]

* 曼	mandala
	Sun ... eye ... crotch. [11]
	曰　　　㬓　　曼

892 慢	ridicule
	State of mind . . . mandala. [14]

893 漫	loose
	Water . . . mandala. [14]

894 買	buy
	Eye . . . shellfish. [12]

895 置	placement
	Eye . . . straightaway. [13]

896 罰	penalty
	Eye . . . words . . . saber. [14]

897 寧	rather
	House . . . heart . . . eye . . . spike. [14]

898 濁	voiced
	The key word for this kanji connotes the "muddying" effect on a soft consonant brought about by vibrating the vocal chords. For example, in English a "j" is **voiced** while a "sh" is unvoiced. In Japanese, the し is changed to じ when it is **voiced**. The primitives are: *water . . . eye . . . bound up . . . insect.* [16]

899 環	ring
	Jewel . . . eye . . . ceiling . . . mouth . . . scarf. The number of elements is large here, so take care. Learn it in conjunction with the next frame, since these are the only two cases in this book where the combination of elements to the right appears. [17]

900 還	send back
	Road . . . eye . . . ceiling . . . mouth . . . scarf. [16]

901   husband

夫

The kanji for *a* **husband** or "head of the family" is based on the kanji for *large* and an extra line near the top for the "head." Recall the kanji for *heavens* already learned back in FRAME 457, and be sure to keep your story for this kanji different. [4]

一　二　㐄　夫

---

902   aid

扶

Fingers . . . husband. [7]

---

903   mountain stream

渓

Water . . . vulture . . . husband. [11]

---

904   standard

規

Husband . . . see. [11]

---

905   exchange

替

Two husbands . . . day. [12]

---

906   approve

賛

Two husbands . . . shells. [15]

---

907   submerge

潜

Water . . . exchange. [15]

---

908   lose

失

"To **lose**" here takes the sense of "misplace," not the sense of *defeat*, whose kanji we learned in FRAME 67. It pictures a *husband* with something falling from his side as he is walking along, something he **loses**. [5]

ノ　失

* As a primitive, this character can also mean *to drop*.

909 鉄	iron
Metal . . . to drop. [13]	

910 迭	alternate
To drop . . . road. [8]	

911 臣	retainer

This kanji is actually a pictograph for an eye, distorted to make it appear that the pupil is protruding towards the right. This may not be an easy form to remember, but try this: Draw it once rather large, and notice how moving the two vertical lines on the right as far right as possible gives you the pictograph of the eye in its natural form. The "pop-eye" image belongs to an Emperor's **retainer** standing in awe before his ruler. [7]

丨 厂 厂 卢 臣 臣 臣

* As a primitive, the meaning of the key word becomes *slave*.

912 姫	princess
Woman . . . slave. [10]	

913 蔵	storehouse
Flowers . . . parade . . . slaves. [15]	

艹 广 莀 蔵

914 臓	entrails
Part of the body . . . storehouse. [19]	

月 臓

915	intelligent
賢	*Slave . . . crotch . . . shellfish.* [16]

916	kidney
腎	*Slave . . . crotch . . . flesh.* [13]

917	strict
堅	*Slave . . . crotch . . . soil.* [12]

918	look to
臨	*Slave . . . reclining . . . goods.* The key word suggests both **looking** ahead **to** something and "seeing to" what is at hand. Consistent with everything that we have learned about the role of the key word, this means that you must choose ONE meaning and stick to it. [18]

919	perusal
覧	*Slaves . . . reclining . . . floor . . . see.* [17]

920	gigantic
巨	This kanji depicts a **gigantic** "pop-eye," which accounts for its shape. Be sure not to confuse it with the *slave (retainer)* we just learned. [5]

丨 厂 厂 戸 巨

921	repel
拒	*Fingers . . . gigantic.* [8]

922	power
力	With a little imagination, one can see a muscle in this simple, two-stroke character meaning **power**. [2]

フ 力

* As a primitive, either *muscle* or *power* can be used.

923	man
男	*Rice fields . . . power.* This character is the gender-specific **man**, not the generic human *person* of FRAME 951. [7]

924	labor
劳	*Schoolhouse . . . power.* [7]

925	recruit
募	*Graveyard . . . power.* [12]

926	inferiority
劣	*Few . . . muscles.* [6]

927	achievement
功	*Craft . . . power.* [5]

928	persuade
勧	*Pegasus . . . power.* [13]

929	toil
努	*Guy . . . muscle.* [7]

930	uprising
勃	If you think of the *ten* as a little "cross" sitting atop the root of a *house* where we are used to seeing the "chimney" (*drop*), then you have the image of a *chapel*. (This combination will appear once more in this book: FRAME 1465.) To complete the picture for **uprising**, add: *child . . . muscles.* [9]

931	encourage
励	*Cliff . . . ten thousand . . . power.* [7]

932	add
加	*Muscles . . . mouth.* This is the only case in which the primitive for *muscle* appears on the left; note should be taken of the fact in composing one's story. [5]

933	congratulations
賀	*Add . . . shells.* [12]

934	erect
架	*Add . . . trees.* Hint: if you ever *played with* an "**Erector** Set" or "Tinker Toys" as a child, don't pass up the opportunity to relate it to this kanji's key word and the element for *trees*. [9]

935	armpit
脇	*Part of the body . . . muscles* (three of which give us "*triceps*" or "*muscles* on top of *muscles*"). You will want to keep the kanji distinct from the one that follows by paying attention to the positioning of the elements. [10]

936	threaten
脅	*Triceps . . . meat.* [10]

937	co-
協	This prefix should be kept distinct from *inter* (FRAME 222) and *mutual* (FRAME 819). Its elements: *needle . . . triceps*. [8]

938	going
行	By joining the top four strokes, you should get a picture of the front current of a river, the stream trailing behind. Hence the character for **going**. [6]

ノ　ク　彳　彳　行　行

* As a primitive, this character has two forms. Reduced to the
  left side only, 彳, it can mean a *column, going,* or a *line* of some-

thing or other. When the middle is opened up to make room for other elements, it means a *boulevard*.

---

939   **rhythm**

律   This character depicts a calligrapher's *brush* and its **rhythmic** sway as it flows down *a column* writing kanji on the way. [9]

---

940   **restore**

復   *Going . . . double back.* [12]

---

941   **gain**

得   *Column . . . nightbreak . . . glue.* [11]

---

942   **accompany**

従   *Column . . . animal horns . . . mending.* [10]

---

943   **junior**

徒   *Line . . . run.* [10]

---

944   **wait**

待   *Line . . . Buddhist temple.* [9]

---

945   **journey**

往   *Column . . . candlestick.* This character has the special sense of **journeying** to someplace or other. [8]

---

946   **subjugate**

征   *Column . . . correct.* [8]

---

947   **diameter**

径   *Line . . . spool.* [8]

948 彼	he
	Going . . . pelt. This kanji refers to the third person singular personal pronoun, generally in its masculine form. [8]

949 役	duty
	Going . . . missile. [7]

950 德	benevolence
	Going . . . needle . . . eye . . . heart. Refer back now to the note in FRAME 890. [14]

951 徹	penetrate
	Line . . . bring up . . . taskmaster. [15]

952 徵	indications
	Line . . . mountain . . . king . . . taskmaster. [14]
	彳　彳丬　彳丬　徵

953 懲	penal
	Indications . . . heart. [18]

954 微	delicate
	Line . . . mountain . . . ceiling . . . human legs . . . taskmaster. [13]

955 街	boulevard
	This is the character from which the sense of **boulevard** mentioned in FRAME 938 derives. Its elements: *boulevard . . ivy.* [12]

956 桁	girder
	Tree . . . going. [10]

957	equilibrium

衡

Boulevard . . . bound up . . . brains . . . St. Bernard dog. [16]

彳 彳 徉 徫 衡

Lesson 26

WE RETURN ONCE again to the world of plants and growing things, not yet to complete our collection of those primitives, but to focus on three elements that are among the most commonly found throughout the kanji.

Now and again, you will no doubt have observed, cross-reference is made to other kanji with similar key words. This can help avoid confusion if you check your earlier story and the connotation of its respective key word before proceeding with the kanji at hand. While it is impossible to know in advance which key words will cause confusion for which readers, I will continue to point out some of the likely problem cases.

---

*

禾

wheat

This primitive element will be made to stand for **wheat**. It connotes a special grain, more expensive than ordinary rice and so reserved for special occasions. Alternatively, it can mean *cereal*. Its form is like that for *tree*, except for the dot at the top to represent a spike of **wheat** blowing in the wind. [5]

ノ 二 千 禾 禾

958	draft

稿

The key word connotes the preliminary composition of a plan or manuscript. Its elements: *wheat . . . tall.* [15]

959 稼	earnings
	Wheat . . . house. [15]

960 程	extent
	Wheat . . . display . Do not confuse with *extremity* (FRAME 230) or *boundary* (FRAME 523). [12]

961 税	tax
	Wheat . . . devil. [12]

962 稚	immature
	Wheat . . . turkey. [13]

963 和	harmony
	Wheat . . . mouth. [8]

964 移	shift
	Wheat . . . many. [11]

965 秒	second
	The reference here is to a **second** of time. The elements: *wheat . . . few.* [9]

966 秋	autumn
	Wheat . . . fire. [9]

967 愁	distress
	Autumn . . . heart. [13]

968 私	private
	Wheat . . . elbow. Like the characters for *I* (FRAME 17) and *ego* (FRAME 690), this kanji is also representative of the subject, with the special connotation of **privacy**. [7]

969 秩	regularity
	Wheat . . . drop. [10]

970 秘	secret
	Cereal . . . invariably. [10]

971 称	appellation
	Wheat . . . reclining . . . little. [10]

972 利	profit
	Wheat . . . saber. Be careful not to confuse with *gain* (FRAME 941) or *earnings* (FRAME 959). [7]

973 梨	pear tree
	Profit . . . tree. [11]

974 穫	harvest
	Wheat . . . flowers . . . vessels. Compare FRAMES 756 and 757 for the right side. [18]

975 穂	ear of a plant
	Wheat . . . favor. [15]

976 稲	rice plant
	Wheat . . . vulture . . . olden times. [14]

977 香	incense
	Wheat . . . sun. [9]

978 季	seasons
	Wheat . . . child. [8]

979		committee
委	*Wheat . . . woman.* [8]	

980		excel
秀	*Wheat . . . fist.* [7]	

981		transparent
透	*Excel . . . road-way.* [10]	

982		entice
誘	*Words . . . excel.* Compare *beckon* (FRAME 702), to *urge* (FRAME 300), *seduce* (FRAME 90), and *encourage* (FRAME 931) when choosing your connotation. [14]	

983		training
稽	*Wheat . . . chihuahua with one human leg . . . delicious.* [15]	

984		cereals
穀	*Samurai . . . crown . . . wheat . . . missile.* [14]	

985		germ
菌	*Flowers . . . pent in . . . wheat.* [11]	

986		numb
萎	*Flowers . . . committee.* [11]	

987		rice
米	This kanji has a pictographic resemblance to a number of grains of **rice** lying on a plate in the shape of a star. [6]	

丶　　丷　　⺌　　半　　半　　米

* As a primitive, it keeps its meaning of *rice*, and is meant to connote a very ordinary, commonplace grain, in contrast to

the primitive for *wheat* that we just learned. (This meaning accords well with Japan, where the output of *rice* far exceeds that of *wheat*.)

It occasionally takes the shape 米 when it stands on its own, or is joined to a line above. In this case, we shall have it refer specifically to *grains of rice*. This primitive is not to be confused with the similar-looking primitive for *water*. While the stroke orders are nearly alike, *grains of rice* has 5 strokes, while *water* only has 4 because it joins the second and third strokes into one.

Finally, we may note that by itself the kanji for *rice* is an abbreviation used for the *United States*, which can then also serve as an alternate reading for the main primitive form, if you so wish.

988 粉	flour
Rice . . . part. [10]	

989 粘	sticky
Rice . . . fortune-telling. [11]	

990 粒	grains
Rice . . . vase. [11]	

991 粧	cosmetics
Rice . . . cave . . . soil. [12]	

992 迷	astray
Road . . . United States. [9]	

993 粋	chic
Rice . . . game of cricket. (See FRAME 121.) [10]	

994 謎	riddle
Words . . . astray. [16]	

995 糧	provisions
	Rice . . . quantity. [18]

996 菊	chrysanthemum
	Flower . . . bound up . . . rice. [11]

997 奥	core
	A drop . . . pent in . . . rice . . . St. Bernard dog. Notice that the horizontal line of the bottom primitive doubles up as the final stroke for pent in. [12]

998 数	number
	Rice . . . woman . . . taskmaster. [13]

999 楼	watchtower
	Tree . . . rice . . . woman. [13]

1000 類	sort
	Rice . . . St. Bernard dog . . . head. [18]

1001 漆	lacquer
	Water . . . tree . . . umbrella . . . grains of rice. [14]

1002 膝	knee
	Flesh . . . tree . . . umbrella . . . rice grains. [13]

1003 様	Esq.
	The abbreviation **Esq.** will help associate this character with the honorific form of address to which it belongs. Its elements are: tree . . . sheep . . . grains of rice. Note that the final vertical stroke in the element for sheep is extended to form the first stroke for grains of rice. [14]

才 样 様

1004 **request**

求

Let the *drop* in the upper right-hand corner of this character close the right angle off to make an *arrowhead*. Whenever we find the *needle* with that *drop* in an element that has no other special meaning, we will take advantage of this primitive meaning. At the bottom, we see the *grains of rice*, the vertical line doubling up for the two elements. Do not confuse with *petition* (FRAME 143). [7]

1005 **ball**

球

Ball . . . request. [11]

1006 **salvation**

救

Request . . . taskmaster. [11]

1007 **bamboo**

竹

Bamboo grows upwards, like a straight *nail*, and at each stage of its growth (which legend associates with the arrival of the new moon) there is a jointed rootstock (the first stroke). Two such **bamboo** stalks are pictured here. [6]

* As a primitive, the meaning remains the same, but the vertical lines are severely abbreviated so that they can take their place at the top where, like *flowers*, they are always to be found.

1008 **laugh**

笑

Bamboo . . . heavens. [10]

1009 **bamboo hat**

笠

Bamboo . . . vase. [11]

1010 **bamboo grass**

笹

Bamboo . . . generation. [11]

1011	stationery
箋	*Bamboo . . . float.* Note that the drawing of the primitive for *float* uses the abbreviated form that has become standard in the general-use kanji and as we met it earlier in 桟, 銭, and 浅 (FRAMES 393–95). Until such time as typesetting fonts make the adjustment, only the older form has been approved: 箋. Here we have opted for the simpler, avant garde drawing. [12]

1012	muscle
筋	*Bamboo . . . part of the body . . . power.* Here we see how the primitive meaning of **muscle** was derived from the kanji for *power.* [12]

1013	box
箱	*Bamboo . . . inter-.* [15]

1014	writing brush
筆	*Bamboo . . . brush.* [12]

1015	cylinder
筒	*Bamboo . . . monk.* [12]

1016	etc.
等	*Bamboo . . . Buddhist temple.* [12]

1017	calculate
算	*Bamboo . . . eyes . . . two hands.* [14]

1018	solution
答	*Bamboo . . . fit.* [12]

1019	scheme
策	*Bamboo . . . belted tree* (see FRAME 446). [12]

1020	register
簿	*Bamboo . . . water . . . acupuncturist.* [19]

1021	fabricate
築	*Bamboo . . . craft . . . mediocre . . . wood/tree.* [16]

1022	basket
篭	*Bamboo . . . dragon.* Note that the older (and still official) form of this kanji uses the old character for dragon 龍, which is good to learn and is fun to write in any case. It is made up of five primitive elements: *vase . . . flesh . . . slingshot . . . fishhook* (enclosure) *. . . three.* [16]

Lesson 27

THIS LESSON WILL take us just beyond the halfway mark. From there on, it will all be downhill. The final uphill push will involve what appears to be the simplest of primitive elements. It was withheld until now because of the difficulty it would have caused earlier on.

1023	person
人	The character for *enter* (FRAME 842) showed someone walking inwards (in terms of the direction of writing). The one for **person**, shown here, represents someone walking outwards. [2]

* As a primitive, it can keep its kanji form except when it appears to the left (its normal position), where it is made to stand up in the form ⺅.

The primitive meaning is another matter. The abstract notion of *person* so often has a relation to the meaning of the

kanji that confusion readily sets in. So many of the previous stories have included people in them that simply to use *person* for a primitive meaning would be risky. We need to be more specific, to focus on one particular *person*. Try to choose someone who has not figured in the stories so far, perhaps a colorful member of the family or a friend whom you have known for a long time. That individual will appear again and again, so be sure to choose someone who excites your imagination.

1024	assistant
佐	*Person ... left.* [7]

1025	partner
侶	*Person ... spine.* [9]

1026	however
但	*Person ... nightbreak.* [7]

1027	dwell
住	*Person ... candlestick.* [7]

1028	rank
位	*Person ... vase.* [7]

1029	go-between
仲	*Person ... in.* [6]

1030	body
体	*Person ... book.* [7]

1031	remote
悠	*Person ... walking stick ... taskmaster ... heart.* [11]

1032	affair
件	*Person . . . cow.* [6]

1033	attend
仕	*Person . . . samurai.* The key word means to wait on someone or serve them. [5]

1034	other
他	*Person . . . scorpion.* [5]

1035	prostrated
伏	*Person . . . chihuahua.* [6]

1036	transmit
伝	*Person . . . rising cloud.* Hint: the Amerindians' smoke signals can help provide a good image for this kanji, whose key word is meant to include **transmissions** of all sorts. [6]

1037	Buddha
仏	*Person . . . elbow.* [4]

1038	rest
休	*Person . . . tree.* Do not confuse with *relax* (FRAME 202).[6]

1039	provisional
仮	*Person . . . anti-.* [6]

1040	performing artist
伎	*Person . . . branch.* [6]

1041	chief
伯	*Person . . . white dove.* [7]

1042 俗	vulgar

Person . . . valley. The key word should be taken in its older sense of "popular" or "commonplace." [9]

1043 信	faith

Person . . . words. [9]

1044 佳	excellent

Person . . . ivy. To distinguish from *excel* (FRAME 980), *eminent* (FRAME 52), *esteem* (FRAME 196), and *exquisite* (FRAME 130), give the key word its own unique connotation. [8]

1045 依	reliant

Person . . . garment. [8]

1046 例	example

Person . . . file. [8]

1047 個	individual

Person . . . harden. [10]

1048 健	healthy

Person . . . build. [11]

亻 律 健

1049 側	side

Person . . . rule. See FRAME 92 for help. [11]

1050 侍	waiter

Person . . . Buddhist temple. The key word is deceptively modern, but the kanji is actually another way of writing "samurai." Be careful not to confuse with *attend* (FRAME 1033).[8]

1051	halt
停	*Person . . . pavilion.* [11]

1052	price
値	*Person . . . straightaway.* [10]

1053	emulate
倣	*Person . . . set free.* [10]

1054	arrogance
傲	*Person . . . soil . . . compass . . . taskmaster.* You may, of course, take the character for *emulate* from the previous frame as the basis for this kanji, adding to it only the element for *soil*. [13]

1055	overthrow
倒	*Person . . . arrival.* [10]

1056	spy
偵	*Person . . . upright.* [11]

1057	Buddhist priest
僧	*Person . . . increase.* [13]

1058	hundred million
億	*Person . . . idea.* [15]

1059	ceremony
儀	*Person . . . righteousness.* [15]

1060	reparation
償	*Person . . . prize.* [17]

1061	hermit
仙	*Person . . . mountain.* [5]

1062	sponsor
催	*Hermit . . . turkey.* Note what has happened to the *mountain* in the element for *hermit*. In order to make room for the *turkey*, it was raised and condensed. [13]

1063	humanity
仁	To refer to the fullness of **humanity** that can only be achieved in dialogue with another *(person . . . two)*, Confucius used this character. [4]

1064	scorn
侮	*Every . . . person.* [8]

1065	use
使	*Person . . . officer.* [8]

1066	convenience
便	*Person . . grow late.* Hint: this kanji also means that unmentionable material that one disposes of when one goes to the "**conveniences**." [9]

1067	double
倍	*Person . . . muzzle.* Do not confuse with the kanji for *duplicate* (FRAME 504). [10]

1068	tenderness
優	*Person . . melancholy.* [17]

1069	fell
伐	*Person . . . fiesta.* Hint: recall the German legend of the English missionary, Saint Boniface, who **felled** the sacred oak tree dedi-

cated to Thor at Geismar (in lower Hessia), occasioning a great *fiesta* for the Christians in the neighborhood to mark the defeat of their pagan competition. Be sure to fit your special *person* into the story if you use it. [6]

1070 宿	inn
House . . . person . . . hundred. [11]	

1071 傷	wound
Person . . . reclining . . . piggy bank. [13]	

1072 保	protect
Person . . . mouth . . . tree. [9]	

1073 褒	praise
Top hat and scarf . . . protect. Note that the "tree" in *protect* becomes a *wooden pole* here. [15]	

1074 傑	greatness
Person . . . sunglasses . . . tree. [13]	

1075 付	adhere
Person . . . glue. The few cases in which this character serves as a primitive should include some connotation of "**adhering** to" that distinguishes it from "*glued to.*" Two examples follow. [5]	

1076 符	token
Bamboo . . . adhere. [11]	

1077 府	municipality
Cave . . . adhere. [8]	

1078 任	responsibility
Person . . . porter. [6]	

1079 賃	fare
	Responsibility . . . shells/money. [13]

1080 代	substitute
	Person . . . arrow. [5]

1081 袋	sack
	Substitute . . . garment. [11]

1082 貸	lend
	Substitute . . . shells/money. [12]

1083 化	change
	Person . . . spoon. [4]

1084 花	flower
	Flower . . . change. [7]

1085 貨	freight
	Change . . . shells. [11]

1086 傾	lean
	Change . . . head. The key word has the sense of **leaning** on or toward someone or something. [13]

1087 何	what
	Person . . . can. [7]

1088 荷	baggage
	Flowers . . . what. [10]

1089 俊	sagacious
	Person . . . license . . . walking legs. [9]

1090	bystander
傍	*Person . . . stand . . . crown . . . compass.* [12]

1091	myself
俺	The key word refers to a very familiar way of referring to one-self, typically used by men. Its component elements: *person . . . St. Bernard . . . eel.* [10]

1092	long time
久	This character uses the diagonal sweep of the second stroke to double up for *bound up* and a *person*. Think of a mummy, and the key word will not be far behind. [3]

ノ　ク　久

1093	furrow
畝	Think of the three kinds of **furrows** shown here in this character—a *top hat's* rim, a *rice field's* ridges, and the wrinkles that show you've been around a *long time.* [10]

1094	captured
囚	*Person . . . pent in.* [5]

1095	inside
内	*Person . . belt.* Note that we cannot use the primitive meaning of *hood* here because the *person* runs THROUGH the element, not under it. [4]

冂　内

1096	third class
丙	Those no-frills flights the airlines offer to attract customers should help create an image from *ceiling . . . person . . . belt.* The kanji meaning "*inside*" should not be used because of its proximity to the element for "*in.*" [5]

1097 柄	design
Tree . . . third class. [9]	

1098 肉	meat
Let this doubling of one of the elements for *"inside"* yield the sense of *"insides"* to approach the key word, **meat**. The abbreviated form of this character gave us the primitive meaning of *flesh* or *part of the body* for the kanji 月. [6]	

1099 腐	rot
Municipality . . . meat. [14]	

* 从	assembly line
The duplication of the kanji for *person* gives us this primitive for **assembly line**. Perhaps you can imagine clones of your chosen *person* rolling off an assembly line in a factory. [4]	

1100 座	sit
Cave . . . assembly line . . . soil. [10]	

广 庆 庎 座 座

1101 挫	sprain
Fingers . . . assembly line . . . soil. [10]	

1102 卒	graduate
Top hat . . . assembly line . . . needle. [8]	

1103 傘	umbrella
Umbrella . . . two assembly lines . . . needle. [12]	

八 仐 仐 仐 傘

Lesson 28

IN THIS LESSON we pick up a group of unconnected characters and elements that have fallen between the cracks of the previous lessons, mainly because of the rarity of the characters themselves, of their primitive elements, or of the way in which they are written. In a later lesson, we will do this once again.

1104   *monme*

匁

This character obliges us to use a Japanese key word for want of an English equivalent. It refers to an old unit of weight, equal to about 3.75 grams. The word is only slightly more useful in modern Japanese than cubits and kites are in modern English. Its primitives, if you look closely, are: *bound up . . . arm.* [4]

ク 勺 匁

---

*   **plow**

⌡

Take this as a pictograph of a **plow.** [2]

丨 ⌡

1105   **by means of**

以

Picture a *person* dragging a *plow* behind, and the *drop of* sweat which falls from his brow as he does his work. Think of him (or her, for that matter) making a living "**by means of** the sweat of their brows." [5]

1106   **similar**

似

Be sure to keep this key word distinct from *likeness* (FRAME 104). Its elements: *person . . . by means of.* [7]

---

*   **puzzle**

并

Think of this element as a picture **puzzle** in which the pieces interlock. Its elements: *horns . . . two hands.* [6]

丶 丷 丷 羊 并

1107	join
併	The sense of the key word is one of **joining** things together that were previously separate. Its elements: *person . . . puzzle.* [8]

1108	tile
瓦	*Ceiling . . . plow . . . fishhook . . . a drop of.* [5]

一 丆 丆 瓦 瓦

1109	flower pot
瓶	*Puzzle . . . tile.* [11]

1110	Shinto shrine
宮	Way back in Lesson 2 we learned the character for *spine*. The two other characters in which it is used we can now learn together in this and the following frame. Here a **Shinto shrine** is composed of *house* and *spine*. [10]

1111	occupation
営	*Schoolhouse . . . spine.* [12]

1112	virtuous
善	*Sheep . . . horns . . . mouth.* Pay special attention to the writing of this character. [12]

羊 羊 羔 善

1113	dining tray
膳	*Flesh . . . virtuous.* [16]

1114 **year**

年

In an odd fashion, the kanji for **year** joins together the element for *horse,* on the top, and the right half of the element for *sunglasses.* Think of it as a *horse* wearing *sunglasses with one of the lenses popped out.* We will use this latter image again, so learn it now and save yourself the trouble later. [6]

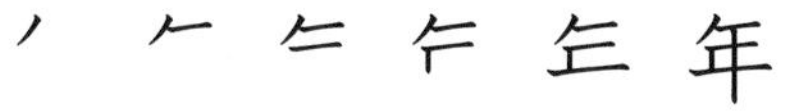

1115 **night**

夜

First of all, be sure not to confuse the connotations of **night** with those of *evening* (FRAME 114) and *nightbreak* (FRAME 30). Its elements: *top hat . . . person . . .walking legs . . . drop.* [8]

1116 **fluid**

液

Water . . . night. [11]

1117 **hillock**

塚

Soil . . . crown . . . sow. Compare FRAME 582. [12]

* **shredder**

敝

The element on the left looks like *rice* with a *belt* running through it, but we would do best to think of it in terms of its writing order: *little . . . belt . . . little.* On the right, of course, the *taskmaster.* [12]

1118 **cash**

幣

Shredder . . . towel. [15]

1119 **cover over**

蔽

Flower . . . shredder. [15]

1120		abuse
弊	*Shredder . . . two hands.* [15]	

1121		yell
唤	The *mouth* on the left is obvious. The rest is harder. Try this: *four St. Bernard dogs bound up* in a bunch. Together they should supply a clear enough portrait of a **yell**, provided you are careful to see all *four* of them. Note how the final stroke of the *four* is supplied by the long horizontal stroke of the *St. Bernard*. [12]	

1122		interchange
换	*Fingers . . . four St. Bernard dogs bound up.* [12]	

1123		dissolve
融	*Ceiling . . . mouth . . . hood . . . human legs . . . spike . . . insect.* This is the maximum number of elements *to appear in* any story in the book. [16]	

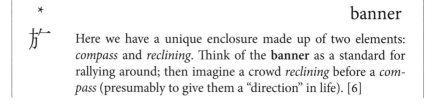

Lesson 29

WE COME NOW TO a rather simple group of primitives, built up from the three elements that represent *banners, knots,* and *flags.*

*		banner
㫃	Here we have a unique enclosure made up of two elements: *compass* and *reclining.* Think of the **banner** as a standard for rallying around; then imagine a crowd *reclining* before a *compass* (presumably to give them a "direction" in life). [6]	

	方　扩

1124 施	alms
	Banner . . . scorpion. [9]

1125 旋	rotation
	A banner . . . a zoo. Hint: think of a merry-go-round. [11]

1126 遊	play
	Banners . . . children . . . road. [12]

1127 旅	trip
	Let the last 4 strokes, which are also the concluding strokes to the character for *garment*, represent a *rag* as its primitive meaning. We shall meet this only on one other occasion. This gives us as our elements: *banner . . . rag.* [10]
	扩　扩　扩　扩　旅

1128 勿	not
	First take the primitive meaning of this character: *knot.* Think of it as the *piglet* minus its body (the horizontal stroke), that is, the curly tail that looks like a *knot.* As an exception, we will use the homonym to remember the abstract key word, **not.** [4]
	ノ　勹　勺　勿

1129 物	thing
	Cow . . . knot. [8]

1130 易	easy
	Sun . . . knot. [8]

1131		grant
賜	*Shells . . . easy.* [15]	

*		flag
尸	The pictographic representation of this element is obvious. Provided you can hold your imagination in check for the first example, you might best imagine your own national **flag** in composing your stories. [3]	

ᄀ ᄏ 尸

1132		urine
尿	*Flag . . . water.* [7]	

1133		nun
尼	*Flag . . . spoon.* [5]	

1134		buttocks
尻	*Flag . . . baseball team.* [5]	

1135		mud
泥	*Water . . . nun.* [8]	

1136		fence
塀	*Soil . . . flag . . . puzzle.* [12]	

1137		footgear
履	*Flag . . . restore.* [15]	

1138		roof
屋	*Flag . . . climax.* Note that this kanji has no relation to the drawing of a "roof" used in the primitive for *house* (page 85). [9]	

1139	grip
握	*Fingers . . . roof.* [12]

1140	yield
屈	*Flag . . . exit.* [8]

1141	dig
掘	*Fingers . . . yield.* [11]

1142	ditch
堀	*Soil . . . yield.* [11]

1143	reside
居	*Flag . . . old.* Do not confuse with *dwell* (FRAME 1027). [8]

1144	set
据	*Fingers . . . reside.* [11]

1145	hem
裾	*Cloak . . . reside.* [13]

1146	stratum
層	*Flag . . . increase.* [14]

1147	bureau
局	*Flag . . . phrase.* Note how the *flag*'s long stroke doubles up for the first stroke of *phrase*. [7]

1148	slow
遅	*Flag . . . sheep . . . road.* [12]

1149 漏	Water . . . flag . . . rain. [14]	leak

1150 刷	Flag . . . towel . . . saber. [8]	printing

1151 尺 *shaku*

The key word *shaku* has actually come into English in the word *shakuhachi*, the ancient Japanese flute that measured "one *shaku* and eight *sun*" (the "sun" being about an inch in length). Since the *shaku* is about one foot in length, this makes about 20 inches. Let the final sweeping stroke be like a tape measure added to the *flag*. [4]

尸 尺

* As a primitive, this will mean the *shakuhachi* flute.

1152 尽	Shakuhachi . . . ice. [6]	exhaust

1153 沢	Water . . . shakuhachi. [7]	swamp

1154 訳	Words . . . shakuhachi. [11]	translate

1155 択	Fingers . . . shakuhachi. [7]	choose

1156 昼	Shakuhachi . . . nightbreak. [9]	daytime

1157 戸	door
	Ceiling . . . flag. [4]

1158 肩	shoulder
	Door . . . flesh. [8]

1159 房	tassel
	Door . . . compass. [8]

1160 扇	fan
	Door . . . wings. [10]

1161 炉	hearth
	Hearth fire . . . door. [8]

1162 戻	re-
	The key word signals a "coming back" or **return** to some place or activity. Its elements: *door . . . St. Bernard dog.* [7]

1163 涙	tears
	Water . . . re-. Do not confuse with *cry* (FRAME 463). [10]

1164 雇	employ
	Door . . . turkey. Be sure to keep distinct from both *employee* (FRAME 59) and *use* (FRAME 1065). [12]

1165 顧	look back
	Employ . . . head. [21]

1166 啓	disclose
	Door . . . taskmaster . . . mouth. [11]

Lesson 30

IN THIS LESSON we pick up a series of primitives related pictographically to one another and based on the image of a seed. But first we include a stray element that does not really fit into any of our other categories but is very useful in forming some common and elementary kanji (in fact, 18 of them already at this point), namely, the *altar*.

1167	show
示	Although the elements *two* and *little* are available for the using, it may be easier to remember this character as a picture of an altar. Something placed atop the altar is put on **show** for all to see. [5]
	* As a primitive, this kanji means *altar*. At the left, the abbreviated form that this element takes is made by chopping the *altar* in half and leaving only one dot behind to represent the right side. The new appearance of this primitive form, 礻, should be kept distinct from that for *cloak*, 衤, identical except for the one final short stroke.

1168	salutation
礼	This key word refers to the polite bows and ceremonious forms of **salutation** so important in Japanese culture. Its elements: *altar . . . fishhook*. [5]

1169	auspicious
祥	*Altar . . . sheep*. [10]

1170	celebrate
祝	*Altar . . . teenager*. [9]

1171	blessing
福	*Altar . . . wealth*. [13]

1172 祉	welfare *Altar . . . footprint.* [8]
1173 社	company *Altar . . . soil.* The **company** referred to here is that of the modern business world. [7]
1174 視	inspection *Altar . . . see.* [11]
1175 奈	Nara We choose the city of **Nara** as the key word in this case because this kanji, frequently used in proper names, appears in **Nara**; and also because of **Nara's** famed religious monuments, which help us with the primitives: *St. Bernard dog . . . altar.* [8]
1176 尉	military officer *Flag . . . altar . . . glue.* [11]
1177 慰	consolation *Military officer . . . heart.* [15]
1178 款	goodwill *Samurai . . . altar . . . yawning.* [12]
1179 禁	prohibition *Grove . . . altar.* [13]
1180 襟	collar *Cloak . . . prohibition.* [18]
1181 宗	religion *House . . . altar.* [8]

1182 崇	adore

Mountain . . . religion. [11]

1183 祭	ritual

Flesh . . . crotch . . . altar. Note how the second element is cut short, giving a tent-like effect to the character. [11]

1184 察	guess

"Guess" here has the sense of a measured conjecture. Its elements: *house . . . ritual.* [14]

1185 擦	grate

Fingers . . . guess. [17]

1186 由	wherefore

The **"wherefore"** of this kanji explains the reason or origin of a thing. It does this graphically by depicting a seed in a *rice field* sending up a single sprout, which is the whole why and **wherefore** of the seed's falling in the earth and dying. (When the *flower* appears, you will recall from FRAME 249, we have a full *seedling.*) [5]

口 巾 由 由

* As a primitive, in conformity to the explanation above, this kanji will be taken to mean *shoot* or *sprout.*

1187 抽	pluck

Fingers . . . sprout. [8]

1188 油	oil

Water . . . sprout. [8]

1189 袖	sleeve *Cloak . . . sprout.* [10]
1190 宙	mid-air *House . . . shoot.* [8]
1191 届	deliver *Flag . . . sprout.* [8]
1192 笛	flute *Bamboo . . . sprout.* [11]
1193 軸	axis *Car . . . shoot.* [12]
1194 甲	armor This kanji reverses the element for *sprout*, giving the image of roots being sent down into the earth by a seed planted in the *rice field*. From there you must invent a connection to the key word, **armor**. [5] 日　甲 * The primitive meaning is *roots*. Important to that word is the image of "pushing downwards," as *roots* do.
1195 押	push *Fingers . . . roots.* Compare and contrast with *pluck* (FRAME 1187). [8]
1196 岬	headland Like the *cape* (FRAME 164) and the *promontory* (FRAME 840), the **headland** refers to a jut of land. Its elements: *mountain . . . roots.* [8]

1197   insert

捗

Fingers . . . thousand . . . roots. Observe how the writing order does not follow the elements in order, because the final stroke is used for two different elements. [10]

扌　扩　拍　挿

1198   speaketh

申

The olde English is used here to indicate a humble form of the third person singular of the verb "to speak." It is written by a *tongue wagging in the mouth* with a *walking stick* rammed through it and coming out at both ends. [5]

日　申

* While this kanji has obvious affinities to the "seed" group, it also happens to be the zodiacal sign of the *monkey* (the one who *speaketh* no evil, among other things). We shall therefore take *monkey* as its primitive meaning.

1199   expand

伸

Person . . . monkey. [7]

1200   gods

神

Altar . . . monkey. [9]

1201   search

捜

Fingers . . . monkey . . . crotch. [10]

1202   fruit

果

The final stage of the seed is reached when the plant has reached its full growth (the *tree*) and comes to fruition, producing **fruit** full of new seeds that can return to the earth and start the process all over again. The main thing to notice here is the element

for *brains* at the top, which might prove more helpful than *rice field* for creating an image. The writing, however, follows the order of a *sun* with a *tree* who trunk runs through the sun. [8]

1203 菓	confectionary
Flowers ... fruits. [11]	

1204 課	chapter
Words ... fruit. [15]	

1205 裸	naked
Cloak ... fruit. [13]	

Lesson 31

BY NOW YOU will have learned to handle a great number of very difficult kanji with perfect ease and without fear of forgetting. Some others, of course, will take review. But let us focus on the ones you are most confident about and can write most fluently, in order to add a remark about what role the stories, plots, and primitives should continue to play even after you have learned a character to your own satisfaction.

This course has been designed to move in steps from the full-bodied story (Part One) to the skeletal plot (Part Two) to the heap of bones we call primitive elements (Part Three). This also happens roughly to be the way memory works. At first the full story is necessary (as a rule, for every kanji, no matter how simple it appears), in that it enables you to focus your attention and your interest on the vivid images of the primitives, which in turn dictate how you write the character. Once the image has strutted through the full light of imagination, it will pass on, leaving its footprints on the interstices of the brain in some mysterious way. And those footprints are often enough of a clue about the nature of the beast to enable you to reconstruct the plot in broad outlines. Should you need to, you can nearly always follow the tracks back to their source and recall your whole story, but that is generally unnecessary. The third stage occurs when

even the plot is unnecessary, and the key word by itself suggests a certain number of primitive meanings; or conversely, when seeing a kanji at once conjures up a specific key word. Here again, the plot is still within reach if needed, but not worth bothering with once it has fulfilled its task of providing the proper primitive elements.

There is yet a fourth stage to be reached, as you have probably realized by now, but one you ought not trust until you have completed the full list of the kanji given here. In this stage, the primitive elements are suggested according to *form* without any immediate association to *meaning*. Quite early on, you will recall, we insisted that visual memory is to be discarded in favor of imaginative memory. It may now be clear just why that is so. But it should also be getting clear that visual memory deserves a suitable role of some sort or other, once it has a solid foundation. This is a process not to be rushed, however appealing its rewards in terms of writing fluency.

Insofar as you have experienced these things in your own study, fears about the inadequacy of the key words should be greatly allayed. For in much the same way that the character slowly finds its way into the fabric of memory and muscular habits, the key word will gradually give way to a key concept distinct from the particular English word used to express it. Hence the substitution of a Japanese word—or even a number of words—will prove no stumbling block. Quite the contrary, it will help avoid confusion between key words with family resemblances.

In short, the number of steps required to learn the Japanese writing system has not been increased by what we have been doing. It has simply become more pronounced than it is in traditional methods of drawing and redrawing the kanji hundreds of times until they are learned, and in that way the whole process has become much more efficient. Pausing to think about just what your mind has been doing through this book should make the ideas mentioned in the Introduction much more plausible now than they must have seemed way back then.

But we must be on our way again, this time down a road marked "tools."

1206	ax

斤 This character represents a picture of an **ax**, the two vertical lines being the handle and the horizontal strokes of the blade. Note the writing order carefully. [4]

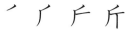

1207 析	chop
	Tree . . . ax. [8]

1208 所	place
	Door . . . ax. [8]

1209 祈	pray
	Altar . . . ax. [8]

1210 近	near
	Ax . . . road. Be careful not to confuse with *draw near* (FRAME 204) or *bystander* (FRAME 1090). [7]

1211 折	fold
	Fingers . . . ax. Hint: make an image out of the Japanese art of "origami" (paper-**folding**). [7]

1212 哲	philosophy
	Fold . . . mouth. [10]

1213 逝	departed
	The connotation is of a "dearly **departed**" who has passed away. The elements: *fold . . . road.* [10]

1214 誓	vow
	Fold . . . words. [14]

1215 斬	chop off
	Car . . . ax. [11]

1216 暫	temporarily
	Chop off . . . days. [15]

1217 漸	steadily
	Water . . . chop off. [14]
1218 断	severance
	Fishhook . . . rice . . . ax. [11]
1219 質	substance
	Two axes . . . shells. [15]
1220 斥	reject
	Ax . . . a drop of. [5]
1221 訴	accusation
	Words . . . reject. [12]
* 乍	saw
	The **saw** in this primitive is distinguished from the primitive for *ax* by the extra "teeth" on the blade. [5]
	ノ 乍 乍 乍 乍
1222 昨	yesterday
	Day . . . saw. [9]
1223 詐	lie
	The **lie** in this character refers to falsehoods and fibs. Its elements: *words . . . saw.* [12]
1224 作	make
	Person . . . saw. [7]

* 彐	**broom** The pictographic representation here is of the bristles on the head of a **broom**. Note that the second stroke stops short without cutting through the second. [3]

フ ヨ ヨ

1225 雪	**snow** *Rain* that undergoes a change so that it can be swept aside with a *broom* is **snow**. [11]

1226 録	**record** *Metal . . . broom . . . grains of rice.* Note how the final stroke of the *broom* is extended slightly when an element below is attached directly to it. [16]

1227 剥	**peel off** *Broom . . . rice grains . . . saber.* [10]

1228 尋	**inquire** *Broom . . . craft . . . mouth . . . glue.* [12]

1229 急	**hurry** *Bound up . . . broom . . . heart.* [9]

1230 穏	**calm** *Wheat . . . vulture . . . broom . . . heart.* [16]

1231 侵	**encroach** *Person . . . broom . . . crown . . . crotch.* Gather the elements on the right into a composite image that can serve you in the next two frames. [9]

1232 浸	**immersed**
	Water ... broom ... crown ... crotch. [10]

1233 寝	**lie down**
	Do not confuse this key word with either the element for *reclining* or the character for *prostrated* (FRAME 1035). Its primitive elements are: *house ... turtle ... broom ... crown ... crotch.* [13]

1234 婦	**lady**
	Woman ... broom ... apron. [11]

1235 掃	**sweep**
	Fingers ... broom ... apron. [11]

1236 当	**hit**
	Little ... broom. [6]

1237 彙	**glossary**
	The top primitive of this character is actually an old form of broom ⺕. The remaining elements are: *crown ... fruit.* [13]

* 尹	**rake**
	A single vertical stroke transforms *broom* into a **rake**. When an element comes BELOW the **rake**, the vertical stroke is shortened, as we have seen before with other similar primitives such as *sheep* and *cow*. Moreover, when something comes ABOVE the **rake** and joins to it at the top, the vertical stroke begins at the top horizontal stroke, as in the following two frames. [4]
	⼅ ⺕ 尹

1238 争	**contend**
	Bound up ... rake. [6]

1239	clean
浄	Water . . . contend. [9]

1240	matter
事	This key word here refers to abstract **matters**. The elements are: *one . . . mouth . . . rake*. Note how the *rake* handle reaches out the top and bottom of the character. [8]

1241	T'ang
唐	The key word here refers of course to the **T'ang** Dynasty in China (and not to the name of the drink astronauts take with them into outer space, though this could be useful for the next frame). Its elements: *cave . . . rake . . . mouth*. [10]

1242	sugar
糖	*Rice . . . T'ang.* [16]

*	sieve
隶	A *rake* and the *grains of rice* at the bottom give us a hint of winnowing, which relates clearly to the meaning of a **sieve**. [8]

尹 隶

1243	sane
康	*Cave . . . sieve.* [11]

1244	apprehend
逮	Think of **apprehending** criminals. The elements are: *sieve . . . road*. [11]

*	mop
尹	The only thing distinguishing a **mop** from a *rake* is the bent handle that does not cut through the top horizontal stroke. It depicts the swish-swash motion of a **mop**. [4]

　　　　ㄱ　㇆　㇗　尹

1245	Italy
伊	Used chiefly in proper names, and given the sound "i," this kanji can be remembered as an abbreviation of **Italy**, for which it is still used today in Japan. Its primitives: *person . . . mop.* [6]

1246	old boy
君	The somewhat highbrow British term of address is chosen here to represent the kanji for a form of address used towards one's juniors. It is composed of: *mop . . . mouth.* [7]

1247	flock
群	*Old boys . . . sheep.* [13]

*	comb
而	The pictograph of a **comb** is clearly visible in this primitive element. [6]

　　　一　　㇒　　厂　　币　　而　　而

1248	-proof
耐	The key word is a suffix used to indicate "safe from" or "protected against," as in the words rust**proof**, water**proof**, and fire**proof**. It is composed of: *comb . . . glue.* [9]

1249	demand
需	The sense of **demand** is best captured by thinking of the economic principle of "supply and **demand**." The primitives: *rain . . . comb.* [14]

1250	Confucian
儒	*Person . . . demand.* [16]

1251	edge
端	*Vase . . . mountain . . . comb.* [14]

★	shovel
∪	This enclosure—which embraces its relative primitive from the bottom—is a pictograph of the scoop of a **shovel**. When room permits, the arms are extended upwards to nearly the same height as the relative element it holds. [2]

∟   ∪

1252	both
両	*Ceiling . . . belt . . . mountain.* Note that the writing order follows the order in which the primitives are given here. [6]

1253	full
満	*Water . . . flowers . . . both.* Given the abstract nature of this last primitive, you may want to borrow the image from the previous frame. [12]

1254	brush-stroke
画	In forming an image for the key word, it is helpful to know that this kanji is used both for artistic representations (like a completed painting), and as a counter for the number of **brush-strokes** in a character (as, for instance, in Indexes II and III at the end of this book). Its elements are: *ceiling . . . sprout . . . shovel.* [8]

冂   币   再   甶   画

1255	tooth
歯	*Footprint . . . rice . . . shovel.* [12]

1256   **bend**

曲 Picture yourself grabbing hold of the two strokes poking out the top of the kanji and wrenching them apart, thus giving the sense of **bend**. If you think of them as deriving from the element for *brains* beneath (of course, the middle stroke has been reduplicated and pulled out to where it can be grabbed hold of), you can associate the key word with **bending** someone's mind to your own point of view. [6]

丨　冂　冊　冊　冊　曲

1257   **cadet**

曹 This character is written in the order of its elements: *one . . . bend . . . sun.* [11]

1258   **encounter**

遭 *Cadet . . . road.* [14]

1259   **rowing**

漕 *Water . . . cadet.* [14]

1260   **vat**

槽 *Tree . . . cadet.* [15]

1261   **Big Dipper**

斗 The **Big Dipper** here is of course the constellation of Ursa Major, of which this kanji is a sort of pictographic representation. [4]

丶　冫　二十　斗

* Since we already have a primitive element for a "dipper"—namely, the *ladle*—we shall let this one stand for a *measuring cup.* By the way, it would make a rather large one, since the kanji is also used for a measure of about 18 liters!

1262	fee
料	*Measuring cup . . . rice.* [10]

1263	department
科	Think here of the faculty or **department** you entered in university, using the elements: *measuring cup . . . wheat.* [9]

1264	map
図	*Pent in . . . Big Dipper.* Hint: among the songs dating from the days of slavery that have become part of American folklore is one called "Follow the Drinking Gourd." It referred to the nighttime travel of runaway slaves (those *pent in*) who had no **maps** other than the stars to guide them, among them the bright and predominant *Big Dipper*, the "Drinking Gourd." [7]

1265	utilize
用	*Meat . . . walking stick.* Be sure to keep this key word distinct from that for *use* (FRAME 1065). The stroke order is exactly as you would expect it from the order of the primitive elements as given. [5]
	* As a primitive element, we shall substitute the image of a *screwdriver*, perhaps the most *utilized* of all tools around the house.

1266	comfortable
庸	*Cave . . . rake . . . screwdriver.* [11]

1267	equip
備	*Person . . . flowers . . . cliff . . . screwdriver.* In cases like this you can jumble up the primitive into any order that seems best for the composition of a story, provided you feel confident about the relative position that those primitives take to one another in the completed character. [12]

Lesson 32

IN THIS LESSON we pick up a few primitives of quantity to complement those we learned in Lesson 7, as well as some others related closely to elements learned earlier.

* 艹		**salad**
	The element for *flowers* joins with the long horizontal stroke beneath it to create the picture of a bowl of **salad**. [4]	

1268 昔		**once upon a time**
	Salad . . . days. This is the character with which Japanese fairy tales commonly begin. [8]	

1269 錯		**confused**
	Metal . . . once upon a time. [16]	

1270 借		**borrow**
	Person . . . once upon a time. [10]	

1271 惜		**pity**
	State of mind . . . once upon a time. The sense of the key word is that of a lost opportunity or bad turn of affairs, as in the phrase "What a **pity**!" [11]	

1272 措		**set aside**
	Fingers . . . once upon a time. [11]	

1273 散		**scatter**
	Salad . . . flesh . . taskmaster. [12]	

1274	twenty

廿

The two *tens* joined at the bottom by a short line is actually the old character for **twenty**, which we might as well learn since we need its primitive form. It is written the same as *salad,* except for the shorter final stroke. [4]

一　十　廾　廿

*	caverns

庐

The primitive for **caverns** differs from that for *cave* by the presence of the primitive for *twenty,* suggesting a maze of underground *caves.* [7]

1275	commoner

庶

Caverns . . . oven fire. [11]

1276	intercept

遮

Commoner . . . road. [14]

1277	seat

席

Caverns . . . towel. [10]

1278	degrees

度

This key word refers to a gradation of measurement, not to academic diplomas. Its primitives: *caverns . . . crotch.* [9]

1279	transit

渡

Water . . . degrees. [12]

*	haystack

卉

The three *needles* stacked up give us a **haystack** (in which it may be harder to find the hay than the *needles*). In the rare case in which there is nothing underneath this element, as in the following frame, the last three strokes are written virtually the

same as *two hands*—that is, the second stroke sweeps down slightly to the left. [5]

十　土　卉

1280	bustle
奔	The hustle and **bustle** of this character is depicted by a *St. Bernard dog* and a *haystack*. [8]

1281	erupt
噴	*Mouth . . . haystack . . . clams.* [15]

1282	tomb
墳	*Soil . . . haystack . . . clams.* In order not to confuse this kanji with that for a *grave* (FRAME 246), something like the image of an Egyptian **tomb** should be adopted, with all its special connotations. [15]

1283	aroused
憤	*State of mind . . . haystack . . . clams.* [15]

---

*	straw man
尭	The two *human legs* added to the *haystack* (with the horizontal stroke to keep the two parts distinct from one another and avoid an ugly tangle) give us a **straw man**. [8]

十　垚　尭

1284	bake
焼	*Hearth . . . straw man.* Take care to distinguish this kanji from *cook* (FRAME 507) and *burn* (FRAME 549) when you compose your story. [12]

1285	daybreak
暁	*Sun . . . straw man.* [12]

1286 半 **half**

Although the writing order is different, one can remember the appearance of this character by seeing it as a *little needle*—the kind used for splitting hairs in **half**. (Again, according to rule, *little* takes a stroke beneath it in order to be placed over an element that has no horizontal line at the top.) [5]

1287 伴 **consort**

Person . . . half. [7]

1288 畔 **paddy ridge**

Rice field . . . half. The key word here refers to the **ridges** that rise up between the sections of a rice **paddy**. [10]

1289 判 **judgment**

Half . . . saber. You might recall the famous **judgment** of King Solomon, who offered to slice a baby in two with a *saber* to give *half* to each of the mothers who claimed it as her own. [7]

* 龹 **quarter**

This character simply splits the vertical stroke of a *half* in half once again, to get a **quarter**. In so doing, it spreads the split stroke out to form a sort of enclosure under which its main relative primitive will be placed. It can be used either in its substantive or verbal meaning. [6]

1290 拳 **fist**

Quarter . . . hand. Be careful to keep this key word distinct from the primitive element of the same meaning we met back on page 221. [10]

1291	ticket
券	*Quarter . . . dagger.* [8]

1292	scroll
巻	*Quarter . . . snake.* The key word refers to a manuscript rolled up into a **scroll**, not to a *hanging scroll* (FRAME 435). [9]

1293	sphere
圏	This key word refers to a realm or orbit, not to a ball. Its elements: *pent in . . . scroll.* [12]

1294	victory
勝	*Moon . . . quarter . . . muscle.* [12]

1295	wisteria
藤	*Flower . . . moon . . . quarter . . . rice grains.* [18]

1296	facsimile
謄	*Moon . . . quarter . . . words.* [17]

1297	one-sided
片	This kanji is based on the pictograph of a tree with some branches going upwards and others hanging down, split right down the middle. When that picture's right side is isolated, it becomes the kanji for **one-sided**, in the sense of only one part of a whole. [4]
	丿 丿丶 丿ㅏ 片

1298	printing block
版	Although this character also carries the sense of an "edition" of a publication, the elements, *one-sided* and *anti-*, more readily suggest its other meaning of a **printing block**. [8]

1299	of

之

This character is now used chiefly in proper names, and is best learned as the character closest to the hiragana え, though in fact it has no relation to it. [3]

* In order to give this kanji a more concrete meaning when it is used as a primitive element, think of it as referring to *building blocks* with the hiragana written on them, much the same as the A-B-C blocks you played with as a child.

1300	destitution

乏

Drop of . . . building blocks. [4]

1301	turf

芝

Flowers . . . building blocks. [6]

1302	negative

不

You may play with the primitives of this kanji as you wish *(ceiling . . . person . . . a drop of), but* you will probably find that its simplicity, and its frequency, make it easy to remember just as it is. [4]

一 フ 不 不

1303	negate

否

Negative . . . mouth. [7]

1304	cupfuls

杯

Tree . . . negative. [8]

Lesson 33

WE TURN NOW TO the weapons that remain to be examined. To the *saber*, the *dagger*, and the *arrow*, we add three more primitives to complete the list: the *spear*, the *snare*, and the *slingshot*.

1305 矢		**dart**
	When shot high into the *heavens*, the **dart** gets so small it looks like a mere *drop*. Although this character could as well mean "arrow," it has no connection with the primitive of that meaning. Hence the new key word. [5]	
1306 矯		**rectify**
	Dart . . . angel. Compare your stories for *correct* (FRAME 405), *revise* (FRAME 362), and *reformation* (FRAME 567). [17]	
1307 族		**tribe**
	Banner . . . dart. [11]	
1308 知		**know**
	Dart . . . mouth. [8]	
1309 智		**wisdom**
	Know . . . sun. [12]	
1310 挨		**shove**
	Fingers . . . elbow . . . dart. [10]	
1311 矛		**halberd**
	The **halberd's** battle-ax head and long shaft are depicted here. Take care with the number and order of the strokes. [5]	
	⁻ ⁻ 予 矛	

1312	tender
柔	*Halberd . . . tree.* [9]

1313	task
務	*Halberd . . . taskmaster . . . muscle.* [11]

1314	fog
霧	*Weather/rain . . . task.* [19]

*	spear
刂	This weapon, which has the appearance of the long *saber* but is drawn slightly differently, depicts a **spear**. It appears very rarely—in fact, only twice and both instances are given in the following frames. [2]

1315	squad
班	*Spear . . . two balls.* [10]

1316	homecoming
帰	*Spear . . . broom . . . apron.* The character for *lady* (FRAME 1234) shares the same right side as this character, which does not bode for a very happy **homecoming**. [10]

1317	bow
弓	This character pictures the bent wooden **bow**. Later we will learn how to make the *bowstring* that goes with it (FRAME 1490). If you stretch this character out and see the indentation on the left as its handle, the pictography should be clearer. [3]

ㄱ ㄱ 弓

1318	pull
引	*Bow . . . walking stick.* [4]

1319 弔	condolences A *bow* . . . wrapped around a *walking stick*. [4]
1320 弘	vast Bow . . . *elbow*. [5]
1321 強	strong *Vast* . . . *insect*. Note how the *elbow* of *vast* is shrunken and elevated to make room for the *insect* beneath. [11]
1322 弥	more and more *Bow* . . . *reclining* . . . *little*. [8]
1323 弱	weak Two *bows* . . with *ice* on them. [10]
1324 溺	drowning *Water* . . . *weak*. Do not confuse the meaning of this key word with 没 (FRAME 763), which is closer to "founder." [13]
* 弗	dollar sign Composed of two *walking sticks* running through a *bow*, this character is infrequent as a primitive, and yet easy to remember for what it looks like (which is also what the Japanese adopted it to mean in days gone by): the **dollar sign**, $. When it is written under another element, the first vertical stroke is abbreviated to a short "tail" as the final stroke, and the second vertical stroke is cut off at the top. Examples follow in FRAMES 1327 and 1328. [5] フ 弓 弗 弗
1325 沸	seethe *Water* . . . *dollar sign*. [8]

1326	expense
費	*Dollar sign . . . shells/money.* [12]

1327	No.
第	The key word **No.** is the abbreviation for "number." Its elements: *bamboo . . . dollar sign.* [11]

1328	younger brother
弟	*Horns . . . dollar sign.* [7]

*	snare
丂	The simple **snare** composed of a piece of vine and a bent twig is depicted here as a sort of abbreviation of the *bow,* to which it is related. [2]

$$ー \quad 丂$$

1329	adroit
巧	*Craft . . . snare.* [5]

1330	nickname
号	*Mouth . . . snare.* [5]

1331	decay
朽	*Tree . . . snare.* Do not confuse with *rot* (FRAME 1099). [6]

1332	boast
誇	*Words . . . St. Bernard dog . . . ceiling . . . snare.* [13]

1333	chin
顎	*Two mouths . . . ceiling . . . snare . . . head.* [18]

1334	dirty

汚   *Water . . . two . . . snare.* Note that the first stroke for *snare* doubles up with the first stroke for *two.* [6]

氵 氵 汚

*	slingshot

与   The **slingshot** differs from the *snare* by virtue of the first stroke, which you may take as the strip of rubber you pull back on, to make the **slingshot** sling. [2]

一 与

1335	bestow

与   *Slingshot . . . one.* Later we will meet the character for *give* (FRAME 2046), but even so, it is a good idea already at this point to distinguish this key word from *impart* (FRAME 795) and *grant* (FRAME 1131). [3]

与 与

1336	copy

写   *Crown . . . bestow.* [5]

Lesson 34

ALTHOUGH WE still have a number of primitives left relating to human activities, we may at this point pick up what remain of those having to do specifically with people and parts of the human body.

1337	somebody

The key word **somebody** was chosen to convey the double meaning of this kanji: body and person. Its composition is based on the *nose* (which, you will recall, is also the kanji for *oneself*). The extension of the bottom and far right strokes of that element, together with the unusual diagonal stroke, forms the pictograph of **somebody** with a prominent paunch. [7]

´　丨　冂　冎　月　身　身

1338	shoot

射

"I **shot** an arrow into the air, And it landed I know not where" goes the poem. (The poor poet obviously loses a lot of arrows.) This kanji, however, tells us where it did land. Its elements: *somebody . . . glued to.* [10]

1339	apologize

謝

Words . . . shoot. [17]

1340	old man

老

First, do not confuse this character with *venerable old man* (FRAME 849), which is far more rarely used. The character for an **old man** begins with an abbreviation of the character for *somebody*, the *nose* having been shortened into a simple criss-cross of lines. But there is another, simpler way to remember it all: the *soil* drawn first indicates that one has come close to the age when "dust to dust" begins to take on a personal meaning; the diagonal *walking stick* for getting around; and the *spoon* for being spoon-fed. [6]

　　土　耂　老

* As a primitive, the meaning is the same, but the final two strokes are omitted so that they can be replaced with other elements: 耂.

1341	consider
考	*Old man . . . slingshot.* Remember: you already have kanji for *discriminating* (FRAME 521), *deliberation* (FRAME 692), and *think* (FRAME 651). [6]

1342	filial piety
孝	*Old man . . . child.* [7]

1343	teach
教	*Filial piety . . . taskmaster.* [11]

1344	torture
拷	*Fingers . . . consider.* [9]

1345	someone
者	*Old man . . . sun.* This key word looks difficult because of its proximity to *somebody.* In fact, it is a very common kanji that will cause you no difficulty at all. Its meaning should be seen as the human referent for the abstract noun "something." [8] * As a primitive it means a *puppet*-on-a-string.

1346	boil
煮	*Puppet . . . oven fire.* [12]

1347	renowned
著	*Flowers . . . puppet.* [11]

1348	chopsticks
箸	*Bamboo . . . puppet.* [14].

1349	signature
署	*Eye . . . puppet.* [13]

1350 暑	**sultry** The key word refers to the heat of summer. Its elements: *sun . . . puppet*. [12]
1351 諸	**various** *Words . . . puppet*. Do not confuse with *miscellaneous* (FRAME 604). [15]
1352 猪	**boar** *Pack of wild dogs . . . puppet*. [11]
1353 渚	**strand** The **strand** referred to here is the stretch of land along a beach or shoreline. Its elements are: *water . . . puppet*. [11]
1354 賭	**gamble** *Shells/money . . . puppet*. [15]
* 夹	**scissors** This primitive is based on that for *husband*. The two extra strokes represent a pair of **scissors** he is carrying around. [6]

一　　一ワ　　エ　　夹

1355 峡	**gorge** *Mountain . . . scissors*. [9]
1356 狭	**cramped** *Pack of wild dogs . . . scissors*. [9]
1357 挟	**sandwiched** *Fingers . . . scissors*. Do not confuse with the kanji for *pinch* (FRAME 709). [9]

1358 頼	**cheek**
	Scissors . . . head. [15]

✻ 自	**maestro**
	To remember with this primitive meaning, you might picture a tuxedo-clad **maestro** waving his baton about wildly. The baton is, of course, the little *drop* at the top. And the two boxes attached to the long vertical stroke may represent his tuxedo tails, if you wish. [6]

′ 亅 亇 宀 宀 自

1359 追	**chase**
	Maestro . . . road. [9]

1360 阜	**large hill**
	Maestro . . . needle. [8]

1361 師	**expert**
	Maestro . . . ceiling . . . towel. [10]

1362 帥	**commander**
	Maestro . . . towel. [9]

1363 官	**bureaucrat**
	By replacing the *maestro*'s baton (the *drop*) with the roof of a *house*, we have his equivalent in the institutional world of big government: the **bureaucrat**. [8]

1364 棺	**coffin**
	Wood . . . bureaucrat. [12]

1365 管	**pipe**
	Bamboo . . . bureaucrat. [14]

1366	father
父	The kindness and hard work of the ideal **father** is seen in this abbreviation of the *taskmaster* that leaves off his rod or whip (the first stroke) and replaces it with the sweat of the **father's** brow (the two *drops* at the top). [4]

ノ　ハ　ケ　父

1367	cauldron
釜	*Father . . . metal.* Note the stroke overlap between *father* and *metal.* [10]

1368	mingle
交	*Top hat . . . father.* [6]

1369	merit
効	*Mingle . . . power.* Note the distinct connotations that separate **merit** from *achievement* (FRAME 927). [8]

1370	contrast
較	*Cars . . . mingle.* [13]

1371	exam
校	*Tree . . . mingle.* [10]

1372	leg
足	*Mouth . . . mending.* Note that the last stroke of *mouth* and the first of *mending* overlap. [7]

* As a primitive on the left, it is amended to ⻊. Its meaning remains *leg*, but should be thought of as a *wooden leg* in order to avoid confusion with other similar elements, namely *human legs, animal legs,* and *walking legs.*

1373 促	*Person . . . leg.* [9]	stimulate

1374 捉	*Fingers . . . wooden leg.* [10]	nab

1375 距	*Wooden leg . . . gigantic.* [12]	long-distance

1376 路	*Wooden leg . . . each.* [13]	path

1377 露	*Rain . . . path.* [21]	dew

1378 跳	*Wooden leg . . . portent.* [13]	hop

1379 躍	*Wooden leg . . . feathers . . . turkey.* [21]	leap

1380 践	*Wooden leg . . . parade float.* [13]	tread

1381 踏	The meaning of this character is virtually identical with that of the last frame. Be sure to come up with distinct connotations suggested by phrases in which each is commonly used. *Wooden leg . . . water . . . sun.* [15]	step

1382 踪	*Person . . . soil . . . compass . . . taskmaster.* The key word refers to a **trail** of footprints or tracks left behind.[13]	trail

1383	skeleton

骨 This kanji and primitive refers to the *part of the body* composed of the bones and their joints. The top part of the kanji, terminating in the element for *crown*, is a pictograph of a bone joint. I leave it to you to put the pieces together, so to speak. [10]

〡　冂　冂　冎　凸　骨

1384	slippery

滑 *Water . . . skeleton.* [13]

1385	marrow

髄 *Skeleton . . . possess . . . road.* [19]

*	jawbone

咼 The meaning of this primitive is taken from the combination of "the joint" above and the *mouth* in the *cowl* below. [9]

〡　冂　冂　冎　冎　咼　咼

1386	calamity

禍 *Altar . . . jawbone.* [13]

1387	whirlpool

渦 *Water . . . jawbone.* [12]

1388	pot

鍋 *Metal . . . jawbone.* [17]

1389	overdo

過 *Jawbone . . . road.* [12]

Lesson 35

THE NEXT GROUP OF primitives we shall consider has to do with topography and exhausts the list of those remaining in that category.

| ★ 阝 | **pinnacle** |

This key word has been chosen because of its connotation of "the highest point," thereby suggesting the image of the highest point in a village, that is, a hill or mountain on which sacred or festive events take place. If you have a clear image of the Athenian acropolis, you might use it to express this element for a **pinnacle**. Note that this primitive appears only on the left. On the right, as we shall see later, the same form takes a different meaning. [3]

フ　３　阝

1390

阪　**Heights**

This character is used for proper names, much as the English word "**Heights**" is. Its primitives: *pinnacle . . . anti-*. [7]

1391

阿　**Africa**

This kanji, an abbreviation for **Africa**, is now used chiefly for its sound, "a," not unlike the kanji for *Italy* and the sound "i" that we met earlier (FRAME 1245). Its composite elements are: *pinnacle . . . can*. [8]

1392

際　**occasion**

Pinnacle . . . ritual. [14]

1393

障　**hinder**

Pinnacle . . . badge. [14]

1394	chink

隙 *Pinnacle . . . little . . . sun . . . little.* Note that the form of the first element for *little* given here is the simpler form that has become standard in general-use characters (see FRAME 110). For the time being, until typesetting fonts have made the adjustment, the officially approved drawing is this: 隙. [12]

1395	follow

随 *Pinnacle . . . possess . . . road.* [12]

1396	auxiliary

陪 *Pinnacle . . . muzzle.* [11]

1397	sunshine

陽 Different from the primitive for *sun* (which figures in the character) and the kanji for *ray* (FRAME 125), the key word **sunshine** is meant to convey the meaning of the masculine principle in nature, or "Yang." (The dark is viewed mythically as the feminine principle; see FRAME 1718.) From there it comes to mean *sun* also. The elements are: *pinnacle . . . piggy bank.* [12]

1398	line up

陳 *Pinnacle . . . east.* [11]

1399	ward off

防 *Pinnacle . . . compass.* [7]

1400	affixed

附 *Pinnacle . . . adhere.* [8]

1401	Inst.

院 This key word, the abbreviation for **Institution**, represents the use of that word as a suffix affixed to certain buildings and organizations. Its primitive elements: *pinnacle . . . perfect.* [10]

1402		camp
陣	*Pinnacle . . . car.* [10]	

1403		regiment
隊	*Pinnacle . . . animal horns . . . sow.* [12]	

1404		crash
墜	*Regiment . . . ground.* [15]	

1405		descend
降	*Pinnacle . . . walking legs . . . sunglasses with a lens popped out.* Distinguish from *fall* (FRAME 320) and *crash*, which we considered in the previous frame. [10]	

1406		story
階	The **story** of this character refers to floors in a building. The elements: *pinnacle . . . all.* [12]	

1407		highness
陛	This key word indicates a title of address to royalty. Its elements: *pinnacle . . . compare . . . ground.* [10]	

1408		neighboring
隣	*Pinnacle . . . rice . . . sunglasses.* [16]	

1409		isolate
隔	*Pinnacle . . . ceiling . . . mouth . . . glass canopy . . . human legs . . . spike.* You might want to compare the kanji for *dissolve* (FRAME 1123). [13]	

1410		conceal
隠	*Pinnacle . . . vulture . . . broom . . . heart.* Compare the elements at the right to the kanji for *calm* (FRAME 1230). [14]	

1411 堕	degenerate
	Pinnacle . . . possess . . . ground. [12]

1412 陥	collapse
	Pinnacle . . . bound up . . . olden times. [10]

1413 穴	hole
	House . . . eight. [5]
	* As a primitive, this kanji uses an alternate form: the primitive for *eight* is replaced with that for *human legs*.

1414 空	empty
	Hole . . . craft. [8]

1415 控	withdraw
	Fingers . . . empty. [11]

1416 突	stab
	Hole . . . St. Bernard dog. [8]

1417 究	research
	Hole . . . baseball. [7]

1418 窒	plug up
	Hole . . . climax. [11]

1419 窃	stealth
	Hole . . . cut. [9]

1420 窟	cavern
	Hole . . . yield. [13]

1421 窪	depression

Hole . . . water . . . ivy. The **depression** referred to here is a sunken place in the ground, rather than in one's spirits. [14]

1422 搾	squeeze

Fingers . . . hole . . . saw. [13]

1423 窯	kiln

Hole . . . sheep . . . oven fire. [15]

1424 窮	hard up

Hole . . . somebody . . . bow. [15]

★ 兀	paper punch

This primitive simply discards the first stroke of that for *hole* to become a **paper punch**. When found at the top of its relative primitive, it undergoes the same change, the *eight* becoming *human legs* (see FRAME 1413). [4]

1425 探	grope

Fingers . . . paper punch . . . tree. [11]

1426 深	deep

Water . . . paper punch . . . tree. [11]

1427 丘	hill

Since this supposedly pictographic representation of a **hill** looks like anything but, picture a row of *axes* driven into the ground up to their heads, and see if that doesn't present you with a more memorable image of **hill**—at least a riskier one sliding down! [5]

1428	Point
岳	Think of the key word as referring to proper names of mountains, but do not confuse with *mountain pass* (FRAME 835). The elements are: *hill . . . mountain.* [8]

1429	soldier
兵	*Hill . . . animal legs.* [7]

1430	seacoast
浜	*Water . . . soldier.* [10]

Lesson 36

THE PRIMITIVE FOR *thread* is one of the most common in all the kanji. This means that you are likely to be putting it where it doesn't belong and forgetting to include it where it does—all the more reason to give it a vivid image each time. Fortunately, nearly all the thread-related kanji to be covered in this book will appear in this lesson, so you can learn them all at once.

1431	thread
糸	Remember when your granny used to ask you to bend your arms at the *elbows* and hold them out so that she could use them like a rack to hold a skein of string or yarn (here **thread**) while she rolled it up into a *little* ball? Now can you see the two *elbows* (with the second stroke doubling up) at the top, and the character for *little* below? [6]

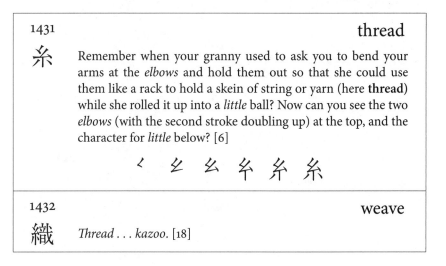

1432	weave
織	*Thread . . . kazoo.* [18]

| 1433 繕 | *Thread . . . virtuous.* [18] | darning |

| 1434 縮 | *Thread . . . inn.* [17] | shrink |

| 1435 繁 | *Cleverness . . . thread.* [16] | luxuriant |

| 1436 縦 | *Thread . . . accompany.* [16] | vertical |

| 1437 緻 | The key word should be taken to mean minute, detailed, or nuanced. Its primitive elements are: *thread . . . doth.* [16] | fine |

| 1438 線 | *Thread . . . spring.* [15] | line |

| 1439 綻 | *Thread . . . determine.* [14] | come apart at the seams |

| 1440 締 | *Thread . . . sovereign.* [15] | tighten |

| 1441 維 | *Thread . . . turkey.* [14] | fiber |

| 1442 羅 | *Eye . . . fiber.* [19] | gauze |

1443 練	practice
	Thread . . . east. [14]

1444 緒	thong
	Thread . . . puppet. Although we usually think of a **thong** as coming at the end of a piece of string, this character's meaning allows for it to come at the beginning as well. [14]

1445 続	continue
	Thread . . . sell. [13]

1446 絵	picture
	Thread . . . meeting. [12]

1447 統	overall
	Thread . . . allot. [12]

1448 絞	strangle
	Thread . . . mingle. [12]

1449 給	salary
	Thread . . . fit. [12]

1450 絡	entwine
	Thread . . . each. [12]

1451 結	tie
	Thread . . . aerosol can. [12]

1452 終	end
	Thread . . . winter. [11]

1453 級	class
	Threads . . . outstretched hands. [9]
1454 紀	chronicle
	Thread . . . snake. [9]
1455 紅	crimson
	Thread . . . craft. [9]
1456 納	settlement
	Thread . . . inside. [10]
1457 紡	spinning
	For the kanji that means the *spinning* of *thread* and other fibers we have the elements: *thread . . . compass.* [10]
1458 紛	distract
	Thread . . . part. [10]
1459 紹	introduce
	Thread . . . seduce. [11]
1460 経	sūtra
	Thread . . . spool. [11]
1461 紳	sire
	Thread . . . monkey. [11]
1462 約	promise
	Consider for a moment the etymology of the word "**promise**" in order to notice its roots in the activity of putting one thing (e.g., one's word of honor) in place of another (e.g., the fulfillment of a task). For as it turns out, this character also means "to abridge,

economize, and abbreviate"—all activities that involve putting one thing in place of another. With that in mind, we may now work with the elements: *thread . . . ladle.* [9]

1463

dainty

細

Thread . . . brains. [11]

1464

accumulate

累

Rice field . . . threads. Make use of the position of the elements to distinguish this kanji from that of the previous frame. [11]

1465

cord

索

Chapel (see FRAME 930) *. . . thread.* [10]

1466

general

総

This kanji, meaning universal or widespread, is composed of three elements: *thread . . . public . . . heart.* [14]

1467

cotton

綿

Thread . . . white . . . towels. [14]

1468

silk

絹

Thread . . . mouth . . . flesh. [13]

1469

winding

繰

Thread . . . goods . . . tree. [19]

1470

inherit

継

Thread . . . rice . . . fishhook. Compare FRAME 1218. [13]

1471

green

緑

Thread . . . broom . . . rice grains. [14]

1472 縁	affinity
Thread . . . broom . . . sow. [15]	

1473 網	netting
Thread . . . glass canopy . . . animal horns . . . perish. [14]	

1474 緊	tense
Slave . . . crotch . . . thread. [15]	

1375 1475 紫	purple
Footprint . . . spoon . . . thread. [12]	

1476 縛	truss
Threads . . . acupuncturist. [16]	

1477 縄	straw rope
Thread . . . eels. [15]	

* 幺	cocoon
The two triangular shapes here and their final stroke are intended as a pictograph of a **cocoon**, spun in circles and tied up at the end. It is like the character for *thread*, except that the silkworm's actual product has not yet emerged clearly at the bottom. [3]	
く 幺 幺	

1478 幼	infancy
Cocoon . . . muscle. [5]	

1479 後	behind
Line . . . cocoon . . . walking legs. [9]	

1480	faint

幽

Two cocoons . . . mountain. Observe how the two vertical strokes of *the mountain* are extended upwards to serve as a kind of enclosure. [9]

丨 幺 幺幺 幽 幽

1481	how many

幾

Two cocoons . . . person . . . fiesta. [12]

幺幺 幺幺 幺幺 幾

* As a primitive, this kanji will mean an *abacus*, the bead-instrument used in the Orient to calculate *how many*.

1482	mechanism

機

Tree . . . abacus. [16]

1483	capital suburbs

畿

Two cocoons . . . field . . . fiesta. [15]

1484	mysterious

玄

Top hat . . . cocoon. [5]

1485	livestock

畜

Mysterious . . . rice field. [10]

1486	amass

蓄

Flowers . . . livestock. [13]

1487	bowstring

弦

Bow . . . mysterious. [8]

1488	hug
擁	*Fingers . . . mysterious . . . turkey.* Note that the *top hat* is extended across both elements, though it belongs only to the *cocoon*. This means that you may either use *mysterious*—as we did here—or take the three elements separately. [16]

1489	nourishing
滋	*Water . . . double-mysterious.* Note the doubling up of the element for *top hat* in the primitive for *mysterious* and assign it a special image, as it will come up in the next two frames. [12]

1490	mercy
慈	Double-*mysterious . . . heart.* [13]

1491	magnet
磁	*Stone . . .* double-*mysterious.* [14]

1492	lineage
系	The single stroke added to the beginning of the primitive for *thread* gives the image of threads woven into a single cord. Hence the meaning, **lineage**. [7] * As a primitive, we shall give this kanji the meaning of *yarn*, as the uniting of many threads into a single strand is most obvious with *yarn*.

1493	person in charge
係	*Person . . . yarn.* [9]

1494	grandchild
孫	*Child . . . yarn.* [10]

1495	suspend
懸	*Prefecture . . . yarn . . . heart.* [20]

1496	modest
遜	*Grandchild . . . road.* [13]

Lesson 37

EARLIER WE created an image for *seal* (FRAME 168). Here we come to a set of primitives based on the shape of a seal and deriving their meanings from the notion of stamping or sealing.

⋆	stamp
卩	This character is a kind of pictograph of a **stamp** that may best be imagined as a postage **stamp** to distinguish it from other stamp-like things to come up later. [2]

$$ 丁 \quad 卩 $$

1497	instead
却	*Gone . . . stamp.* [7]

1498	shins
脚	*Part of the body . . . instead.* This character has more or less the same meaning as that for *leg* learned back in FRAME 1372. It can also indicate the part of the legs from the **shins** down, which explains the choice of the key word. [11]

1499	wholesale
卸	The left primitive is a union of *a horse* and *footprint*. To the right, the *stamp*. [9]

午 午 牛 牟 卸

1500   honorable

御   *Line ... wholesale.* [12]

1501   clothing

服   *Flesh ... stamp ... crotch.* Note how the *stamp* is stretched out here. [8]

1502   fate

命   This character connotes life in general, but also the particular life to which one is **fated** by virtue of the distinctive character with which one is born. Its elements are: *fit ... stamp.* The bottom portion of *fit* is nudged to the left in order to make room for the *stamp.* [8]

---

*   chop-seal

卩   The **chop-seal** is the engraved piece of wood or stone used in the Orient to certify documents. Unlike the *stamp*, the top stroke here reaches a good distance to the left of its vertical stroke. When it appears at the top of another primitive, it is abbreviated to ⴲ. [2]

フ 卩

1503   orders

令   *Meeting ... chop-seal.* [5]

1504   zero

零   *Rain ... orders.* [13]

1505   age

齢   This character is used to express the years of one's **age.** Its elements: *teeth ... orders.* [17]

1506		cool
冷	Ice . . . orders. [7]	
1507		jurisdiction
領	Orders . . . head. [14]	
1508		small bell
鈴	Gold . . . orders. [13]	
1509		courage
勇	Chop-seal . . . male. [9]	
1510		bubble up
湧	Water . . . courage. [12]	
1511		traffic
通	Chop-seal . . . utilize . . . road. By combining the first two primitives into a single image, you will be able to use that image in a few instances later, one of which comes immediately. [10]	
1512		jump
踊	Wooden leg . . . chop-seal . . . utilize. [14]	
1513		doubt
疑	Spoon . . . dart . . . chop-seal . . . zoo. [14]	
1514		mimic
擬	Fingers . . . doubt. [17]	
1515		congeal
凝	Ice . . . doubt. [16]	

*	**fingerprint**
巳	The primitive for **fingerprint** is like that for *stamp* except that the second stroke bends back towards the right, like an arm. [2]

コ　巳

1516	**pattern**
範	*Bamboo . . . car . . . fingerprint.* [15]

1517	**crime**
犯	*Wild dogs . . . fingerprint.* [5]

1518	**widespread**
氾	*Water . . . fingerprint.* [5]

1519	**unlucky**
厄	*Cliff . . . fingerprint.* [4]

1520	**dangerous**
危	*Bound up . . . unlucky.* [6]

*	**mailbox**
夗	*Evening . . . fingerprint.* [5]

1521	**address**
宛	*House . . . mailbox.* [8]

1522	**arm**
腕	*Part of the body . . . address.* [12]

1523	**garden**
苑	*Flowers . . . mailbox.* [8]

1524	grudge
怨	Mailbox . . . heart. [9]

*	receipt
仏	This primitive element is actually the mirror-image of that for *stamp*, but since Japanese does not permit a stroke to go to the left and bottom in one swoop, the visual similarity is not perfectly clear. If you play with the idea with pen and paper, its logic will become obvious. [3]

´ 𠃊 仏

1525	willow
柳	Tree . . . receipt . . . stamp. [9]

1526	egg
卵	Receipt . . . stamp . . . and *a drop* in each side to represent a little smear of **egg** yoke. The third stroke is drawn slightly higher to close the **egg** up tightly and keep the yoke inside. [7]

´ 𠃊 仾 𠂤 卵 卵 卵

1527	detain
留	Receipt . . . dagger . . . rice field. [10]

1528	marine blue
瑠	Jewel . . . detain. [14]

1529	trade
貿	Receipt . . . dagger . . . shells. Do not confuse with *make a deal* (FRAME 471) or *wholesale* (FRAME 1499). [12]

*	staples
𦣝	This primitive represents a number of small **staples**, like the kind commonly used in an office and at school. [4]

´ ⌐ ⌐ ⌐

1530		stamp
印	At last we come to the general character meaning **stamp**. Its elements: *staples . . . stamp*. [6]	

1531		mortar
臼	The image here is of *back-to-back staples*. The **mortar** referred to in this key word is a stone or wooden basin used for grinding with a pestle. [6]	

1532		break
毀	*Mortar . . . soil . . . missile.* [13]	

1533		entertain
興	*Mortar . . . same . . . tool.* Be careful to make an image that keeps *same* in the middle. [16]	

Lesson 38

THE NEXT CLUSTER of kanji has to do with primitives related to the activities of eating and drinking.

1534		sign of the bird
酉	Though we shall later encounter the kanji for *bird*, we introduce this one for the tenth sign of the zodiac mainly because of its use as a primitive, where it has a different meaning. [7]	

一 厂 冂 丙 丙 酉 酉

* As a primitive, it means *whiskey bottle*. In its pictograph, you can see the loosely corked lid, the bottle, and the contents (about one-third full). You might also think of the Spanish "porrón," a decanter shaped like a long-necked bird.

1535		saké
酒	Water . . . whiskey bottle. [10]	

1536		bartending
酌	Whiskey bottle . . . ladle. [10]	

1537		hooch
酎	This kanji is used for thick, low-grade saké made from various kinds of grains. Its primitives are: *whisky bottle . . . glue*. [10]	

1538		fermentation
酵	Whiskey bottle . . . filial piety. [14]	

1539		cruel
酷	Whiskey bottle . . . revelation. [14]	

1540		repay
酬	Whiskey bottle . . . state. [13]	

1541		dairy products
酪	Whiskey bottle . . . each. [13]	

1542		vinegar
酢	Whiskey bottle . . . saw. [12]	

1543		drunk
酔	Whiskey bottle . . . baseball . . . needle. [11]	

1544	distribute
配	*Whisky bottle . . . snake.* [10]

1545	acid
酸	*Whiskey bottle . . . license . . . walking legs.* [14]

1546	waver
猶	*Wild dogs . . . animal horns . . . whiskey bottle.* [12]

1547	revered
尊	*Animal horns . . . whiskey bottle . . . glue.* [12]

1548	beans
豆	This kanji depicts a pot of **beans**, although it looks more like a table on which the pot is resting. [7]

一　　　口　　　亨　　　豆

* As a primitive, this kanji will also mean *table*.

1549	head
頭	Here we meet at last the full kanji on which the primitive for **head** is based. The elements: *table . . . head.* [16]

1550	short
短	*Dart . . . table.* [12]

1551	bountiful
豊	*Bend . . . table.* Think of a **bountiful** harvest, and you will not be far from the meaning of this character. [13]

* 壴	**drum** The element for **drum** shows a *samurai* over a *table*. The top stroke of the *table* appears to be missing, but actually it has doubled up with the final stroke of the element for *samurai*. [9]
1552 鼓	**drum** The full kanji for the *drum* adds a *branch*, apparently to serve as a **drum**stick, to the primitive for *drum*. [13]
1553 喜	**rejoice** *Drum . . . mouth.* [12]
1554 樹	**timber-trees** *Trees . . . drum . . . glue.* [16]
1555 皿	**dish** The kanji for a **dish** is, clearly, the pictograph of a painted or carved bowl, seen from the side. [5] 丨　冂　冊　冊　皿
1556 血	**blood** The *drop* in the *dish* is **blood**. It is similar to the *drop* we saw earlier on the *dagger* in the character for *blade* (FRAME 88). [6]
1557 盆	**basin** *Part . . . dish.* [9]
1558 盟	**alliance** *Bright . . . dish.* [13]
1559 盗	**steal** *Next . . . dish.* [11]

1560 温	**warm** *Water . . . sun . . . dish.* [12]
1561 蓋	**lid** *Flowers . . . gone . . . dish.* [13]
1562 監	**oversee** *Slaves . . . reclining . . . floor/one . . . dish.* [15]
1563 濫	**overflow** *Water . . . oversee.* [18]
1564 鑑	**specimen** *Metal . . . oversee.* [23]
1565 藍	**indigo** *Flowers . . . oversee.* [18]
1566 猛	**fierce** *Wild dogs . . . child . . . dish.* [11]
1567 盛	**boom** Here **boom** refers to something that is popular and prospering. Its elements: *turn into . . . dish.* [11]
1568 塩	**salt** *Ground . . . reclining . . . mouth . . . dish.* [13]
* 艮	**silver** We give this element the meaning of **silver** from the kanji in the following frame. Both the original pictographic representation and the primitive elements that make it up are more trouble to hunt out than they are worth. It is best simply to learn it as is. In doing so, take careful note of the stroke order, and also the

fact that when this element appears on the left, the penultimate stroke is omitted, giving us simply 艮. [6]

フ フ ヨ ヨ 臣 艮 艮

1569 銀	silver *Metal . . . silver.* [14]

金 銀

1570 恨	resentment *State of mind . . . silver.* [9]

1571 根	root *Tree . . . silver.* [10]

1572 即	instant *Silver . . . stamp.* [7]

1573 爵	baron *Vulture . . . eye . . . silver . . . glue.* [17]

1574 節	node *Bamboo . . . instant.* [13]

1575 退	retreat *Road . . . silver.* [9]

1576 限	limit *Pinnacle . . . silver.* [9]

1577 眼	eyeball *Eye . . . silver.* [11]

1578		good
良	*Drop of . . . silver.* [7]	

> * As a primitive, use the image of a saint's *halo*. As with *silver*, when this element is drawn on the left, the penultimate stroke is omitted, giving us 𠄌.

1579		melodious
朗	*Halo . . . moon.* [10]	

1580		wandering
浪	*Water . . . halo.* [10]	

1581		daughter
娘	*Woman . . . halo.* [10]	

1582		eat
食	If *halo* and *umbrella* aren't enough, break the *halo* down into *drop* and *silver*—or "silverware," an additional primitive. [9]	

> * As a primitive the kanji means *eating* or *food*. As with *silver*, on the left the final two strokes are combined into one.

1583		meal
飯	*Food . . . anti-.* [12]	

1584		drink
飲	*Food . . . yawn.* [12]	

1585		hungry
飢	*Food . . . wind.* [10]	

1586		starve
餓	*Food . . . ego.* [15]	

1587 飾	decorate

Food . . . reclining . . . towel. [13]

1588 餌	feed

Food . . . ear. The sense of the key word here is that of bait or **feed** for animals. [14]

1589 館	Bldg.

The abbreviation of **Building** suggests that this kanji is used in proper names, as indeed it often is. Keep your connotation distinct from *Inst.* (FRAME 1401) when working with the elements: *food . . . bureaucrat.* [16]

1590 餅	*mochi*

Mochi is the glutinous rice the Japanese pound into cakes. Its primitives are: *food . . . puzzle.* [14]

1591 養	foster

Sheep . . . food. The key word has the sense of promoting the development of something, especially in a psychological or spiritual sense. [13]

1592 飽	sated

Eat . . . wrap. [13]

⋆ 旡	waitress

If you draw this character once, you will see that its first three strokes resemble the form for *receipt* (except that the second stroke ends more parallel to the first), with its last stroke stretched to form the first of the two *human legs*. From this we give it its meaning of a **waitress** (who should not be confused with the *waiter* back in FRAME 1050). [4]

一 ㄷ 乓 旡

1593	previously
既	*Silver . . . waitress.* Do not confuse this kanji's key word with *before* (FRAME 263). [10]

1594	outline
概	*Roots . . . waitress.* Note that the kanji meaning of the two primitives to the right is not used here because we shall later meet a primitive meaning *beforehand* and want to preempt any confusion. The same holds true in the following frame. [14]

1595	rue
慨	*Resentment . . . waitress.* [13]

Lesson 39

A NUMBER OF primitives relating to plant life remain to be considered, and we shall devote the next two pages to doing so. In the following pages, as indeed in the rest of the book, we shall meet several elements whose use is quite limited. Nevertheless, it is better to learn them as primitives both in order to acquaint yourself better with the way the Japanese writing system repeats certain combinations of elements, and in order later to facilitate the learning of characters outside the compass of these pages.

1596	even
平	This character is easiest remembered as a pictograph of a water lily floating on the surface of the water, which gives it its meaning of **even**. The fourth stroke represents the calm, smooth surface of a pond, and the final stroke the long stem of the plant reaching underwater. [5]

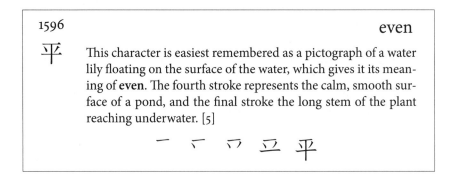

* As a primitive, this kanji can keep its pictographic meaning of a *water lily*.

1597

呼

call

Mouth . . . water lily. Note: this is the one time that the "stem" has a barb at the end. Work this fact into your story. [8]

1598

坪

two-mat area

This kanji belongs to an old Japanese system of measurement and indicates an area of about 36 square feet, or the **area** taken up by **two** tatami **mats**. Its elements: *ground . . . water lily.* [8]

1599

評

evaluate

Words . . . water lily. [12]

---

*

乂

sheaf

These two strokes are a crude drawing of a bundle of stalks bound together into a **sheaf**. [2]

ノ 乂

1600

刈

reap

Sheaf . . . saber. [4]

1601

刹

moment

The key word here is the noun meaning "a brief moment." Its elements: *sheaf . . . tree . . . saber.* [8]

1602

希

hope

Sheaf . . . linen. [7]

1603

凶

villain

Sheaf . . . shovel. [4]

乂 凶

1604	bosom
胸	*Part of the body . . . bound up . . . villain.* [10]

1605	detach
離	*Top hat . . . villain . . . belt . . . elbow . . . turkey.* This is potentially one of the most difficult characters to remember. Tackle it positively and let the image "sink in" by carrying it around with you today and calling it up in your spare moments. [18]

1606	crystal
璃	This kanji refers to one of the seven classical stones of China. Its elements: *jewel . . . top hat . . . villain . . . belt . . . elbow.* [14]

1607	kill
殺	*Sheaf . . . tree . . . missile.* [10]

1608	bracing
爽	The sense of the key word is of something refreshing and invigorating. It is made up of the *St. Bernard* and a pair of *sheaves* on each side. [11]

⋆	earthworm
屯	*Drop of . . . shovel . . . fishhook.* [4]

一 亡 屮 屯

1609	genuine
純	*Thread . . . earthworm.* [10]

1610	immediate
頓	*Earthworm . . . head.* [13]

1611	dull
鈍	*Metal . . . earthworm.* [12]

1612	spicy

辛

The character in this frame pictures food whose taste is so hot and **spicy** that it makes the hairs on your body *stand* up as straight as *needles*. [7]

* As a primitive, we shall use this meaning of *spicy*, except when the two extra strokes are added to the bottom, giving it the form of a tree: 辛. Then we take its alternate meaning of a *red pepper* plant. The connection is obvious.

1613	resign

辞

Tongue . . . spicy. [13]

1614	catalpa

梓

Tree . . . spicy. [11]

1615	superintend

宰

House . . . spicy. [10]

*	ketchup

辟

One way American children learn to cope with food they are forced to eat against their will is to smother it with **ketchup**. We can see this depicted in the *mouth* with the *flag* over it (in this case, the Stars and Stripes), set alongside the element for *spicy* (all of which is not far removed from the original meaning it had as a character on its own: "false"). [13]

尸　居　辟

1616	wall

壁

Ketchup . . . ground. [16]

1617	holed gem

璧

The **holed gem** to which this kanji refers is a flat, circular object of about a foot in length, made of stone or glass and having a large hole in the middle. Its elements: *ketchup . . . ball.* [18]

1618	evade
避	*Ketchup . . . road.* [16]

1619	new
新	*Red pepper . . . ax.* [13]

1620	firewood
薪	*Flowers . . . new.* [16]

1621	parent
親	*Red pepper . . . see.* [16]

1622	happiness
幸	Simply by turning the dot at the top of the primitive for *spicy* into a cross shape, we move from things bitter and *spicy* to things **happy**. [8]

1623	tenacious
執	*Happiness . . . fat man.* [11]

1624	clasp
摯	Of the many and widely different meanings of this kanji, we select the verbal meaning of **clasp**, which fits in well with its primitive elements: *tenacious . . . hand.* [15]

1625	report
報	*Happiness . . . stamp . . . crotch.* Compare FRAME 1501. [12]

*	cornucopia
屮	Considering the lack of circular lines, this kanji is not a bad pictograph of a **cornucopia**. Despite the appearance of the printed form, what looks like the first two strokes are actually written as one. [2]

ㄴ ㅛ

1626	shout
叫	Mouth . . . cornucopia. [5]

1627	twist
糾	Thread . . . cornucopia. [8]

1628	income
収	Cornucopia . . . crotch. Keep distinct from both *fare* (FRAME 1079) and *salary* (FRAME 1449). [4]

1629	lowly
卑	A drop of . . . brains . . . cornucopia. [8]

1630	tombstone
碑	Rock . . . lowly. [13]

*	rice seedling
朮	As we mentioned back in FRAME 249, **rice seedlings** get an element all their own: *soil* and *human legs* becomes an ideograph of the spikelets of rice bunched together for implanting in the muddy soil of the paddy. [5]

1631	land
陸	The sense of **land** carried by this kanji is distinct from *soil* (FRAME 161) and *ground* (FRAME 554) in that it is meant to represent **land** seen from a distance, that is, *land* as opposed to "water." Its elements: *pinnacle . . . rice seedlings . . . ground*. [11]

1632	intimate
睦	Eye . . . rice seedlings . . . ground. [13]

1633 勢	forces
Rice seedlings . . ground . . . fat man . . . muscle. [13]	

1634 熱	heat
Rice seedlings . . . ground . . . fat man . . . oven fire. [15]	

1635 菱	diamond
Named after a **diamond**-shaped flower (the water caltrop), this key word refers to things shaped like a **diamond**. Its elements: *flower . . . rice seedlings . . . walking legs.* [11]	

1636 陵	mausoleum
Pinnacle . . . rice seedlings . . . walking legs. [11]	

1637 亥	sign of the hog
This kanji is the 12th sign of the Chinese zodiac: the **sign of the hog**. It is best learned by thinking of an acorn-eating **hog** in connection with the primitive meaning given below. [6]	

丶 亠 ㇗ 亥 亥 亥

* The *top hat* represents the external shape of the *acorn,* and the unusual but easily written complex of strokes beneath it (which you might also see as distortions of an *elbow* and *person*) stands for the mysterious secret whereby the *acorn* contains the oak tree in a nutshell.

1638 核	nucleus
Tree . . . acorn. [10]	

1639 刻	engrave
Acorn . . . saber. [8]	

1640 該	above-stated *Words . . . acorn.* [13]
1641 骸	remains *Skeleton . . . acorn.* [16]
1642 劾	censure *Acorn . . . muscle.* [8]

* 朮	resin This *tree* has become a *pole* (that is, a *tree* with its branches not touching) because most of its branches have been pruned off by a naive but greedy gardener anxious to siphon off its **resin** (the drop at the top, written as the final stroke) as quickly as possible. [5]

十 オ 朮 朮

1643 述	mention *Resin . . . road.* [8]
1644 術	art *Boulevard . . . resin.* [11]

* 圭	celery This primitive looks very close to that for *salad*, except that an extra horizontal line has been included, reminiscent I should think of the long **celery** sticks in your *salad*. [5]

一 廿 井 圭

1645 寒	cold *House . . . celery . . . animal legs . . . ice.* [12]

---

*

襄 grass skirt

This unusual looking **grass skirt** is composed of a *top hat* and *scarf*, and *eight celery* sticks. [13]

亠　六　窜　襄

1646

塞 block up

House . . . celery . . . animal legs . . . soil. [13]

1647

醸 brew

Whiskey bottle . . . grass skirt. [20]

1648

譲 defer

Words . . . grass skirt. [20]

1649

壌 lot

Ground . . . grass skirt. The **lot** of this key word refers to a portion of land. [16]

1650

嬢 lass

Woman . . . grass skirt. [16]

Lesson 40

THE REMAINDER OF PLANT-RELATED primitives are built up from combinations of vertical and horizontal lines, representing respectively plants and the earth from which they spring. Accordingly it would be a good idea to study the remaining elements of this section at a single sitting, or at least so to review them before passing on to the next grouping.

| ★ 圭 | grow up |

As the plant **grows up** it sprouts leaves and a stalk, which are depicted here over a single horizontal stroke for the *soil*. Think of something (its relative primitive) **growing up** in a flash to many times its normal size, much like little Alice in Wonderland, who **grew up** so fast she was soon larger than the room in which she was sitting. [4]

一 十 キ 圭

1651

毒 · poison

Grow up . . . breasts. [8]

1652

素 · elementary

Grow up . . . thread. [10]

1653

麦 · barley

Grow up . . . walking legs. [7]

1654

青 · blue

Grow up . . . moon. [8]

1655

精 · refined

Rice . . . blue. [14]

1656

請 · solicit

Words . . . blue. [15]

1657

情 · feelings

State of mind . . . blue. Do not confuse with *emotion* (FRAME 662). [11]

1658 晴	clear up
	Take the key word in its associations with the weather (unless that tempts you to include the primitive for *weather*, which doesn't belong here). Its elements: *sun . . . blue*. [12]

1659 清	pure
	Water . . . blue. [11]

1660 静	quiet
	Blue . . . contend. Do not confuse with *calm* (FRAME 1230). [14]

1661 責	blame
	Grow up . . . oyster. [11]

1662 績	exploits
	Thread . . . blame. [17]

1663 積	volume
	Wheat . . . blame. This key word has to do with measurement, and should be kept distinct from the kanji for *quantity* (FRAME 189)—even though the meanings are similar. [16]

1664 債	bond
	Person . . . blame. The key word refers to financial **bonds**. [13]

1665 漬	pickling
	Water . . . blame. [14]

1666 表	surface
	Grow up . . . scarf. This character represents the "outside" of a garment, just as the kanji for *back* (FRAME 426) depicted the "inside" or lining. [8]

1667 俵	bag
	Keep this kanji distinct from that for *sack* (FRAME 1081). Its elements are: *person . . . surface*. [10]

1668 潔	undefiled
	Water . . . grow up . . . dagger . . . thread. Do not confuse with *upright* (FRAME 58). [15]

1669 契	pledge
	Grow up . . . dagger . . . St. Bernard dog. The connotation of this character should be kept distinct from that for *vow* (FRAME 1214) and *promise* (FRAME 1462). [9]

1670 喫	consume
	Mouth . . . pledge. [12]

1671 害	harm
	House . . . grow up . . . mouth. [10]

1672 轄	control
	Car . . . harm. Hint: the image of an auto going "out of **control**" may help keep this key word distinct from others like it, such as *manipulate* (FRAME 864). [17]

1673 割	proportion
	Harm . . . saber. [12]

1674 憲	constitution
	The key word refers to the fundamental guiding principles of a government or other organization. Its elements: *House . . . grow up . . . eyes . . . heart*. [16]

1675 生	life
	A single *drop* added to the element for *grow up* gives us the character for **life**. [5]

* As a primitive, we may think of a microscopic *cell*, that miraculous unit that *grows up* to become a living being.

1676		star
星	*Sun . . . cell.* [9]	

1677		awakening
醒	*Whisky bottle . . . star.* [16]	

1678		surname
姓	*Woman . . . cell.* [8]	

1679		sex
性	*State of mind . . . cell.* [8]	

1680		animal sacrifice
牲	*Cow . . . cell.* [9]	

1681		products
産	*Vase . . . cliff . . . cell.* [11]	

1682		hump
隆	This character, used for everything from little **humps** of hills to camel **humps**, easily suggests the hunch on the pig's back and hind parts where the best cuts of meat are to be found (and hence the English expression for luxury, "living high off the hog"). The elements we have to work with are: *pinnacle . . . walking legs . . . cell.* [11]	

*		bushes
丰	Whatever image you contrived for the character meaning *hedge* (FRAME 165), choose something different and clearly distinguishable for this primitive for **bushes**. The element itself differs from that for *grow up* only in the extension of the single vertical stroke beneath the final horizontal stroke and in the order	

of writing. Though we shall meet only one instance of it in this chapter and one more later on, it is worth noting that when this element appears on the side, the final stroke is sloped somewhat to the left: 耒. [4]

三 丰

| 1683 | summit |
| 峰 | Mountain . . . walking legs . . . bushes. [10] |

| 1684 | bee |
| 蜂 | Insect . . . walking legs . . . bushes. [13] |

| 1685 | sew |
| 縫 | Thread . . . walking legs . . . bushes . . . road. [16] |

| 1686 | worship |
| 拝 | Fingers . . . bush . . . suspended from the ceiling. [8] |

| 1687 | longevity |
| 寿 | Bushes . . . glue. [7] |

| 1688 | casting |
| 鋳 | Metal . . . longevity. As you probably guessed from the elements, the key word refers to the casting of metals. [15] |

| * | Christmas tree |
| 耒 | The addition of the final two strokes to the element for bushes gives the sense of a tree that is also a bush. Hence, the Christmas tree. [6] |

丰 耒

1689		enroll
籍	Bamboo . . . Christmas tree . . . once upon a time. [20]	

*		bonsai
夫	The element for *bushes* has an extra stroke added (drawn from the point where the second and fifth strokes touch when it "encloses" something beneath, otherwise from the point where the fourth and fifth strokes intersect) to give the image of the crutches Japanese gardeners use to hold up a tree that is being bent into shape. From there it is but a short leap to the small *bonsai* plants that imitate this art in miniature. [5]	

一　二　三　夫　夫

1690		springtime
春	Bonsai . . . sun. [9]	

1691		camellia
椿	Tree . . . springtime. [13]	

1692		peaceful
泰	Bonsai . . . rice grains. [10]	

1693		play music
奏	Bonsai . . . heavens. [9]	

1694		reality
実	House . . . bonsai. [8]	

*		cornstalk
丰	The element for *bushes* extended the vertical stroke beneath the final horizontal stroke; the **cornstalk** omits that final stroke altogether, leaving only the **stalk** and the leaves bursting forth on all sides. [3]	

一 二 キ

1695	dedicate
奉	*Bonsai . . . cornstalk.* Use a ritualistic, religious meaning. [8]

1696	stipend
俸	*Person . . . dedicate.* [10]

1697	rod
棒	*Tree . . . dedicate.* [12]

★	cabbage
菫	The *flower*, the *mouth*, and the element for *grow up* combine here to create the primitive for **cabbage**. [10]

艹 苫 苹 苹 堇 菫

1698	discreet
謹	*Words . . . cabbage.* [17]

1699	trifle
僅	*Person . . . cabbage.* [12]

1700	diligence
勤	*Cabbage . . . muscle.* [12]

★	scarecrow
荑	By twisting the final two strokes of our *cabbage* into a pair of legs, we get a **scarecrow** with a *cabbage* for a head. [10]

艹 苫 苫 荁 荑 荑

1701	Sino-
漢	*Water . . . scarecrow.* The key word has come to refer to things Chinese in general, including the kanji themselves (for which this character is used). [13]

1702	sigh
嘆	*Mouth . . . scarecrow.* [13]

1703	difficult
難	*Scarecrow . . . turkey.* [18]

*	silage
卉	The drawing of this element is difficult to do smoothly, and should be practiced carefully. It is a pictograph of all sorts of plants and grasses thrown together to make **silage**. The vertical stroke is drawn here with a broken line to indicate that it will always double up with another primitive element's vertical stroke. [6]

一　二　干　卅　母　卉

1704	splendor
華	*Flower . . . silage . . . needle.* [10]

1705	droop
垂	*A drop of . . . silage . . . walking stick . . . floor.* The character is written in the order of its elements. [8]

1706	saliva
唾	*Mouth . . . droop.* [11]

1707	drowsy
睡	*Eyes . . . droop.* [13]

1708		spindle
錘	*Metal . . . droop.* [16]	

1709		ride
乗	The simplest way to remember this character is to find the sprig of *wheat* in it, hidden because it doubles up with one stroke of *silage.* [9]	

1710		surplus
剰	*Ride . . . saber.* [11]	

Lesson 41

ONLY A FEW OF THE primitives relating to time and direction remain. It is to these that we turn our attention in this lesson.

1711		now
今	The final stroke of this kanji is a rare shape, which we have not met before and will only meet in this character and others that include it as a primitive. We are more accustomed to seeing it straightened out as part of other shapes—for instance, as the second stroke of *mouth*. If you need any help at all with this character, you may picture it as two hands of a clock pointing to what time it is **now**. The element above it, *meeting*, should easily relate to that image. [4]	
	* We shall use *clock* as the primitive meaning of this character, in line with the above explanation.	

1712		include
含	*Clock . . . mouth.* [7]	

1713		covet
貪	Clock . . . shellfish. [11]	

1714		versify
吟	As we have already learned characters for *poem* (FRAME 370), *chant* (FRAME 21), and *song* (FRAME 508), it is important to protect this key word with an image all its own. Its elements are the same as those above; only the position has changed: *mouth . . . clock.* [7]	

1715		wish
念	Clock . . . heart. [8]	

1716		wrench
捻	This kanji does not refer to the tool but to the act of twisting. Its elements: *fingers . . . wish.* [11]	

1717		harp
琴	A pair of *jewels . . . clock.* [12]	

1718		shade
陰	Just as the *sunshine* (FRAME 1397) represents the masculine principle in nature (Yang), the **shade** stands for the feminine principle (Yin). Its elements are: *pinnacle . . . clock . . . rising cloud.* [11]	

1719		beforehand
予	Think of this character as identical to the *halberd* (FRAME 1311) except that the final stroke has been omitted. Return to that character and devise some image to take this difference into account. [4]	

1720		preface
序	Cave . . . beforehand. [7]	

1721	deposit
預	*Beforehand . . . head.* [13]

1722	plains
野	This character refers to rustic life and rustic fields primarily, and from there gets derived meanings. Its elements: *computer . . . beforehand.* [11]

1723	concurrently
兼	At the top we have *the animal horns* and the single horizontal stroke to give them something to hang onto. Below that, we see one *rake* with two handles. Finally, we see a pair of strokes splitting away from each of the handles, indicating that they are both splitting under the pressure. The composite picture is of someone holding down two jobs **concurrently**, using the same kit of tools to move in two different directions and ending up in a mess. Take the time to find this sense in the kanji and it will be easy to remember, despite initial appearances. [10]

丶 丷 丷 当 当 当 羊 羊
兼 兼

1724	dislike
嫌	*Woman . . . concurrently.* [13]

1725	sickle
鎌	*Metal . . . concurrently.* [18]

1726	self-effacing
謙	*Words . . . concurrently.* [17]

1727	bargain
廉	*Cave . . . concurrently.* [13]

1728	west

西

To our way of counting directions, the **west** always comes fourth. So it is convenient to find the character for *four* in this kanji. But since we want only *one* of the *four* directions, the **west** adds the *one* at the top and sucks the *human legs* a bit out of their *mouth* in the process. [6]

一 冂 丙 西

* As a primitive, the meaning of *west* can be expanded to refer to the *Old West* of cowboy-movie fame, just as the meaning of the character for *east* was expanded into *the East*. Note, however, that in its primitive form the *legs* are straightened out and reach down to the bottom of the *mouth*. Hence, we get the shape 覀. With the exception of one kanji, given in the following frame, this element always appears at the top of its relative primitives.

1729	value

価

Person . . . Old West. [8]

1730	need

要

Old West . . . woman. [9]

1731	loins

腰

Part of the body . . . need. [13]

1732	ballot

票

Old West . . . altar. [11]

1733	drift

漂

Water . . . ballot. [14]

1734	signpost

標

Tree . . . ballot. [15]

1735 栗	chestnut
	Old West . . . tree. [10]

1736 慄	shudder
	State of mind . . . chestnut.. [13]

1737 遷	transition
	West . . . St. Bernard dog . . . snake . . . road. [15]

1738 覆	capsize
	West . . . restore. [18]

1739 煙	smoke
	Hearth . . . Old West . . . ground. [13]

1740 南	south
	Belt . . . happiness. Note how the *belt* runs through the middle of *happiness*. [9]
	十　冂　南

1741 楠	camphor tree
	Tree . . . south. [13]

1742 献	offering
	South . . . chihuahua. [13]

Lesson 42

THIS NEXT COLLECTION OF characters is based on the primitive for *gates*. From there we shall go on to consider other elements related to entrances and barriers in general.

1743

門

gates

The pictograph of two swinging **gates** is so clear in this kanji that only its stroke order needs to be memorized. In case you should have any trouble, though, you might doodle with the shapes on a piece of paper, taking care to note the difference in the stroke order of the two facing doors. The **gates** usually serve as an enclosure, and are written BEFORE whatever it is they enclose. [8]

| 「 「 「 「 「 「 「 門 門 門

* As a primitive, we shall continue to give it the meaning of *gates*, but recommend the image of swinging doors (like the kind once common at entrances to saloons) to distinguish it from the primitive for *door*.

1744

問

question

Gates . . . mouth. [11]

1745

閲

review

Gates . . . devil. Keep the connotation of this key word distinct from those of *inspection* (FRAME 1174), *revise* (FRAME 362), and *perusal* (FRAME 919). [15]

1746

閥

clique

Gates . . . fell. [14]

1747 間	interval
	Gates . . . sun/day. This **interval** applies to time and space alike, but the latter is better for creating an image. [12]

1748 闇	pitch dark
	Gates . . . sound. [17]

1749 簡	simplicity
	Bamboo . . . interval. [18]

1750 開	open
	Gates . . . two hands. [12]

1751 閉	closed
	Gates . . . genie. [11]

1752 閣	tower
	Gates . . . each. [14]

1753 閑	leisure
	Gates . . . tree. [12]

1754 聞	hear
	Gates . . . ear. Compare the story you invented for the kanji meaning *listen* (FRAME 890). [14]

1755 潤	wet
	Water . . . gates . . . king. [15]

1756 欄	column
	Tree . . . gates . . . east. [20]

1757		**fight**
闘	*Gates . . . table . . . glue.* Do not confuse with *contend* (FRAME 1238). [18]	

1758		**godown**
倉	The single *gate* is used here not in order to represent one *gate*, but many of them, indeed a *meeting of gates.* Add *mouth* (as an entrance here) and you end up with **godown**. That should help keep this character distinct from *warehouse* (FRAME 633). [10]	

1759		**genesis**
創	*Godown . . . saber.* [12]	

1760		**un-**
非	This key word, a negating prefix, is a doodle of a heavy iron pole with bars extending in both directions, to create the picture of a jail cell. From there to "**un-**" is but a short step. [8]	

丿　丿　彐　彐　刲　非　非　非

* As a primitive, we shall draw on the explanation above for the meaning of *jail cell.*

1761		**haiku**
俳	This character is used for the **haiku**, the 17-syllable poem that is one of Japan's best-known literary forms. Its elements: *person . . . jail cell.* [10]	

1762		**repudiate**
排	*Fingers . . . jail cell.* [11]	

1763		**sad**
悲	*Jail cell . . . heart.* [12]	

1764 罪	guilt *Eye . . . jail cell.* [13]
1765 輩	comrade *Jail cell . . . car.* [15]
1766 扉	front door *Door . . . jail cell.* [12]
* ユ	key This element gets its name and meaning from its pictographic representation of a **key**. The shape should be familiar: it is none other than the third and fourth strokes of the kanji for *five*. [2] ユ ユ
1767 侯	marquis *Person . . . key . . . dart.* Hint: the pun suggested by the pronunciation of the key word and the primitive for *key* may come in helpful. [9]
1768 喉	throat *mouth . . . marquis.* [12]
1769 候	climate *Marquis . . . walking stick.* Note where the *walking stick* is positioned in this kanji. [10]
* 夬	guillotine This element depicts a large, sharpened *key* coming down on the head of a criminal *St. Bernard*. [4] ユ ユ 夬

1770 決	decide
	The etymology of **decide** (de-cidere = cut off) will help here; the elements are: *water . . . guillotine*. [7]

1771 快	cheerful
	State of mind . . . guillotine. [7]

* 韋	locket
	The vertical stroke added here (the third stroke) turns the primitive element for a *key* into a **locket**. Below that, we find a square container (the *mouth*) and *sunglasses with one of the lenses popped out*. Note that in the primitive element for **locket** the final vertical stroke of *sunglasses* reaches all the way through to touch the *mouth*. [10]

龶　吾　韋

1772 偉	admirable
	Person . . . locket. [12]

1773 違	difference
	Locket . . . road. [13]

1774 緯	horizontal
	Thread . . . locket. [16]

1775 衛	defense
	Boulevard . . . locket. Do not confuse with *ward off* (FRAME 1399), *protect* (FRAME 1072), *guard* (FRAME 198), or *safeguard* (FRAME 756). [16]

1776 韓	Korea
	As with *Italy* (FRAME 1245) and *Africa* (FRAME 1391), this character simply abbreviates the full name of **Korea**. Its elements: *mist . . . locket*. [18]

Lesson 43

THE NEXT FEW PRIMITIVES are only loosely related in the sense that they all have to do with qualities of material objects in one way or another.

1777 干	**dry**
	It is best to see this kanji as a pictograph of a revolving circular clothesline (viewed from the side). Spin it around quickly in your mind's eye to give it the connotation of to **dry**. [3]

一　二　干

* The primitive meaning is *clothesline*.

1778 肝	**liver**
	Part of the body . . . dry. [7]

1779 刊	**publish**
	Dry . . . saber. [5]

1780 汗	**sweat**
	Water . . . dry. [6]

1781 軒	**flats**
	This kanji, a counter for houses, is made up of *cars . . . dry.* [10]

1782 岸	**beach**
	Mountain . . . cliff . . . dry. [8]

1783 幹	**tree trunk**
	Mist . . . umbrella . . . dry. The meaning of this key word extends beyond **tree trunks** to represent the main stem or line of anything from railway lines to managerial staffs. This should help

distinguish it from the stories used earlier for *book* (FRAME 224) and *body* (FRAME 1030), both of which made use of the image of a **tree trunk**, as well as the kanji for *trunk* (FRAME 194). [13]

---

*

于

potato

Note how this element differs from *dry* in virtue of the small hook at the end of the third stroke. [3]

一　二　于

1784

芋

potato

Flowers . . . potato. [6]

1785

宇

eaves

House . . . potato. [6]

1786

余

too much

Umbrella . . . potato . . . little. The last stroke of *potato* and the first of *little* coincide in this character. [7]

* Since the phrase "*too much*" is overly abstract, we shall take the image of a *scale* whose indicator spins round and round on the dial because *too much* weight has been set on it. It will help to use this image in learning the kanji itself.

1787

除

exclude

Pinnacle . . . scale. [10]

1788

徐

gradually

Line . . . scale. [10]

1789

叙

confer

Scale . . crotch. The key word has to do with **conferring** ranks, titles, and awards. It should not be confused with *bestow* (FRAME 1335) or *impart* (FRAME 795). [9]

1790 途	route
	Scale . . . road. [10]

1791 斜	diagonal
	Scale . . . measuring cup. [11]

1792 塗	paint
	Water . . . scale . . . ground. [13]

1793 束	bundle
	In the same way that we were able to see the *sun* in the *tree* within the kanji for *east*, here we see a square container in the shape of a *mouth*. [7]

1794 頼	trust
	Bundle . . . head. [16]

1795 瀬	rapids
	Water . . . bundle . . . head. [19]

1796 勅	imperial order
	In order to keep this character distinct from that for an *imperial edict* (FRAME 366), we must draw again on a pun. Think of the **order** here as a mail **order** or an **order** of pizza phoned in by the Emperor for delivery to the **imperial** palace. Then it will not be hard to put together *bundle* and *muscle* to form a story about an **imperial order**. [9]

1797 疎	alienate
	Zoo . . . bundle. Note that the element for *zoo* is flattened out on the left just as *leg* (FRAME 1372) had been. This is the only time we will meet this form in this book. [12]

1798	bitter
辣	Spicy . . . bundle. [14]

1799	quick
速	Bundle . . . road. [10]

1800	organize
整	Bundle . . . taskmaster . . . correct. [16]

*	awl
僉	We include this element here because of its visible similarity to the element for *bundle*. Be sure to make a distinct image out of its composite ingredients: *meeting . . . mouth . . . person.* The stroke order follows the order of the elements exactly, but note how the *person* runs through the *mouth.* [8]

亼　合　争　僉

1801	saber
劍	Awl . . . saber. As we promised way back in FRAME 87, here at last is the kanji on which the primitive element of the same name is based. [10]

1802	precipitous
險	Pinnacle . . . awl. [11]

1803	examination
検	Tree . . . awl. [12]

1804	frugal
倹	Person . . . awl. [10]

1805	heavy
重	*Thousand . . . ri.* Note how the long vertical stroke doubles up to serve both elements. [9]

一 一 仁 仨 肻 肻 重 重 重

1806	move
動	*Heavy . . . muscle.* [11]

1807	tumor
腫	*Flesh . . . heavy.* [13]

1808	meritorious deed
勳	*Move . . . oven fire.* So as not to confuse this kanji with the general character for *merit* (FRAME 1369), you may associate the key word with military decorations and medals of distinction, both of which it is used for. [15]

1809	work
働	*Person . . . move.* Do not confuse with *labor* (FRAME 924). [13]

1810	species
種	*Wheat . . . heavy.* [14]

1811	collide
衝	*Boulevard . . . heavy.* [15]

1812	fragrant
薫	*Flowers . . . heavy . . . oven fire.* Do not confuse with *incense* (FRAME 977) or *perfumed* (FRAME 532). [16]

Lesson 44

WE MAY NOW PICK UP the remainder of the enclosure primitives, leaving only a few related to animals, which we will take up in Lesson 55. This lesson should give you a chance to review the general principles governing enclosures.

疒	★	sickness

The enclosure shown in this frame is composed of a *cave* with *ice* outside of it. It is used for a number of kanji related to **sickness**. If you want to picture a *cave*man nursing a hangover with an *ice*-pack, that should provide enough help to remember the shape of this element and its meaning. [5]

广　广　疒

1813 病		ill

Sickness . . . third class. [10]

1814 痴		stupid

Sickness . . . know. [13]

1815 痘		pox

Sickness . . . beans. [12]

1816 症		symptoms

Sickness . . . correct. [10]

1817 瘍		carbuncle

Sickness . . . piggy bank. [14]

1818 瘦		lose weight

Sickness . . . monkey . . . crotch. [12]

1819	rapidly
疾	Be sure to keep this character distinct from *quick* (FRAME 1799) and *swift* (FRAME 298). Picture a succession of poison *darts* (the sort that inflict *sickness*) flying out **rapid**-fire from a blowgun, so that "**rapid**-fire" can conjure up the proper image. [10]

1820	envy
嫉	*Woman . . . rapidly.* [13]

1821	diarrhea
痢	*Sickness . . . profit.* [12]

1822	scar
痕	*Sickness . . . silver.* [11]

1823	tired
疲	*Sickness . . . pelt.* [10]

1824	epidemic
疫	*Sickness . . . missile.* [9]

1825	pain
痛	*Sickness . . . chop-seal . . . utilize.* [12]

1826	mannerism
癖	*Sickness . . . ketchup.* [18]

*	box
匚	This enclosure, open at the right, represents a **box** lying on its side. When it is not used as an enclosure, its form is cramped to look like this: 匚. You may distinguish its meaning by picturing it then as a very small **box**. [2]

一　匚

1827

匿

Box ... young. [10]

hide

一 若 匿

1828

匠

Box ... ax. [6]

artisan

1829

医

Box ... dart. [7]

doctor

1830

匹

Box ... human legs. [4]

equal

1831

区

The **ward** referred to here is a subdivision of a large city. Its elements: *box ... sheaves.* When used as a primitive element, it may be helpful at times to break it up into these same composite elements. [4]

ward

1832

枢

Tree ... ward. [8]

hinge

1833

殴

Ward ... missile. [8]

assault

1834

欧

Ward ... yawn. Like the kanji of FRAME 1776, this character is an abbreviation of the name of a geographical region. [8]

Europe

1835

抑

Fingers ... box ... stamps. [7]

repress

1836	faceup
仰	This character is used both for lying on one's back **faceup**, and for looking up to someone with respect and awe. Its elements: *person . . . box . . . stamps.* [6]

1837	welcome
迎	*Box . . . stamps . . . road.* [7]

★	teepee
癶	The dots at the top of this tent are the wooden poles protruding outside the canvas walls of a **teepee**. [5]

フ　　ア　　ブ′　　癶　　癶

1838	ascend
登	*Teepee . . . table.* Do not confuse with *rise up* (FRAME 43). [12]

1839	lucidity
澄	*Water . . . ascend.* [15]

1840	discharge
発	This key word refers to the **discharging** of guns, trains, people, and even words. The elements: *teepee . . . two . . . human legs.* Contrast the writing with FRAME 63. [9]

1841	abolish
廃	*Cave . . . discharge.* [12]

★	pup tent
寮	The *St. Bernard dog* and its overlapping with the element for *teepee* are enough to suggest the meaning of this primitive element: a **pup tent**. The combination of *sun* and *little* at the bottom can be seen as a *little* opening or flap through which the *sun* shines in the morning to let you know it's time for getting up. [12]

大 大 容 寮

1842	colleague
僚	*Person . . . pup tent.* Choose some connotation of the key word that will keep it distinct for you from *companion* (FRAME 19), *friend* (FRAME 760), *consort* (FRAME 1287), and *comrade* (FRAME 1765). [14]
1843	obvious
瞭	*Eye . . . pup tent.* [17]
1844	dormitory
寮	*House . . . pup tent.* [15]
1845	heal
療	*Sickness . . . pup tent.* [17]

Lesson 45

WE COME NOW TO A CLASS OF elements loosely associated with shape and form. We then append what remains of elements having to do with color.

*	shape
彡	The three simple strokes of this element actually represent the form or **shape** of the hair of one's beard. But we keep the simple sense of a **shape**, or its verb "to **shape**," in order to avoid confusion later when we meet an element for *hair*. When using this element, be sure to visualize yourself **shaping** the thing in question, or better still, twisting it out of **shape**. [3]

1846 彫	**carve** The two primitives here, *circumference* and *shape*, belong naturally to the special connotations that differentiate **carving** from *engrave* (see FRAME 1639). [11]
1847 形	**shape** *Two hands . . . shape.* [7]
1848 影	**shadow** *Scenery . . . shape.* [15]
1849 杉	**cedar** *Tree . . . shape.* [7]
1850 彩	**coloring** *Vulture . . . tree . . . shape.* [11]
1851 彰	**patent** *Badge . . . shape.* The key word is synonymous with "clear" or "openly expressed." [14]
1852 彦	**lad** *Vase . . . cliff . . . shape.* [9] 立　产　彦
1853 顔	**face** *Lad . . . head.* [18]
1854 須	**ought** *Shape . . . head.* This is the only time that *shape* is placed to the left of its relative element, the *head*. [12]

1855	swell
膨	*Part of the body . . . drum . . . shape.* Compare *expand* (FRAME 1199). [16]

1856	visit
参	*Elbow . . . St. Bernard dog . . . shape.* [8]

1857	wretched
惨	*A state of mind . . . visit.* [11]

1858	discipline
修	*Person . . . walking stick . . . taskmaster . . . shape.* [10]

1859	rare
珍	*Jewel . . . umbrella . . . shape.* [9]

1860	checkup
診	*Words . . . umbrella . . . shape.* The key word refers to a medical examination. [12]

1861	sentence
文	Under the familiar *top hat* we see a crisscross pattern or design, like that found on woodwork or garments. This should make an ugly enough image to help remember it. It can be associated with **sentence** by thinking of a **sentence** as a grammatical pattern. [4]

丶　亠　ナ　文

* The primitive meaning for this character will be *plaid*, the familiar crisscross pattern frequently used in textiles.

1862	vis-à-vis
対	*Plaid . . . glue.* [7]

1863 紋	family crest
	Thread ... plaid. [10]

1864 蚊	mosquito
	Insect ... plaid. [10]

1865 斑	speckled
	Ball ... plaid ... ball. [12]

* 丿丨	fenceposts
	This element means just what it looks like: two **fenceposts**. They enclose whatever comes between them, as distinct from a pair of *walking sticks* (see FRAME 265). [2]

1866 斉	adjusted
	Plaid ... fenceposts ... two. Do not confuse with *just so* (FRAME 414). [8]

1867 剤	dose
	Adjust ... saber. Think of this as a **dose** of medicine. [10]

1868 済	finish
	Water ... adjust. Do not confuse with *complete* (FRAME 101), *end* (FRAME 1455\2), or *perfect* (FRAME 199). [11]

1869 斎	purification
	Plaid ... fenceposts ... altar. This is a "religious" **purification**, which distinguishes it from the simple kanji for *pure* (FRAME 1659). [11]

1870 粛	solemn
	Rake ... rice ... fenceposts. Take special care to draw this character in the same order as the primitive. Note, too, that the fourth stroke for *rice* is already taken care of by the fourth stroke of *rake*. [11]

肀 聿 肃 肅

sparkler

*

义

As the pictograph itself immediately suggests, this element depicts spreading out or scattering from a focal point. To capture this meaning, we choose the image of a **sparkler**. It will often have another primitive put at its center point. [4]

丶 丷 丷 义

1871 bases

塁

The kanji of this frame refers to the four **bases** that are placed at the corners of a baseball infield. The elements: *field . . . sparkler . . . ground.* [12]

1872 music

楽

Dove . . . sparkler . . . tree. [13]

1873 medicine

薬

Flowers . . . music. [16]

1874 ratio

率

Mysterious . . . sparkler . . . ten. Do not confuse with *proportion* (FRAME 1673). [11]

1875 astringent

渋

Water . . . footprint . . . sparkler. [11]

1876 vicarious

摂

Fingers . . . ear . . . sparkler. Do not confuse with *substitute* (FRAME 1080). [13]

1877 央	center

The elements depict a *St. Bernard* with its head and paws keeping their stick-like form, but with the middle or **center** of its body filled out in a box-like shape. [5]

1878 英	England

Flowers . . . center. This is another abbreviation used to identify a country by the pronunciation of the kanji. [8]

1879 映	reflect

Sun . . . center. [9]

1880 赤	red

Ground . . . dagger . . . little. The two strokes of the *dagger* take the place of the middle stroke of *little*. [7]

土 亦 亦 赤

* As a primitive on the left, this kanji keeps the same form. Elsewhere, the first two strokes are abbreviated to a single dot, giving us 亦. This latter form will take the meaning of an *apple*.

1881 赦	pardon

Red . . . taskmaster. [11]

1882 変	unusual

Apple . . . walking legs. [9]

1883 跡	tracks

Wooden leg . . . apple. [13]

1884 蛮	barbarian

Apple . . . insects. [12]

| 1885 恋 | romance | Apple . . . heart. [10] |

1885		romance
恋	Apple . . . heart. [10]	
1886		**gulf**
湾	Water . . . apple . . . bow. [12]	
1887		**yellow**
黄	Salad . . . sprout . . . animal legs. [11]	
1888		**sideways**
横	Tree . . . yellow. [15]	
★		**mosaic**
巴	This element is shaped roughly like the *snake*, but pay attention to the difference when writing it. [4]	
	コ 刁 巴 巴	
1889		**grasp**
把	Fingers . . . mosaic. [7]	
1890		**color**
色	Bound up . . . mosaic. [6]	
1891		**discontinue**
絶	Thread . . . color. [12]	
1892		**glossy**
艶	Bountiful . . . color. [19]	
1893		**fertilizer**
肥	Flesh . . . mosaic. [8]	

Lesson 46

A NUMBER OF CONTAINERS of various sorts can be gathered together here. Most of them have limited use as primitives, but none of them should cause any particular difficulty.

1894	sweet

甘   This kanji is a pictograph of a small wicker basket. (The extra short stroke in the middle helps keep it distinct from the character for *twenty*.) All one needs to add is some image of **sweet** cakes or breads carried in the basket, and the union of picture and meaning is complete. Take care not to confuse with *confectionary* (FRAME 1203). [5]

一 十 卄 廿 甘

* As a primitive, the pictograph's meaning of a *wicker basket* is used, a small one like the kind used for picnics.

1895	navy blue

紺   *Thread . . . wicker basket.* [11]

1896	so-and-so

某   The key word here refers to the adjective for an unspecified person or thing. Its elements: *wicker basket . . . tree.* [9]

1897	conspire

謀   *Words . . . so-and-so.* [16]

1898	mediator

媒   *Woman . . . so-and-so.* [12]

* 其	**bushel basket**

As the two *legs* at the bottom suggest, this **bushel basket** is a large container, standing on the floor. Its first four strokes indicate that it is made of wicker, much like the small *wicker basket* introduced just above. To make room for something inside of the **bushel basket**, the legs at the bottom are attached to the final horizontal stroke and extended to make an enclosure. [8]

一　十　廾　廾　甘　其　其

1899	**deceit**
欺	*Bushel basket . . . yawn.* [12]

1900	**chess piece**
棋	*Tree . . . bushel basket.* [12]

1901	**national flag**
旗	*Banner . . . bushel basket.* [14]

1902	**period**
期	*Bushel basket . . . month.* As the *month* indicates, this has to do with **periods** of time. [12]

1903	**Go**
碁	*Bushel basket . . . stones.* The key word refers to the Japanese game played with black and white colored *stones* on a lined board. [13]

1904	**fundamentals**
基	*Bushel basket . . . soil.* [11]

1905	**tremendously**
甚	*Bushel basket . . . equal.* Note how the first stroke of *equal* doubles up with the sixth stroke of the *bushel basket,* and how the

animal legs of the *bushel basket* are dropped to make room for the *human legs* of *equal*. [9]

1906 勘	intuition
	Tremendously . . . muscle. [11]

1907 堪	withstand
	Soil . . . tremendously. [12]

* 串	purse
	By adding a single stroke at the bottom of the kanji for *in*, we get a sort of pictograph of a **purse**. [5]

1908 貴	precious
	Purse . . . shells. [12]

1909 遺	bequeath
	Precious . . . road. [15]

1910 遣	dispatch
	This kanji takes away the *maestro*'s baton and replaces it with a *purse*. The *road* represents his being **dispatched** on his way as an obvious misfit. You will remember that when he did have his baton, he was being *chased* down the road by his fans. All of which shows what a difference a single stroke can make! [13]

1911 潰	defile
	Water . . . precious. [15]

1912 舞	dance
	The top two strokes show someone *reclining*, and the next six are a pictograph of an oaken *tub* ribbed with metal strips, like the kind once used for bathing. At the bottom, the *sunglasses* round off the character. [15]

一　⌐　卌　無　舞

1913　nothingness

無

This character is the Japanese character for the supreme philosophical principle of much Oriental thought: **nothingness**. Make use of the oaken *tub* from the previous frame, and add to that the *oven fire* at the bottom. [12]

Lesson 47

THE SEVERAL PRIMITIVES we turn to next are all related to the position and disposition of things. The classification is somewhat arbitrary since we are getting hard pressed to organize the leftover primitives into tidy categories. In addition, from this lesson on, most references to key words with possibly confusing similarities will be omitted. Try to think of them yourself as you are going through these characters.

---

*　shelf

且

The pictographic representation in the primitive shown here is a small stand with horizontal **shelves**. Thus we give it the general meaning of a **shelf**. It differs from the kanji and primitive for an *eye* only in its final stroke, which extends beyond the two vertical strokes at both ends. Think of it as a **shelf** for special keepsakes or a glass bureau for knickknacks, keeping it distinct from the kanji we learned in FRAME 214. [5]

1914　association

組

Thread . . . shelf. [11]

1915　coarse

粗

Rice . . . shelf. [11]

1916	tariff
租	*Wheat . . . shelf.* [10]

1917	aim at
狙	*Pack of wild dogs . . . shelf.* [8]

1918	ancestor
祖	*Altar . . . shelf.* [9]

1919	thwart
阻	*Pinnacle . . . shelf.* [8]

1920	investigate
査	*Tree . . . shelf.* [9]

1921	help
助	*Shelf . . . power.* The reason why the *shelf* appears on the left here is that the right side is the normal position for *power*, the stronger primitive. Indeed, the only exception in all the kanji is the character for *add* (FRAME 932). [7]

1922	best regards
宜	This kanji is a polite way of expressing one's **best regards** to another. Its elements: *house . . . shelf.* [8]

1923	tatami mat
畳	*Rice field . . . crown . . . shelf.* [12]

1924	row
並	This character represents a slightly stylized duplication of the kanji for *stand up*. By lengthening the sixth and seventh strokes, you will see how this is done. [8]
	丶　　丷　　丷　　ㅛ　　並　　並　　並　　並

* The primitive meaning remains the same as that of the kanji, but special attention has to be given to the varieties of shape this element can undergo. It is the most difficult one you will meet in this book. When it appears BENEATH its relative primitive, the top three strokes are omitted, though the third horizontal stroke may be doubled up with the bottom horizontal stroke of the element above it: 业. ATOP its relative primitive, it can keep its kanji shape. When it does not, the top three strokes are removed and all of them are replaced BELOW the primitive's bottom line: 业. We shall acknowledge this latter transformation by changing its meaning to *upside down in a row*.

1925 **universal**

普 *Row . . . sun.* [12]

1926 **musical score**

譜 *Words . . . universal.* [19]

1927 **damp**

湿 *Water . . . sun . . . row.* [12]

1928 **appear**

顕 *Sun . . . row . . . heads.* [18]

1929 **slender**

繊 *Thread . . . Thanksgiving . . . row.* [17]

1930 **spirits**

霊 *Rain . . . two . . . row.* This character will refer only to the inhabitants of the "**spirit** world," and not to moods or temperaments, for which we will learn another character in FRAME 2030. [15]

1931 **profession**

業 *In a row upside down . . . not yet.* [13]

業

1932

撲

slap

Fingers . . . upside down in a row . . . husbands. [15]

1933

僕

me

This key word is yet another synonym for "I," somewhat more familiar in tone. As a rule, it is a word that boys and men use to refer to themselves. Its elements: *person . . . husbands . . . in a row upside down.* [14]

1934

共

together

Salad . . . animal legs. [6]

* The primitive retains the meaning of *together*. Imagine things *strung together* like fish on a line, beads on a thread, or whatever. The main thing is to avoid putting them in a straight row, which would confound this element with the previous one. As we saw with *bushel basket*, this primitive can join its legs to the final horizontal stroke and stretch them to form an enclosure.

1935

供

submit

Submit here is a transitive verb, meaning to offer or present. Its elements: *person . . . strung together.* [8]

1936

異

uncommon

Brains . . . together. [11]

1937

翼

wing

Feathers . . . uncommon. [17]

1938

戴

accept humbly

Thanksgiving . . . uncommon. [17]

1939 洪	Water . . . strung together. [9]	deluge
1940 港	Deluge . . . snakes. [12]	harbor
1941 暴	Sun . . . strung together . . . rice grains. [15]	outburst
1942 爆	Fire . . . outburst. [19]	bomb
1943 恭	Strung together . . . valentine. [10]	respect
1944 選	Two snakes . . . strung together . . . road. [15]	elect
1945 殿	Flags . . . strung together . . . missile. [13]	Mr.

Lesson 48

THIS NEXT lesson *is* composed of characters whose primitives are grouped according to shape rather than meaning. Each of them makes use, in one way or another, of squares and crossing lines. While this might have brought confusion earlier, we know enough primitives at this stage to introduce them together without risking any confusion.

1946	well
井	Recalling that there are no circular strokes, and that the shape of the square and the square within a square (FRAME 630) have already been used, it should be relatively easy to see how this character can be consider a pictograph of a **well**. [4]

$$一 \quad 二 \quad 丰 \quad 井$$

1947	*donburi*
丼	*Donburi* is a bowl of rice with eel or meat on it. The character is a pictograph, perhaps designed by someone who felt that the portion of meat he was served with his bowl of rice looked to be no more than a tiny *drop* in a *well*. [5]

1948	surround
囲	*Well . . . pent in.* [7]

1949	till
耕	*Christmas tree . . . well.* [10]

1950	Asia
亜	In this kanji, the abbreviation for **Asia**, you should be able to see the character for *mouth* behind the Roman numeral II. [7]

$$一 \quad 日 \quad 田 \quad 亜$$

1951	bad
悪	*Asia . . . heart.* [11]

1952	circle
円	This kanji, also used for Yen, is one you are not likely to need to study formally, since you can hardly get around in Japan without it. The connection is that the yennies, like pennies, are **circular** in shape. In any case, the elements are: *glass canopy . . . walking stick . . . one.* [4]

丨 冂 冂 円

1953 **angle**

角

Bound up . . . glass canopy . . . walking stick . . . two. If you write the character once, you will see why we avoided using the element for *soil*, which would prompt you to write it in improper order. [7]

ク 尹 角 角

* As a primitive, imagine the tool used by draftsmen and carpenters to draw right-*angles*.

1954 **contact**

触

Angle . . . insect. [13]

1955 **unravel**

解

Angle . . . dagger . . . cow. [13]

1956 **again**

再

Jewel . . . with a *belt* hung on it. Note how the *belt* is drawn right after the first stroke of *jewel*. [6]

一 冂 冇 再 再

---

* **funnel**

冓

Celery . . . again. [10]

丰 冉 冉 冓 冓

1957 **lecture**

講

Words . . . funnel. [17]

1958	subscription
購	*Shells . . . funnel.* The key word is meant to suggest magazine **subscriptions** and the like. [17]

1959	posture
構	*Tree . . . funnel.* [14]

1960	gutter
溝	*Water . . . funnel.* [13]

★	scrapbook
冊	*Glass canopy . . . flower.* It is most rare to see the *flower* come under its relative element. Note how it is straightened out to fill the space available. [5]

| | 丨 冂 冄 冊 冊 |

1961	argument
論	*Words . . . meeting . . . scrapbook.* The **argument** here is a process of academic reasoning, not a personal quarrel or spat. [15]

1962	ethics
倫	*Person . . . meeting . . . scrapbook.* [10]

1963	wheel
輪	*Car . . . meeting . . . scrapbook.* [15]

1964	partial
偏	*Person . . . door . . . scrapbook.* The sense of the key word is that of having a bias or preference for someone or something. [11]

1965	everywhere
遍	*Door . . . scrapbook . . . a road.* [12]

1966	compilation
編	*Thread . . . door . . . scrapbook.* [15]

1967	tome
冊	This key word is a counter for books. It differs from *scrapbook* both in the writing order and in the extension of the second horizontal stroke. [5]

冂　冊　冊

1968	palisade
栅	*Tree . . . tome.* [9]

1969	code
典	We introduce this character here because of its connection to the book-related kanji treated above. It is based on the character for *bend* (FRAME 1256), whose last stroke is lengthened to coincide with the first stroke of the element for *tool.* [8]

Lesson 49

A FEW PRIMITIVES HAVING to do with groupings and classifications of people remain to be learned, and we may bring them all together here in this short lesson.

1970	family name
氏	Pay close attention to the stroke order of the elements when learning to write this character. The elements: a long *drop . . . fishhook . . .* a *one . . . fishhook.* [4]

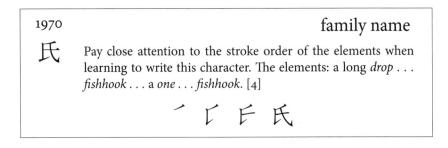

1971 紙	paper
	Thread . . . family name. [10]

1972 婚	marriage
	Woman . . . family name . . . day. [11]

★ 氏	calling card
	Family name . . . floor. [5]

1973 低	lower
	Person . . . calling card. [7]

1974 抵	resist
	Fingers . . . calling card. [8]

1975 底	bottom
	Cave . . . calling card. [8]

1976 民	people
	In place of the *drop* at the start of the character for *family name*, we have a *mouth*, which makes you think of the "vox populi." [5]
	乛 コ ア ア 民

1977 眠	sleep
	Eyes . . . people. [10]

★ 甫	dog tag
	This primitive refers to all sorts of identification tags, but **dog tag** is chosen for its descriptiveness. On the top we see the *arrowhead*, joined to the *screwdriver* below by the lengthened vertical stroke. [7]

一 冂 冃 甫 甫

1978		catch
捕	*Fingers . . . dog tag.* [10]	

1979		suckle
哺	*Mouth . . . dog tag.* [10]	

1980		bay
浦	*Water . . . dog tag.* [10]	

1981		bullrush
蒲	*Flowers . . . bay.* [13]	

1982		shop
舗	*Cottage . . . dog tag.* The key word refers to the noun, not the verb. [15]	

1983		supplement
補	*Cloak . . . dog tag.* [12]	

*		city walls
阝	On the left, and rather more pressed in its form, this element meant the high spot of a village, or its *pinnacle*. On the right side, in the form shown here, it means the lowest part of the city, around which its walls rise up as a protection against invaders. Hence we nickname this element: **city walls**. [3]	

1984		residence
邸	*Calling card . . . city walls.* [8]	

1985		enclosure
郭	*Receive . . . city walls.* [11]	

1986 郡	county
	Old boy . . . city walls. [10]
1987 郊	outskirts
	Mingle . . . city walls. [9]
1988 部	section
	Muzzle . . . city walls. [11]
1989 都	metropolis
	Someone . . . city walls. [11]
1990 郵	mail
	Droop . . . city walls. [11]
1991 邦	home country
	Bushes . . . city walls. [7]
1992 那	interrogative
	Sword . . . two . . . city walls. Used classically to indicate an **interrogative** part of speech, this character is used chiefly now for its sound. [7]
1993 郷	hometown
	Cocoon . . . silver . . . city walls. [11]
1994 響	echo
	Hometown . . . sound. [20]
1995 郎	son
	Halo . . . city walls. [9]

1996	corridor
廊　　*Cave . . . son.* [12]	

Lesson 50

IN THIS LESSON we simply present an assortment of leftover primitives that were not introduced earlier for want of a proper category or because we had not enough elements to give sufficient examples of their use.

*	drag
厂	Although not a pictograph in the strict sense, this primitive depicts one stroke pulling another along behind it. Note how it differs from *cliff* and *person* because of this **dragging** effect, not to mention the fact that the first stroke is written right to left, almost as if it were a long *drop*. When this element comes under a different element, the strokes are drawn apart like this: ⌕. [2]

⌐ 厂

1997	shield
盾　　*Dragging . . . ten eyes.* [9]	

1998	sequential
循　　*Line . . . shield.* [12]	

1999	faction
派	*Water . . . drag . . . rag.* Back in FRAME 1127 we indicated that this latter primitive would come up once again, as it does in this and the following two frames. [9]

2000 脈	vein
	Part of body . . . drag . . . rag. [10]

2001 衆	masses
	Blood . . . drag . . . rag. [12]

2002 逓	parcel post
	Drag . . . cornstalk . . . belt . . . road. [10]

2003 段	grade
	The kanji connoting rank or class shows us a new element on the left: the familiar primitive for *staples* with an additional stroke cutting through the vertical stroke. It is easiest in these cases to make a primitive related to what we already know. Hence, we call it a *staple gun.* To the right, *missile.* [9]

　 ′ 亻 仃 仨 仨 仐 仐 段 段

2004 鍛	forge
	Metal . . . grade. [17]

2005 后	empress
	Drag . . . one . . . mouth. [6]

* 刁	clothes hanger
	This element, which looks something like a backwards *hook,* we will call a **clothes hanger.** Used as an enclosure, it begins further to the left. [1]

2006 幻	phantasm
	Cocoon . . . clothes hanger. [4]

2007 司	director
	Clothes hanger . . . one . . . mouth. [5]

2008

伺

pay respects

This honorific form of *call on* (FRAME 534) is made up of: *person . . . director*. [7]

2009

詞

parts of speech

The key word, **parts of speech**, refers to nouns, verbs, adjective, adverbs, and so on. The elements: *words . . . directors*. [12]

2010

飼

domesticate

Eat . . . director. The sense is of rearing of animals. [13]

2011

嗣

heir

Mouth . . . scrapbook . . . director. [13]

2012

舟

boat

After the *drop* and the *glass canopy*, we come to a combination of three strokes that we met only once before, in the character for *mama* (FRAME 105). The pictographic meaning we gave it there has no etymological relationship to this character, but use it if it helps. [6]

′ 丿 凢 凢 凢 舟

2013

舶

liner

The type of *boat* connoted by this key word is a large ocean-going **liner**. The important thing here is to work with the elements *boat* and *dove* to make an image distinct from that of the former frame. Don't count on size alone to distinguish the *boat* from the **liner**. [11]

2014

航

navigate

Boat . . . whirlwind. [10]

2015

舷

gunwale

boat . . . mysterious. [11]

2016 般	carrier
	Boat . . . missile. [10]
2017 盤	tray
	Carrier . . . dish. [15]
2018 搬	conveyor
	Fingers . . . carrier. [13]
2019 船	ship
	Boat . . . gully. [11]
2020 艦	warship
	Boat . . . oversee. [21]
2021 艇	rowboat
	Boat . . . courts. [13]
2022 瓜	melon
	The only thing that distinguishes this from the *claw* is the *elbow*, made by doubling up the third stroke and adding a fourth. [5]
	一　厂　几　瓜　瓜
2023 弧	arc
	Bow . . . melon. [8]
2024 孤	orphan
	Child . . . melon. [8]

Lesson 51

As we said we would do back in Lesson 28, we now leave the beaten path to gather up those characters left aside because they form exceptions to the rules and patterns we have been learning. The list is not large and has a number of repeating patterns. Aside from the few others we shall interpose in the next section where they belong, and three characters appended at the very end, this will complete our collection of special characters. This is probably the most difficult lesson of the book.

2025	cocoon
繭	Though it's a good thing that the primitive for **cocoon** has been radically abbreviated from this, its full form as a kanji, the story it holds is a charming one. The silkworm (*insect*) eats the leaves of the mulberry bush (the *flowers*), digests them and transforms them into *thread* with which it spins about itself, in mystic wisdom, its own coffin (the *hood*). The dividing line that separates the two elements helps the picture of the little worm cutting itself off from contact with the outside world, but as a character stroke, it is a clear exception. [18]

艹 芇 芇 繭 繭

2026	benefit
益	Poised over the *dish* is a pair of *animal horns* that are attached to a pair of *animal legs* by a single horizontal stroke. [10]

丷 䒑 益

2027	spare time
暇	The element for *day* on the left is logical enough. Next to it we see *staples* being held in a *mouth* (one stroke is doubled up), indicating working on one's hobby or handicrafts at home in one's **spare time**. The small *box* at the top right is facing backwards, or more properly "inside out." Finally, we have the *crotch* at the bottom. [13]

日⁷ 旷 旷 旷 暇

2028

敷

spread

At the top we have the *arrowhead* whose vertical line joins it to the *rice field* (or *brains*) below it. Beneath it, the *compass*; and to the right, the *taskmaster*. [15]

甫 尃 敷

2029

来

come

This odd but common kanji is built up of the character for *not yet* into which a pair of *animal horns* has been inserted. [7]

一 ㇡ 丆 ㄓ 平 来 来

2030

気

spirit

The **spirit** in this character refers to the changeable moods and airs of one's personality as well as to the more essential combination of vital forces that distinguish things and individuals one from the other. Its elements are: *reclining . . . floor . . . fishhook . . . sheaf*. Do not confuse with *spirits* (FRAME 1930). [6]

2031

汽

vapor

Think of this character as a sibling of that for *spirit*. Simply replace *sheaves* with drops of *water* on the left in order to get *vapor*. [7]

2032

飛

fly

The two *large hooks* have little propellers (the two *drops* on each hook) attached to them for **flying**. Beneath is the *measuring box*, which serves as the body of this **flying** contraption. The stroke order will cause some problems, so take care with it. [9]

乁 乁 飞 飞 飞 飛 飛 飛 飛

2033   **sink**

沈

The technique for **sinking** used in this kanji is unique. Rather than the biblical image of tying a millstone about the victim's neck, here we see a *crown* tied about one *leg* before the unfortunate party is tossed into the *water*. [7]

2034   **pillow**

枕

Tree . . . crown tied around leg of person. [8]

2035   **wife**

妻

Ten . . . rakes . . . woman. [8]

2036   **nifty**

凄

Ice . . . wife. [10]

2037   **decline**

衰

Let this key word connote the **decline** and fall of the Roman Empire. It shows a fellow in a *top hat* and *scarf*, trying hard to look happy by putting a *walking stick* in his *mouth* sideways to twist his face into a grotesque but semipermanent smile. [10]

2038   **inmost**

衷

Between the *top hat* and the *scarf* you will see the character for *in* which is truncated at the bottom so as not to interfere with the *scarf*. You can think of this character as forming a pair with the one just learned in the last frame: there the *in* (the *walking stick* in the *mouth*) was set on its side; in this character it is set upright. [10]

2039	mask
面	Imagine a **mask** over your head with *eyes* peeping out from all over the head, a *hundred* in all (the element for *eye* displacing the fifth stroke of that for *hundred*). [9]

一　一　厂　百　帀　而　而　面　面

2040	noodles
麺	*Barley . . . mask.* [16]

2041	leather
革	After the *flowers* at the top (painted on the **leather** for decoration), we see the element for *car* with the middle stroke left out. Think of the seats having been taken out so that they can be reupholstered with this decorated **leather**. [9]

一　十　艹　艹　莒　莒　莒　莒　革

2042	shoes
靴	*Leather . . . change.* [13]

2043	hegemony
覇	*Old West . . . leather . . . moon.* [19]

2044	voice
声	The *samurai* at the top is familiar enough. The combination beneath, which looks like a *flag* with a line running through it, is not. Try to devise some way to take note of it, and pay attention to the writing. [7]

士　吉　声　声　声

2045	eyebrow
眉	The *flag* here has an extra vertical stroke in it. Think of it as an **eyebrow** pencil stuck in the *eye*. [9]

2046

give

呉

The complex of strokes in this kanji is unusual and difficult, because of the fourth stroke, which is rare (see FRAMES 33 and 34). The *mouth* and *tool* are already familiar. [7]

口　呙　呉

2047

recreation

娯

Woman . . . give. [10]

2048

mistake

誤

Words . . . give. [14]

2049

steam

蒸

The *flower* at the top and the *floor* with the *oven fire* beneath are familiar. The problem is what comes in between. It is formed by the character for *complete*, whose vertical stroke doubles up as the first stroke of *water*. [13]

艹　艻　茏　莁　蒸

2050

acquiesce

承

The sense of passive acceptance or reception of information is contained in this key word. The form is based on the middle portion of the preceding character, with three additional strokes, best thought of as the kanji for *three*. [8]

　了　孑　子　手　手　承　承

2051

bin

函

This is the character from which the element for *shovel* derives. Within it comes the element for *snare,* with the *sparkler* surrounding it. [8]

一　丂　丂　丒　丒　承　函　函

2052	poles

極 The **poles** this key word refers to are the extremities of the earth or the terminals of an electric field. The elements are: *tree . . . snare . . . mouth . . . crotch . . . floor.* [12]

杆 杆 杆 杆 柯 極 極 極

Lesson 52

THE FINAL grouping of kanji revolves about elements related to animals. It is a rather large group, and will take us all of four lessons to complete. We begin with a few recurring elements related to parts of animal bodies.

2053	tusk

牙 If you play with this primitive's form with pencil and paper, you will see that it begins with a *box*-like shape, and ends with the final two strokes of the *halberd*, a convenient combination for the **tusk** protruding from the mouth of an animal. [4]

一 匚 牙 牙

* Since this kanji has 4 strokes, you would expect that as a primitive it would also have 4—but in fact it has 5 in the following two frames (the second stroke between divided into 2 strokes) and reverts to 4 again in FRAME 2056.

2054	bud

芽 *Flowers . . . tusk.* [8]

2055	wicked

邪 *Tusk . . . city walls.* [8]

2056 雅	**gracious**
	Tusk . . . an old turkey. [12]

* 采	**animal tracks**
	Having already met the primitive for human *footprints*, we now introduce the one for **animal tracks**. Its elements are simply: *a drop of . . . rice.* [7]

2057 釈	**interpretation**
	Animal tracks . . . shakuhachi. [11]

2058 番	**turn**
	This key word has been chosen for its overlay of several meanings similar to those of the kanji: a **turn** of duty, a round, a number, and so forth. Its composite elements: *animal tracks . . . rice field.* [12]
	* As a primitive element, we choose the image of a pair of *dice* which it is your *turn* to throw.

2059 審	**hearing**
	The **hearing** referred to in this character relates to trials in the courts. The elements: *house . . . dice.* [15]

2060 翻	**flip**
	Dice . . . feathers. [18]

2061 藩	**clan**
	Flowers . . . water . . . dice. [18]

2062 毛	**fur**
	This character simply reverses the direction of the final stroke of *hand* to produce **fur**. If you reverse your *hand* and put its palm down, you will have the side on which **fur** grows. [4]

ノ　二　三　毛

2063 耗	**decrease**
	Christmas tree . . . fur. [10]

2064 尾	**tail**
	Flag . . . fur. [7]

⋆ 毛	**lock of hair**
	This element is clearly derived from that for *fur*. By leaving out the second stroke, we get simply a **lock of hair**. [3]

2065 宅	**home**
	House . . . lock of hair. [6]

2066 託	**consign**
	Words . . . lock of hair. [10]

⋆ 灬	**tail feathers**
	So as not to confuse this primitive element with the character for *feathers*, think of the extravagant **tail-feather** plumage of the peacock. The form itself is too pictographic to need breaking down further. [5]

フ　灬

2067 為	**do**
	This character rightly belongs to the previous lesson, but we held it until now because of the final element, the *tail feathers*. After the *drop* at the outset, the next three strokes are completely novel and should be given special attention. [9]

丶　ノ　为　为　為　為

2068	falsehood
偽	Person . . . do. [11]

---

*	hairpin
伏	Here we have a quasi-pictograph of the colorful and decorated clips used to bind up long hair. Note its similarity to the *scarf*, which differs only by the addition of one stroke. [4]

一 厂 厂 伏

2069	apprehensive
畏	Field . . . hairpin. [9]

2070	long
長	In line with the story of the preceding frame, the *hair* that needs the *hairpin* is **long**. [8]

丨 厂 F 上 毛 長

* The primitive of this kanji has two more shapes in addition to that of the kanji itself. Above its relative primitive, it is abbreviated to the form 镸 and will mean *hair*. Further abbreviated to 彐, it will mean the long, mangy *mane* of an animal.

2071	lengthen
張	Bow . . . long. [11]

2072	notebook
帳	Towel . . . long. [11]

2073	dilate
脹	Flesh . . . long. [12]

2074	hair of the head
髪	Hair . . . shape . . . friend. [14]

2075 展 **unfold**

Flag . . . salad . . . hairpin. [10]

2076 喪 **miss**

Soil . . . two *mouths . . . hairpin.* Hint: see *spit* (FRAME 162). The key word carries the wide range of meanings readily associated with it: error, loss, absence, and so on. [12]

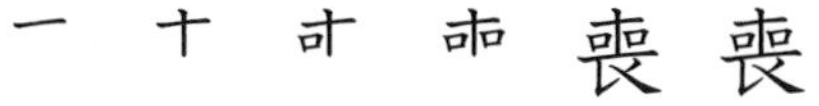

Lesson 53

WE TURN NOW to the animals themselves, beginning with the smaller animals. Because of the fair number of limited-use primitives, this lesson will supply a larger than normal number of stories in complete or semi-complete form.

* ⺍ **owl**

We have met these three strokes before. When they come under another stroke, they represent a *claw,* and thence a *vulture.* And when placed atop a roof structure, they create a *schoolhouse.* The **owl** has something to do with both: it is a bird of prey, and it has come to be associated with learning. [3]

2077 巣 **nest**

Owl . . . fruit. [11]

2078 単 **simple**

Owl . . . brain . . . needle. The sense is "not complex." [9]

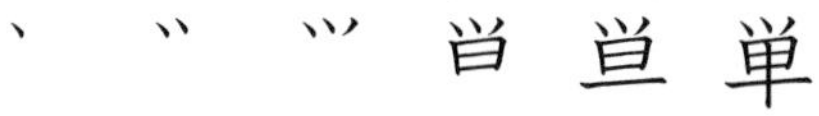

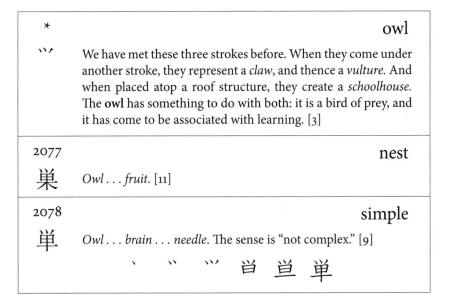

2079	war
戦	*Simple . . . fiesta.* [13]

2080	Zen
禅	*Altar . . . simple.* [13]

2081	bullet
弾	*Bow . . . simple.* [12]

2082	cherry tree
桜	*Tree . . . owl . . . woman.* [10]

2083	animal
獣	*Owl . . . rice field . . . one . . . mouth . . . chihuahua.* [16]

2084	brain
脳	*Part of the body . . . owl . . . villain.* By way of exception, the kanji for **brain** has no connection with the primitive for *brains*. [11]

2085	trouble
悩	*State of mind . . . owl . . . villain.* [10]

2086	stern
厳	*Owl . . . cliff . . . daring.* [17]

2087	chain
鎖	*Metal . . . little . . . shells.* We have saved this character until now in order to draw attention to the visual difference between the *owl* and *little*. By now your eyes should be so accustomed to these apparently infinitesimal differences that the point is obvious. [18]

2088	raise
挙	*Owl . . . tool . . . hand.* [10]

2089	reputation
誉	*Owl . . . tool . . . saying.* [13]

2090	game hunting
猟	*Pack of wild dogs . . . owl . . . wind . . . cornstalk.* [11]

2091	bird
鳥	*Dove . . . one . . . tail feathers.* This is, of course, the character from which we derived the primitive meaning of *dove*. Note the lengthening of the second stroke. [11]

尸　尸　鸟　鸟　鳥

2092	chirp
鳴	*Mouth . . . bird.* [14]

2093	crane
鶴	*Turkey house . . . bird.* The first element appears on only one other occasion, back in FRAME 609. [21]

2094	crow
烏	The only thing that distinguishes this character from that for *bird* is the omission of the one stroke that makes it *white*. Which is logical enough, when you consider that there are no **crows** of that color. [10]

2095	vine
蔦	*Flower . . . bird.* [14]

2096	pigeon
鳩	*Baseball . . . bird.* [13]

2097	chicken
鶏	*Vulture . . . husband . . . bird.* [19]

2098	island
島	The *bird's tail* is tucked under here, because it has come to stop on a *mountain* to rest from its journey across the waters. Thus the kanji comes to mean an **island**. [10]

*	migrating ducks
爰	This primitive is simplicity itself. It depicts bird *claws* that are joined to one another. Note the extra horizontal stroke in *friendship*, which gives the appearance of a "two" in the middle of the kanji, further emphasizing the togetherness of the **migrating ducks**. [9]

爫　　ᴗ　　爭　　爰

2099	warmth
暖	Unlike the connotation of *warm* weather learned for an earlier key word, (FRAME 1560), this key word will be used to refer to the **warmth** of human congeniality. Its elements are: *sun . . . migrating ducks.* [13]

2100	beautiful woman
媛	*Woman . . . migrating ducks.* [12]

2101	abet
援	*Fingers . . . migrating ducks.* [12]

2102	slacken
緩	*Thread . . . migrating ducks.* [15]

2103	belong
属	*Flag . . . gnats* (see FRAME 563) *. . . with a belt.* [12]

尸 尸 尸 属 属

2104	entrust
嘱	Mouth . . . belong. [15]

2105	accidentally
偶	The *person* on the left is familiar. As for the right side, we may combine the *insect* with a *brain* (observe the writing) and a *belt* to create the *Talking Cricket* who served as Pinocchio's conscience. (*The belt* is there because he pulls it off to give unrepentant little Pinocchio a bit of "strap" now and again.) [11]

亻 侣 偶 偶 偶

2106	interview
遇	Talking Cricket . . . road. [12]

2107	foolish
愚	Talking Cricket . . . heart. [13]

2108	corner
隅	Pinnacle . . . Talking Cricket. [12]

*	mountain goat
屰	The *animal horns* and *mountain* unite, quite naturally, to give us a **mountain goat**. The extension of the final stroke indicates its tail, which only shows up when it has something under it. In an overhead enclosure, it is to be pictured as standing still, so that its tail droops down and out of sight. [6]

䒑 䒑 屰

2109	inverted
逆	Mountain goat . . . road. [9]

2110		model

塑

This kanji depicts the art of **modeling** clay or wood into a figure of your choice. The elements for composing it are: *mountain goat . . . moon . . . soil.* [13]

2111		go upstream

遡

Mountain goat . . . moon . . . road. [13]

2112		Mount

岡

Here we see a *mountain goat* "**mounted**" under a *glass canopy*. In this and the following frames, think of a particular **Mount** you know. [8]

2113		steel

鋼

Metal . . . Mount. [16]

2114		hawser

綱

Thread . . . Mount. [14]

2115		sturdy

剛

Mount . . . saber. [10]

2116		tin can

缶

Though the meaning has no reference to animals, the parts do: *horse* with a *mountain* underneath. [6]

2117		pottery

陶

Pinnacle . . . bound up . . . tin can. [11]

★		condor

䍃

Vulture . . . king . . . mountain. By now you should be used to finding two elements double up on a stroke, as is the case here with *king* and *mountain*. [9]

宀　亝　䍃

2118	swing
揺	*Fingers . . . condor.* [12]

2119	Noh chanting
謡	*Words . . . condor.* [16]

2120	gloom
鬱	Learning this character will take a little doing. Before we start, it is a good idea to keep the key word distinct from *melancholy* (FRAME 663), with which it combines to create the psychological condition of depression (a metaphor based on the hollow or sinking of the material *depression* we met in FRAME 1421).

The picture of **gloom** begins with a small *grove* of trees, under which we see a *crown* made out of used *tin cans*. Next (the lower half of the kanji) we find a combination that appears only a few times in modern characters and only once in those treated in the volumes of *Remembering the Kanji*. It is composed of a *shovel* with a *sheaf* dotted with small *drops* on all sides. Think of it as the large scoop *shovel* attached to the front of a bulldozer, whose driver is singing: 𝄞 "Bulldozing in the *sheaves*, bulldozing in the *sheaves*…" ♪ The *drops* represent the chaff flying about as the *sheaves* are tossed about by the heavy machinery.

There is *someone sitting on the ground* alongside, watching as the machinery makes its way around the neighboring farmland—and it's you, wearing your *tin-can crown*. You feel overwhelmed by the impending doom as the invasion of agro-business draws closer and closer to the *grove*, the only patch of woods that remains of what once was a vast forest. The whole scene represents a re-*shaping* of the natural environment that brings the heavy weight of **gloom** down upon you.

A bit much, perhaps, but there are enough elements to allow for any number of other combinations. [29]

木　　柏　　柏木　　欛桝　　欛桝　　欛桝　　欛桝　　欛桝

欛桝　　鬱　　鬱　　鬱

2121	concerning
就	*Capital . . . chihuahua* with a *human leg* in place of one of its paws. [12]

2122	kick
蹴	*Wooden leg . . . concerning.* [19]

*	skunk
豸	This primitive represents a **skunk** by combining the *claw* with the first part of the element for a *sow*. Note how the final stroke of *claw* is turned and lengthened to double up with the first stroke of the *sow*. [7]

ノ イ ⺅ ⺋ 乎 乊 豸

2123	sociable
懇	*Skunk . . . silver . . . heart.* [17]

2124	groundbreaking
墾	The **groundbreaking** referred to here is not for the erection of new buildings but for the opening of farmlands. The elements: *skunk . . . silver . . . soil.* [16]

2125	countenance
貌	*Skunk . . . white . . . human legs.* [14]

2126	excuse
免	This character is used for **excusing** oneself for a failure of courtesy. The elements are: *bound up . . . sun* (oddly enough, laid on its side) *. . . human legs.* [8]

ノ ⺈ ⼾ 宀 免 免 免 免

* For the primitive meaning, we shall refer to this character as a *rabbit*, for which the old form of the character is 兔. [8]

2127 逸	**elude**
	Rabbit . . . road. [11]

2128 晩	**nightfall**
	Sun . . . rabbit. [12]

2129 勉	**exertion**
	Rabbit . . . muscle. Notice how the last stroke of *rabbit* is stretched out to underlie the element for *muscle.* [10]

2130 象	**elephant**
	A *rabbit's* head with the body of a *sow* represents an **elephant**. Little wonder that the kanji also means "phenomenon"! [12]

2131 像	**statue**
	Person . . . elephant. [14]

Lesson 54

NOW THAT WE have come as far as the elephant, we may continue on with more of the larger animals. Fortunately, this group will cause us much less of a head-ache than the preceding series, since there are fewer new primitives and their use is more frequent.

2132 馬	**horse**
	Let the extra vertical stroke in the *mane* combine with the first vertical stroke to give an image of the **horse's** long neck. The only odd thing is the *tail feathers* at the end, but that should present a good image to remember the character by. The fact that the last stroke of *mane* and the first of *tail feathers* coincide should no longer surprise you. [10]

｜ 厂 厂 厍 斤 토 馬 馬 馬
馬 馬

* As a primitive, this kanji will mean a *team of horses* as distinct
from the single *horse* whose primitive we met earlier.

2133 駒	pony

Team of horses . . . phrase. In American slang, a **pony** is an
underground translation of a classical text, which students who
cannot manage the difficult *phrases* of the original language
consult and pass on from one generation to the next. [15]

2134 験	verification

Team of horses . . . awl. [18]

2135 騎	equestrian

Team of horses . . . strange. [18]

2136 駐	parking

Team of horses . . . candlestick. [15]

2137 駆	drive

Team of horses . . . ward. [14]

2138 駅	station

Team of horses . . . shakuhachi. [14]

2139 騒	boisterous

Team of horses . . . crotch . . . insect. [18]

2140 駄	burdensome

Team of horses . . . plump. [14]

2141 驚	**wonder**
	Awe . . . team of horses. [22]
2142 篤	**fervent**
	Bamboo . . . team of horses. [16]
2143 罵	**insult**
	Eyeball . . . team of horses. [15]
2144 騰	**inflation**
	Meat . . . quarter . . . team of horses. [20]

2145

虎

tiger

The kanji in this frame recalls the famous Bengali fable about the group of magicians (the *magic wand*) who decided to make a **tiger**. It seems that each of them knew how to make one part of the beast, so they pooled their talents and brought all the pieces (*diced* into pieces) together, at which point the fabricated *tiger* promptly ate its makers up (the bodiless *human legs*). Whatever the parable's significance for modern civilization and its arsenals, it should help with this kanji.

Oh yes, we should not forget that cliff-like element. Think of it as an abbreviation of the primitive for *zoo* (the first and fourth strokes, actually), in order to fit the **tiger** somewhere into the picture. In fact, the abbreviation is perfectly logical, since the bottom elements usurp the room for the rest of the primitive for *zoo*. [8]

　ㅣ　ㅏ　广　广　户　声　虍　虎

* As a primitive element itself, the *human legs* are also swallowed up, but the meaning of *tiger* is kept, and the whole serves as a roof for what comes beneath, 虍, giving the *tiger* something else to eat.

2146	captive
虜	*Tiger . . . male.* [13]

2147	skin
膚	*Tiger . . . stomach.* [15]

2148	void
虚	*Tigers . . . row.* [11]

2149	frolic
戯	*Void . . . fiesta.* [15]

2150	uneasiness
虞	*Tiger . . . give.* [13]

2151	prudence
慮	*Tiger . . . think.* [15]

2152	drama
劇	*Tiger . . . sow . . . saber.* [15]

2153	tyrannize
虐	*Tiger . . . box* with a *one* in it (or a backwards *broom,* if that makes it easier). [9]

2154	deer
鹿	Drawn on the walls of a complex of *caves* near Niaux in southern France are a number of animal likenesses dating from the Upper Paleolithic period. Among them we find pictures of **deer,** some of them showing men in **deer** masks. By *comparing* their drawings to real **deer,** Stone Age people hoped to acquire power over the animal in the hunt; and by *comparing* themselves to the **deer,** to take on that animal's characteristics. But time has locked with a "double-*key*" (the extra stroke through the ele-

ment for *key*) the real secret of this art form from us, and we can only surmise such meanings. But more important than the enigmas of the troglodytic mind is the way in which *caves*, a double-*key*, and *comparing* gives us the kanji for **deer**. [11]

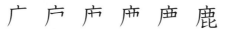

* As a primitive, this kanji is abbreviated much the same as the *tiger* was: the lower element is dropped to leave room for a replacement: 声. Its meaning, however, remains the same. There are a very few cases (see FRAME 2158) in which there is no abbreviation. When this happens, we may keep the image suggested by the above explanation: *painting of a deer*.

2155	foot of a mountain
麓	*Grove . . . deer.* [19]

2156	recommend
薦	*Flowers . . . deer . . . one . . . tail feathers.* Note the doubling up in these last two elements as in FRAME 2091. [16]

2157	jubilation
慶	*Deer . . . crown* (note the doubling up) *. . . heart . . . walking legs.* You may recall that we met the relative primitives at the bottom here before, in the kanji for *melancholy* (FRAME 663). [15]

2158	lovely
麗	The painting of a *deer* itself with its form and color is enough to fill the bill for an image of something **lovely**. But to give a bit of contrast, we see two *mediocre* drawings from a later age on two patches of *ceiling* above. Note that the drop in *mediocre* has been lengthened somewhat and the second stroke drawn down straight. [19]

2159	bear
熊	*Elbow . . . meat . . . spoon* ATOP *spoon . . . oven fire.* [14]

2160	ability
能	Try relating this kanji to that of the previous frame. For instance, you might imagine that the test of **ability** envisioned here is removing the *bear* from the oven fire. [10]

2161	attitude
態	*Ability . . . heart.* [14]

Lesson 55

THE FINAL GROUPING of kanji is based on primitives related to fantastical animals and beings. We begin with two animals belonging to the zodiac.

2162	sign of the tiger
寅	*House . . . ceiling . . . sprout . . . animal legs.* Compare, and do not confuse with, the kanji in FRAME 1887. [11]

2163	performance
演	*Water . . . sign of the tiger.* [14]

2164	sign of the dragon
辰	*Cliff . . . two . . . hairpins.* [7]

2165	embarrass
辱	*Sign of the dragon . . . glue.* [10]

2166	quake
震	*Weather . . . sign of the dragon.* [15]

2167	shake
振	*Fingers . . . sign of the dragon.* [10]

2168	with child
娠	*Woman . . . sign of the dragon.* The key word is a synonym for *pregnant*, whose character we met earlier (FRAME 546). Although the two kanji are often used together, they should be kept distinct. [10]

2169	lips
唇	*Sign of the dragon . . . mouth.* [10]

2170	agriculture
農	*Bend . . . sign of the dragon.* [13]

2171	concentrated
濃	Among other things, the key word refers to the thick consistency of liquids. Its elements: *water . . . agriculture.* [16]

*	golden calf
关	The story is told of the people of the Exodus that, disstisfied with Moses' leadership, they colleted their gold ornaments and melted them down to fashion a **golden calf** for an idol. The *animal horns* and *heavens* here represent that god of theirs. [6]

2172	send off
送	*Road . . . golden calf.* [9]

2173	connection
関	*Gates . . . golden calf.* [14]

2174	blossom
咲	*Mouth . . . golden calf.* [9]

2175	ghost
鬼	*Drop of . . . brains . . . human legs . . . elbow.* [10]
2176	ugly
醜	*Whiskey bottle . . . ghost.* [17]
2177	soul
魂	*Rising cloud of . . . ghosts.* [14]
2178	witch
魔	*Hemp . . . ghost.* Take care not to confuse with the primitive of the same name learned earlier (page 164). [21]
2179	fascination
魅	*Ghost . . . not yet.* [15]
2180	clod
塊	*Soil . . . ghost.* [13]
2181	attack
襲	*Vase . . . meat . . . slingshot* (doubled up with) *snake . . . three . . . garment.* The top half of this character is the old form for the kanji in FRAME 575. [22]
	立　音　音　音　龍　龍　龍　龍　襲

Lesson 56

THIS FINAL LESSON is intended to complete preparations for learning new kanji not treated in these pages. A group of 19 such kanji has been reserved for this purpose and arranged in four groups typifying the kinds of problems you can

run into. Aside from help with unusual stroke order and the indication of the total number of strokes in square brackets, no hints will be given.

The first and simplest group will be composed of those whose parts you will recognize immediately from characters already learned. We list seven examples, each representing one of the principles governing primitives.

2182 嚇 [17]		upbraid
2183 朕 [10]		majestic plural
2184 雰 [12]		atmosphere
2185 箇 [14]		item
2186 錬 [16]		tempering
2187 遵 [15]		abide by
2188 罷 [15]		quit

Secondly, you may run into characters that you learned as primitives, but whose meaning is completely unrelated to the primitive meaning we adopted. In learning the meaning of the kanji, be careful not to forget what it stands for when used as a primitive element.

2189	barracks
屯 [4]	

2190	moreover
且 [5]	

In the third place, you will meet kanji using combinations of elements that you can make into a new primitive with its own particular meaning. Recall a previous kanji in which this combination appears and adjust your story to reinforce your new invention.

2191	seaweed
藻 [19]	

2192	slave
隷 [16]	

2193	healing
癒 [18]	

2194	imperial seal
璽 [19]	

Finally, there are shapes that were not covered in this book. You are on your own here, but it may help to consult a kanji dictionary to see whether any of the parts might not be a character with a specific and useful meaning. In many cases, as in the following two frames, the unfamiliar pieces will turn out to be parts of known characters or primitives (the *bird* in FRAME 2195 and the *boat* in FRAME 2196).

| 2195 | | lagoon |
| 潟 | [15] | |

| 2196 | | cinnabar |
| 丹 | [4] | |

Scattered here and there throughout the foregoing 55 lessons several figures of the Sino-Japanese zodiac were introduced. We conclude this lesson, and the book, with the remaining figures. In all, there are twelve animals, several of which take their writing from other characters quite unrelated in meaning. So far, then, we have learned the following: *rat* (子), *tiger* (寅), *dragon* (辰), *horse* (午), *ram* (未), *monkey* (申), *bird* (酉), *dog* (戌), and *hog* (亥). This leaves three for the learning, and one new associated kanji.

2197		sign of the cow
丑	[4]	
	フ　丁　开　丑	

| 2198 | | humiliate |
| 羞 | *Wool . . sign of the cow.* [11] | |

| 2199 | | sign of the hare |
| 卯 | [5] | |

| 2200 | | sign of the snake |
| 巳 | [3] | |

Valeant benefici,
Poenas dent malefici!

Indexes

INDEX I

Kanji

The following Index includes all the kanji presented in this book, in the order of their appearance. They are printed in one of the typical block-form type styles used in Japan to teach children the proper form for drawing kanji by hand with a pen or pencil—the same form used in this book to show proper stroke order.

一	二	三	四	五	六	七	八	九	十
1	2	3	4	5	6	7	8	9	10
口	日	月	田	目	古	吾	冒	朋	明
11	12	13	14	15	16	17	18	19	20
唱	晶	品	呂	昌	早	旭	世	胃	旦
21	22	23	24	25	26	27	28	29	30
胆	亘	凹	凸	旧	自	白	百	中	千
31	32	33	34	35	36	37	38	39	40
舌	升	昇	丸	寸	肘	専	博	占	上
41	42	43	44	45	46	47	48	49	50
下	卓	朝	嘲	只	貝	唄	貞	員	貼
51	52	53	54	55	56	57	58	59	60
見	児	元	頁	頑	凡	負	万	句	肌
61	62	63	64	65	66	67	68	69	70
旬	勺	的	首	乙	乱	直	具	真	工
71	72	73	74	75	76	77	78	79	80

左	右	有	賄	貢	項	刀	刃	切	召
81	82	83	84	85	86	87	88	89	90
昭	則	副	別	丁	町	可	頂	子	孔
91	92	93	94	95	96	97	98	99	100
了	女	好	如	母	貫	兄	呪	克	小
101	102	103	104	105	106	107	108	109	110
少	大	多	夕	汐	外	名	石	肖	硝
111	112	113	114	115	116	117	118	119	120
砕	砂	妬	削	光	太	器	臭	嗅	妙
121	122	123	124	125	126	127	128	129	130
省	厚	奇	川	州	順	水	氷	永	泉
131	132	133	134	135	136	137	138	139	140
腺	原	願	泳	沼	沖	汎	江	汰	汁
141	142	143	144	145	146	147	148	149	150
沙	潮	源	活	消	況	河	泊	湖	測
151	152	153	154	155	156	157	158	159	160
土	吐	圧	埼	垣	填	圭	封	涯	寺
161	162	163	164	165	166	167	168	169	170
時	均	火	炎	煩	淡	灯	畑	災	灰
171	172	173	174	175	176	177	178	179	180
点	照	魚	漁	里	黒	墨	鯉	量	厘
181	182	183	184	185	186	187	188	189	190
埋	同	洞	胴	向	尚	字	守	完	宣
191	192	193	194	195	196	197	198	199	200

宵	安	宴	寄	富	貯	木	林	森	桂
201	202	203	204	205	206	207	208	209	210
柏	枠	梢	棚	杏	桐	植	椅	枯	朴
211	212	213	214	215	216	217	218	219	220
村	相	机	本	札	暦	案	燥	未	末
221	222	223	224	225	226	227	228	229	230
昧	沫	味	妹	朱	株	若	草	苦	苛
231	232	233	234	235	236	237	238	239	240
寛	薄	葉	模	漠	墓	暮	膜	苗	兆
241	242	243	244	245	246	247	248	249	250
桃	眺	犬	状	黙	然	荻	狩	猫	牛
251	252	253	254	255	256	257	258	259	260
特	告	先	洗	介	界	茶	脊	合	塔
261	262	263	264	265	266	267	268	269	270
王	玉	宝	珠	現	玩	狂	旺	皇	呈
271	272	273	274	275	276	277	278	279	280
全	栓	理	主	注	柱	金	銑	鉢	銅
281	282	283	284	285	286	287	288	289	290
釣	針	銘	鎮	道	導	辻	迅	造	迫
291	292	293	294	295	296	297	298	299	300
逃	辺	巡	車	連	軌	輸	喩	前	煎
301	302	303	304	305	306	307	308	309	310
各	格	賂	略	客	額	夏	処	条	落
311	312	313	314	315	316	317	318	319	320

冗	冥	軍	輝	運	冠	夢	坑	高	享
321	322	323	324	325	326	327	328	329	330
塾	熟	亭	京	涼	景	鯨	舎	周	週
331	332	333	334	335	336	337	338	339	340
士	吉	壮	荘	売	学	覚	栄	書	津
341	342	343	344	345	346	347	348	349	350
牧	攻	敗	枚	故	敬	言	警	計	詮
351	352	353	354	355	356	357	358	359	360
獄	訂	訃	討	訓	詔	詰	話	詠	詩
361	362	363	364	365	366	367	368	369	370
語	読	調	談	諾	諭	式	試	弐	域
371	372	373	374	375	376	377	378	379	380
賊	栽	載	茂	戚	成	城	誠	威	滅
381	382	383	384	385	386	387	388	389	390
減	蔑	桟	銭	浅	止	歩	渉	頻	肯
391	392	393	394	395	396	397	398	399	400
企	歴	武	賦	正	証	政	定	錠	走
401	402	403	404	405	406	407	408	409	410
超	赴	越	是	題	堤	建	鍵	延	誕
411	412	413	414	415	416	417	418	419	420
礎	婿	衣	裁	装	裏	壊	哀	遠	猿
421	422	423	424	425	426	427	428	429	430
初	巾	布	帆	幅	帽	幕	幌	錦	市
431	432	433	434	435	436	437	438	439	440

柿	姉	肺	帯	滞	刺	制	製	転	芸
441	442	443	444	445	446	447	448	449	450
雨	雲	曇	雷	霜	冬	天	妖	沃	橋
451	452	453	454	455	456	457	458	459	460
嬌	立	泣	章	競	帝	諦	童	瞳	鐘
461	462	463	464	465	466	467	468	469	470
商	嫡	適	滴	敵	匕	叱	匂	頃	北
471	472	473	474	475	476	477	478	479	480
背	比	昆	皆	楷	諧	混	渇	謁	褐
481	482	483	484	485	486	487	488	489	490
喝	葛	旨	脂	詣	壱	毎	敏	梅	海
491	492	493	494	495	496	497	498	499	500
乞	乾	腹	複	欠	吹	炊	歌	軟	次
501	502	503	504	505	506	507	508	509	510
茨	資	姿	諮	賠	培	剖	音	暗	韻
511	512	513	514	515	516	517	518	519	520
識	鏡	境	亡	盲	妄	荒	望	方	妨
521	522	523	524	525	526	527	528	529	530
坊	芳	肪	訪	放	激	脱	説	鋭	曽
531	532	533	534	535	536	537	538	539	540
増	贈	東	棟	凍	妊	廷	染	燃	賓
541	542	543	544	545	546	547	548	549	550
歳	県	栃	地	池	虫	蛍	蛇	虹	蝶
551	552	553	554	555	556	557	558	559	560

独 561	蚕 562	風 563	己 564	起 565	妃 566	改 567	記 568	包 569	胞 570
砲 571	泡 572	亀 573	電 574	竜 575	滝 576	豚 577	逐 578	遂 579	家 580
嫁 581	豪 582	腸 583	場 584	湯 585	羊 586	美 587	洋 588	詳 589	鮮 590
達 591	羨 592	差 593	着 594	唯 595	堆 596	椎 597	誰 598	焦 599	礁 600
集 601	准 602	進 603	雑 604	雌 605	準 606	奮 607	奪 608	確 609	午 610
許 611	歓 612	権 613	観 614	羽 615	習 616	翌 617	曜 618	濯 619	日 620
困 621	固 622	錮 623	国 624	団 625	因 626	咽 627	姻 628	園 629	回 630
壇 631	店 632	庫 633	庭 634	庁 635	床 636	麻 637	磨 638	心 639	忘 640
恣 641	忍 642	認 643	忌 644	志 645	誌 646	芯 647	忠 648	串 649	患 650
思 651	恩 652	応 653	意 654	臆 655	想 656	息 657	憩 658	恵 659	恐 660
惑 661	感 662	憂 663	寡 664	忙 665	悦 666	恒 667	悼 668	悟 669	怖 670
慌 671	悔 672	憎 673	慣 674	愉 675	惰 676	慎 677	憾 678	憶 679	惧 680

憧 681	憬 682	慕 683	添 684	必 685	泌 686	手 687	看 688	摩 689	我 690
義 691	議 692	犠 693	抹 694	拭 695	拉 696	抱 697	搭 698	抄 699	抗 700
批 701	招 702	拓 703	拍 704	打 705	拘 706	捨 707	拐 708	摘 709	挑 710
指 711	持 712	拶 713	括 714	揮 715	推 716	揚 717	提 718	損 719	拾 720
担 721	拠 722	描 723	操 724	接 725	掲 726	掛 727	捗 728	研 729	戒 730
弄 731	械 732	鼻 733	刑 734	型 735	才 736	財 737	材 738	存 739	在 740
乃 741	携 742	及 743	吸 744	扱 745	丈 746	史 747	吏 748	更 749	硬 750
梗 751	又 752	双 753	桑 754	隻 755	護 756	獲 757	奴 758	怒 759	友 760
抜 761	投 762	没 763	股 764	設 765	撃 766	殻 767	支 768	技 769	枝 770
肢 771	茎 772	怪 773	軽 774	叔 775	督 776	寂 777	淑 778	反 779	坂 780
板 781	返 782	販 783	爪 784	妥 785	乳 786	浮 787	淫 788	将 789	奨 790
采 791	採 792	菜 793	受 794	授 795	愛 796	曖 797	払 798	広 799	勾 800

拡 801	鉱 802	弁 803	雄 804	台 805	息 806	治 807	冶 808	始 809	胎 810
窓 811	去 812	法 813	会 814	至 815	室 816	到 817	致 818	互 819	棄 820
育 821	撤 822	充 823	銃 824	硫 825	流 826	允 827	唆 828	出 829	山 830
拙 831	岩 832	炭 833	岐 834	峠 835	崩 836	密 837	蜜 838	嵐 839	崎 840
崖 841	入 842	込 843	分 844	貧 845	頒 846	公 847	松 848	翁 849	訟 850
谷 851	浴 852	容 853	溶 854	欲 855	裕 856	鉛 857	沿 858	賞 859	党 860
堂 861	常 862	裳 863	掌 864	皮 865	波 866	婆 867	披 868	破 869	被 870
残 871	殉 872	殊 873	殖 874	列 875	裂 876	烈 877	死 878	葬 879	瞬 880
耳 881	取 882	趣 883	最 884	撮 885	恥 886	職 887	聖 888	敢 889	聴 890
懐 891	慢 892	漫 893	買 894	置 895	罰 896	寧 897	濁 898	環 899	還 900
夫 901	扶 902	渓 903	規 904	替 905	賛 906	潜 907	失 908	鉄 909	迭 910
臣 911	姫 912	蔵 913	臓 914	賢 915	腎 916	堅 917	臨 918	覧 919	巨 920

拒	力	男	労	募	劣	功	勧	努	勃
921	922	923	924	925	926	927	928	929	930
励	加	賀	架	脇	脅	協	行	律	復
931	932	933	934	935	936	937	938	939	940
得	従	徒	待	往	征	径	彼	役	徳
941	942	943	944	945	946	947	948	949	950
徹	徴	懲	微	街	桁	衡	稿	稼	程
951	952	953	954	955	956	957	958	959	960
税	稚	和	移	秒	秋	愁	私	秩	秘
961	962	963	964	965	966	967	968	969	970
称	利	梨	穫	穂	稲	香	季	委	秀
971	972	973	974	975	976	977	978	979	980
透	誘	稽	穀	菌	萎	米	粉	粘	粒
981	982	983	984	985	986	987	988	989	990
粧	迷	粋	謎	糧	菊	奥	数	楼	類
991	992	993	994	995	996	997	998	999	1000
漆	膝	様	求	球	救	竹	笑	笠	笹
1001	1002	1003	1004	1005	1006	1007	1008	1009	1010
箋	筋	箱	筆	筒	等	算	答	策	簿
1011	1012	1013	1014	1015	1016	1017	1018	1019	1020
築	篭	人	佐	侶	但	住	位	仲	体
1021	1022	1023	1024	1025	1026	1027	1028	1029	1030
悠	件	仕	他	伏	伝	仏	休	仮	伎
1031	1032	1033	1034	1035	1036	1037	1038	1039	1040

伯	俗	信	佳	依	例	個	健	側	侍
1041	1042	1043	1044	1045	1046	1047	1048	1049	1050
停	値	倣	傲	倒	偵	僧	億	儀	償
1051	1052	1053	1054	1055	1056	1057	1058	1059	1060
仙	催	仁	侮	使	便	倍	優	伐	宿
1061	1062	1063	1064	1065	1066	1067	1068	1069	1070
傷	保	褒	傑	付	符	府	任	賃	代
1071	1072	1073	1074	1075	1076	1077	1078	1079	1080
袋	貸	化	花	貨	傾	何	荷	俊	傍
1081	1082	1083	1084	1085	1086	1087	1088	1089	1090
俺	久	畝	囚	内	丙	柄	肉	腐	座
1091	1092	1093	1094	1095	1096	1097	1098	1099	1100
挫	卒	傘	夊	以	似	併	瓦	瓶	宮
1101	1102	1103	1104	1105	1106	1107	1108	1109	1110
営	善	膳	年	夜	液	塚	幣	弊	蔽
1111	1112	1113	1114	1115	1116	1117	1118	1119	1120
喚	換	融	施	旋	遊	旅	勿	物	易
1121	1122	1123	1124	1125	1126	1127	1128	1129	1130
賜	尿	尼	尻	泥	塀	履	屋	握	屈
1131	1132	1133	1134	1135	1136	1137	1138	1139	1140
掘	堀	居	据	裾	層	局	遅	漏	刷
1141	1142	1143	1144	1145	1146	1147	1148	1149	1150
尺	尽	沢	訳	択	昼	戸	肩	房	扇
1151	1152	1153	1154	1155	1156	1157	1158	1159	1160

炉 1161	戻 1162	涙 1163	雇 1164	顧 1165	啓 1166	示 1167	礼 1168	祥 1169	祝 1170
福 1171	祉 1172	社 1173	視 1174	奈 1175	尉 1176	慰 1177	款 1178	禁 1179	襟 1180
宗 1181	崇 1182	祭 1183	察 1184	擦 1185	由 1186	抽 1187	油 1188	袖 1189	宙 1190
届 1191	笛 1192	軸 1193	甲 1194	押 1195	岬 1196	挿 1197	申 1198	伸 1199	神 1200
捜 1201	果 1202	菓 1203	課 1204	裸 1205	斤 1206	析 1207	所 1208	祈 1209	近 1210
折 1211	哲 1212	逝 1213	誓 1214	暫 1215	斬 1216	漸 1217	断 1218	質 1219	斥 1220
訴 1221	昨 1222	詐 1223	作 1224	雪 1225	録 1226	剥 1227	尋 1228	急 1229	穏 1230
侵 1231	浸 1232	寝 1233	婦 1234	掃 1235	当 1236	彙 1237	争 1238	浄 1239	事 1240
唐 1241	糖 1242	康 1243	逮 1244	伊 1245	君 1246	群 1247	耐 1248	需 1249	儒 1250
端 1251	両 1252	満 1253	画 1254	歯 1255	曲 1256	曹 1257	遭 1258	漕 1259	槽 1260
斗 1261	料 1262	科 1263	図 1264	用 1265	庸 1266	備 1267	昔 1268	錯 1269	借 1270
惜 1271	措 1272	散 1273	廿 1274	庶 1275	遮 1276	席 1277	度 1278	渡 1279	奔 1280

噴	墳	憤	燒	曉	半	伴	畔	判	拳
1281	1282	1283	1284	1285	1286	1287	1288	1289	1290
券	卷	圏	勝	藤	騰	片	版	之	乏
1291	1292	1293	1294	1295	1296	1297	1298	1299	1300
芝	不	否	杯	矢	矯	族	知	智	挨
1301	1302	1303	1304	1305	1306	1307	1308	1309	1310
矛	柔	務	霧	班	帰	弓	引	弔	弘
1311	1312	1313	1314	1315	1316	1317	1318	1319	1320
強	弥	弱	溺	沸	費	第	弟	巧	号
1321	1322	1323	1324	1325	1326	1327	1328	1329	1330
朽	誇	顎	汚	与	写	身	射	謝	老
1331	1332	1333	1334	1335	1336	1337	1338	1339	1340
考	孝	教	拷	者	煮	著	箸	署	暑
1341	1342	1343	1344	1345	1346	1347	1348	1349	1350
諸	猪	渚	賭	峡	狭	挟	頬	追	阜
1351	1352	1353	1354	1355	1356	1357	1358	1359	1360
師	帥	官	棺	管	父	釜	交	効	較
1361	1362	1363	1364	1365	1366	1367	1368	1369	1370
校	足	促	捉	距	路	露	跳	躍	践
1371	1372	1373	1374	1375	1376	1377	1378	1379	1380
踏	踪	骨	滑	髄	禍	渦	鍋	過	阪
1381	1382	1383	1384	1385	1386	1387	1388	1389	1390
阿	際	障	隙	随	陪	陽	陳	防	附
1391	1392	1393	1394	1395	1396	1397	1398	1399	1400

院	陣	隊	墜	降	階	陛	隣	隔	隠
1401	1402	1403	1404	1405	1406	1407	1408	1409	1410
堕	陥	穴	空	控	突	究	室	窃	窟
1411	1412	1413	1414	1415	1416	1417	1418	1419	1420
窪	搾	窯	窮	探	深	丘	岳	兵	浜
1421	1422	1423	1424	1425	1426	1427	1428	1429	1430
糸	織	繕	縮	繁	縦	緻	線	綻	締
1431	1432	1433	1434	1435	1436	1437	1438	1439	1440
維	羅	練	緒	統	絵	統	絞	給	絡
1441	1442	1443	1444	1445	1446	1447	1448	1449	1450
結	終	級	紀	紅	納	紡	紛	紹	経
1451	1452	1453	1454	1455	1456	1457	1458	1459	1460
紳	約	細	累	索	総	綿	絹	繰	継
1461	1462	1463	1464	1465	1466	1467	1468	1469	1470
緑	縁	網	緊	紫	縛	縄	幼	後	幽
1471	1472	1473	1474	1475	1476	1477	1478	1479	1480
幾	機	畿	玄	畜	蓄	弦	擁	滋	慈
1481	1482	1483	1484	1485	1486	1487	1488	1489	1490
磁	系	係	孫	懸	遜	却	脚	卸	御
1491	1492	1493	1494	1495	1496	1497	1498	1499	1500
服	命	令	零	齢	冷	領	鈴	勇	湧
1501	1502	1503	1504	1505	1506	1507	1508	1509	1510
通	踊	疑	擬	凝	範	犯	氾	厄	危
1511	1512	1513	1514	1515	1516	1517	1518	1519	1520

宛	腕	苑	怨	柳	卵	留	瑠	貿	印
1521	1522	1523	1524	1525	1526	1527	1528	1529	1530
臼	毀	興	酉	酒	酌	酎	酵	酷	酬
1531	1532	1533	1534	1535	1536	1537	1538	1539	1540
酪	酢	酔	配	酸	猶	尊	豆	頭	短
1541	1542	1543	1544	1545	1546	1547	1548	1549	1550
豊	鼓	喜	樹	皿	血	盆	盟	盗	温
1551	1552	1553	1554	1555	1556	1557	1558	1559	1560
蓋	監	濫	鑑	藍	猛	盛	塩	銀	恨
1561	1562	1563	1564	1565	1566	1567	1568	1569	1570
根	即	爵	節	退	限	眼	良	朗	浪
1571	1572	1573	1574	1575	1576	1577	1578	1579	1580
娘	食	飯	飲	飢	餓	飾	餌	館	餅
1581	1582	1583	1584	1585	1586	1587	1588	1589	1590
養	飽	既	概	慨	平	呼	坪	評	刈
1591	1592	1593	1594	1595	1596	1597	1598	1599	1600
刹	希	凶	胸	離	璃	殺	爽	純	頓
1601	1602	1603	1604	1605	1606	1607	1608	1609	1610
鈍	辛	辞	梓	宰	壁	璧	避	新	薪
1611	1612	1613	1614	1615	1616	1617	1618	1619	1620
親	幸	執	摯	報	叫	糾	収	卑	碑
1621	1622	1623	1624	1625	1626	1627	1628	1629	1630
陸	睦	勢	熱	菱	陵	亥	核	刻	該
1631	1632	1633	1634	1635	1636	1637	1638	1639	1640

骸	劾	述	術	寒	塞	醸	譲	壌	嬢
1641	1642	1643	1644	1645	1646	1647	1648	1649	1650
毒	素	麦	青	精	請	情	晴	清	静
1651	1652	1653	1654	1655	1656	1657	1658	1659	1660
責	績	積	債	漬	表	俵	潔	契	喫
1661	1662	1663	1664	1665	1666	1667	1668	1669	1670
害	轄	割	憲	生	星	醒	姓	性	牲
1671	1672	1673	1674	1675	1676	1677	1678	1679	1680
産	隆	峰	蜂	縫	拝	寿	鋳	籍	春
1681	1682	1683	1684	1685	1686	1687	1688	1689	1690
椿	泰	奏	実	奉	俸	棒	謹	僅	勤
1691	1692	1693	1694	1695	1696	1697	1698	1699	1700
漢	嘆	難	華	垂	睡	唾	錘	乗	剰
1701	1702	1703	1704	1705	1706	1707	1708	1709	1710
今	含	貪	吟	念	捻	琴	陰	予	序
1711	1712	1713	1714	1715	1716	1717	1718	1719	1720
預	野	兼	嫌	鎌	謙	廉	西	価	要
1721	1722	1723	1724	1725	1726	1727	1728	1729	1730
腰	票	漂	標	栗	慄	遷	覆	煙	南
1731	1732	1733	1734	1735	1736	1737	1738	1739	1740
楠	献	門	問	閲	閥	間	闇	簡	開
1741	1742	1743	1744	1745	1746	1747	1748	1749	1750
閉	閣	閑	聞	潤	欄	闘	倉	創	非
1751	1752	1753	1754	1755	1756	1757	1758	1759	1760

俳 1761	排 1762	悲 1763	罪 1764	輩 1765	扉 1766	侯 1767	喉 1768	候 1769	決 1770
快 1771	偉 1772	違 1773	緯 1774	衛 1775	韓 1776	干 1777	肝 1778	刊 1779	汗 1780
軒 1781	岸 1782	幹 1783	芋 1784	宇 1785	余 1786	除 1787	徐 1788	叙 1789	途 1790
斜 1791	塗 1792	束 1793	頼 1794	瀬 1795	勅 1796	疎 1797	辣 1798	速 1799	整 1800
剣 1801	険 1802	検 1803	倹 1804	重 1805	動 1806	腫 1807	勲 1808	働 1809	種 1810
衝 1811	薫 1812	病 1813	痴 1814	痘 1815	症 1816	瘍 1817	瘦 1818	疾 1819	嫉 1820
痢 1821	痕 1822	疲 1823	疫 1824	痛 1825	癖 1826	匿 1827	匠 1828	医 1829	匹 1830
区 1831	枢 1832	殴 1833	欧 1834	抑 1835	仰 1836	迎 1837	登 1838	澄 1839	発 1840
廃 1841	僚 1842	瞭 1843	寮 1844	療 1845	彫 1846	形 1847	影 1848	杉 1849	彩 1850
彰 1851	彦 1852	顔 1853	須 1854	膨 1855	参 1856	惨 1857	修 1858	珍 1859	診 1860
文 1861	対 1862	紋 1863	蚊 1864	斑 1865	斉 1866	剤 1867	済 1868	斎 1869	粛 1870
塁 1871	楽 1872	薬 1873	率 1874	渋 1875	摂 1876	央 1877	英 1878	映 1879	赤 1880

赦	変	跡	蛮	恋	湾	黄	横	把	色
1881	1882	1883	1884	1885	1886	1887	1888	1889	1890
絶	艶	肥	甘	紺	某	謀	媒	欺	棋
1891	1892	1893	1894	1895	1896	1897	1898	1899	1900
旗	期	碁	基	甚	勘	堪	貴	遺	遣
1901	1902	1903	1904	1905	1906	1907	1908	1909	1910
潰	舞	無	組	粗	租	狙	祖	阻	査
1911	1912	1913	1914	1915	1916	1917	1918	1919	1920
助	宜	畳	並	普	譜	湿	顕	繊	霊
1921	1922	1923	1924	1925	1926	1927	1928	1929	1930
業	撲	僕	共	供	異	翼	戴	洪	港
1931	1932	1933	1934	1935	1936	1937	1938	1939	1940
暴	爆	恭	選	殿	丼	井	囲	耕	亜
1941	1942	1943	1944	1945	1946	1947	1948	1949	1950
悪	円	角	触	解	再	講	購	構	溝
1951	1952	1953	1954	1955	1956	1957	1958	1959	1960
論	倫	輪	偏	遍	編	冊	柵	典	氏
1961	1962	1963	1964	1965	1966	1967	1968	1969	1970
紙	婚	低	抵	底	民	眠	捕	哺	浦
1971	1972	1973	1974	1975	1976	1977	1978	1979	1980
蒲	舗	補	邸	郭	郡	郊	部	都	郵
1981	1982	1983	1984	1985	1986	1987	1988	1989	1990
邦	那	郷	響	郎	廊	盾	循	派	脈
1991	1992	1993	1994	1995	1996	1997	1998	1999	2000

衆	逓	段	鍛	后	幻	司	伺	詞	飼
2001	2002	2003	2004	2005	2006	2007	2008	2009	2010
嗣	舟	舶	航	舷	般	盤	搬	船	艦
2011	2012	2013	2014	2015	2016	2017	2018	2019	2020
艇	瓜	弧	孤	繭	益	暇	敷	来	気
2021	2022	2023	2024	2025	2026	2027	2028	2029	2030
汽	飛	沈	枕	妻	凄	衰	衷	面	麺
2031	2032	2033	2034	2035	2036	2037	2038	2039	2040
革	靴	覇	声	眉	呉	娯	誤	蒸	承
2041	2042	2043	2044	2045	2046	2047	2048	2049	2050
函	極	牙	芽	邪	雅	釈	番	審	翻
2051	2052	2053	2054	2055	2056	2057	2058	2059	2060
藩	毛	耗	尾	宅	託	為	偽	畏	長
2061	2062	2063	2064	2065	2066	2067	2068	2069	2070
張	帳	脹	髪	展	喪	巣	単	戦	禅
2071	2072	2073	2074	2075	2076	2077	2078	2079	2080
弾	桜	獣	脳	悩	厳	鎖	挙	誉	猟
2081	2082	2083	2084	2085	2086	2087	2088	2089	2090
鳥	鳴	鶴	烏	蔦	鳩	鶏	島	暖	媛
2091	2092	2093	2094	2095	2096	2097	2098	2099	2100
援	緩	属	嘱	偶	遇	愚	隅	逆	塑
2101	2102	2103	2104	2105	2106	2107	2108	2109	2110
遡	岡	鋼	綱	剛	缶	陶	揺	謡	鬱
2111	2112	2113	2114	2115	2116	2117	2118	2119	2120

就	蹴	懇	墾	貌	免	逸	晩	勉	象
2121	2122	2123	2124	2125	2126	2127	2128	2129	2130
像	馬	駒	験	騎	駐	駆	駅	騒	駄
2131	2132	2133	2134	2135	2136	2137	2138	2139	2140
驚	篤	罵	騰	虎	虜	膚	虚	戯	虞
2141	2142	2143	2144	2145	2146	2147	2148	2149	2150
慮	劇	虐	鹿	麓	薦	慶	麗	熊	能
2151	2152	2153	2154	2155	2156	2157	2158	2159	2160
態	寅	演	辰	辱	震	振	娠	唇	農
2161	2162	2163	2164	2165	2166	2167	2168	2169	2170
濃	送	関	咲	鬼	醜	魂	魔	魅	塊
2171	2172	2173	2174	2175	2176	2177	2178	2179	2180
襲	嚇	朕	霧	箇	錬	遵	罷	屯	且
2181	2182	2183	2184	2185	2186	2187	2188	2189	2190
藻	隷	癒	璽	丹	潟	丑	羞	卯	巳
2191	2192	2193	2195	2194	2196	2197	2198	2199	2200

INDEX II

Primitive Elements

This Index lists all the primitive elements of this book, except for those treated as kanji on their own. The primitives are arranged according to the number of strokes and the number beneath each entry refers to the page on which the primitive element is first introduced.

1画

丨	ノ	㇄	㇄	コ
27	27	44	44	397

2画

卜	八	儿	几	ク	㇇	゛	ナ	リ
32	35	35	36	36	36	36	46	48

厂	冂	𠆢	冖	亠	口	ツ	氵	⺅
59	83	109	128	130	161	164	164	173

乂	ム	イ	丬	凵	刂	丂	与	卩
222	229	259	269	291	301	303	304	325

卩	⺈	巳	㐅	屮	ユ	匚	㇄	丨丨
325	326	328	339	342	363	371	371	377

厂	丷
396	396

3画

亠	屮	巛	儿	氵	宀	艹	彐	犭
45	57	64	64	65	85	97	104	105

스	辶	夊	弋	又	也	口	广	忄
110	122	125	143	154	191	206	208	209

450

才 216　疒 221　云 231　彳 248　尸 274　ヨ 287　ヨ 287　彑 288　阝 312

幺 322　厶 329　丰 352　于 366　彡 374　阝 394　毛 406　巛 409

4画

毋 54　川 76　朩 88　生 107　亢 130　夂 137　弋 144　戈 144　𧘇 156

云 162　夭 164　壬 185　小 209　开 219　殳 225　宀 227　去 232　歹 240

声 247　从 268　牛 271　仸 273　礻 278　尹 289　尹 289　卅 294　屮 305

罒 316　𦣏 329　无 337　屯 340　圭 347　丰 350　耂 352　夬 363　㐅 378

巴 380　长 408

5画

罒 20　古 131　䒑 135　戊 145　疋 152　足 155　㞢 155　礻 156　帀 160

卋 161　电 195　易 197　圣 226　台 237　禾 251　水 255　乍 286　卉 295

弗 302　弟 302　夗 328　艮 334　先 343　术 345　卄 345　夅 352　广 370

癶 373　毌 383　且 384　冊 391　氐 393　自 397　罒 407　㫐 408

6画

吉 133　聿 136　畫 136　戋 145　戌 147　戔 148　衣 156　羊 198　羽 204

丷	并	广	而	关	夹	自	艮	良
229	269	272	290	297	307	308	334	336
耒	申	西	亦	卌	亜	屰	卢	关
351	354	358	379	384	386	413	419	423

7画

兌	甶	豕	羊	孚	舛	庄	甫	釆
183	193	196	199	228	241	295	393	406
镸	豸	鹿						
408	416	421						

8画

卓	泉	霝	曷	音	隹	尚	隶	堯
34	66	163	171	178	200	238	289	296
籴	其							
368	382							

9画

畐	俞	复	昜	咼	壴	亲	爰	禺
50	125	175	197	311	333	341	412	413
䍃								
414								

10画

專	莫	崔	堇	莫	韋	冓
31	99	202	353	353	364	390

11画

商	竟	隺	曼
167	180	203	242

12画

喬	戠	敝	尞
165	179	271	373

13画

辟	襄
341	346

INDEX III

Kanji in Stroke Order

Here you will find all the kanji treated in this book, grouped by the number of strokes. The ordering within each stroke-number group follows the standard dictionary practice of arranging the kanji according to "radicals."

1画

一	1
乙	75

2画

丁	95
七	7
乃	741
九	9
了	101
二	2
人	1023
八	8
入	842
刀	87
力	922
匕	476
十	10
又	752

3画

万	68
丈	746
三	3
上	50

下	51
与	1335
丸	44
久	1092
之	1299
乞	501
子	99
亡	524
凡	66
刃	88
勺	72
千	40
及	743
口	11
土	161
士	341
夕	114
大	112
女	102
寸	45
小	110
山	830
川	134
工	80
己	564
巾	432

巳	2200
干	1777
弓	1317
才	736

4画

不	1302
丑	2197
中	39
丹	2196
乏	1300
予	1719
互	819
五	5
井	1946
仁	1063
今	1711
介	265
仏	1037
允	827
元	63
公	847
六	6
内	1095
円	1952

冗	321
凶	1603
分	844
切	89
刈	1600
勿	1128
匁	1104
匂	478
勾	800
化	1083
匹	1830
区	1831
升	42
午	610
厄	1519
友	760
双	753
反	779
収	1628
天	457
太	126
夫	901
孔	100
少	111
尺	1151
屯	2189

幻	2006
廿	1274
引	1318
弔	1319
心	639
戸	1157
手	687
支	768
文	1861
斗	1261
斤	1206
方	529
日	12
曰	620
月	13
木	207
欠	505
止	396
比	482
毛	2062
氏	1970
水	137
火	173
爪	784
父	1366
片	1297

牙 2053
牛 260
犬 253
王 271

5 画

且 2190
世 28
丘 1427
丙 1096
主 284
井 1947
以 1105
仕 1033
他 1034
付 1075
仙 1061
代 1080
令 1503
兄 107
冊 1967
写 1336
冬 456
処 318
凸 34
出 829
凹 33
刊 1779
功 927
加 932
包 569
北 480
半 1286
占 49
卯 2199
去 812
古 16
句 69
只 55
叫 1626
召 90

可 97
叱 477
台 805
号 1330
史 747
右 82
司 2007
囚 1094
四 4
圧 163
外 116
央 1877
失 908
奴 758
尼 1133
尻 1134
左 81
巨 1329
市 920
布 440
平 433
幼 1596
庁 1478
広 635
弁 799
弘 803
必 1320
打 685
払 705
斥 798
旦 1220
旧 30
未 35
末 229
本 230
札 224
正 225
母 405
民 105
永 1976
138

永 139
汁 150
氾 1518
瓜 2022
犯 1517
玄 1484
玉 272
瓦 1108
甘 1894
生 1675
用 1265
田 14
由 1186
甲 1194
申 1198
白 37
皮 865
皿 1555
目 15
矛 1311
矢 1305
石 118
示 1167
礼 1168
穴 1413
立 462
辺 302
辻 297
込 843

6 画

両 1252
争 1238
亘 32
交 1368
亥 1637
仮 1039
仰 1836
仲 1029
伎 1040
件 1032

任 1078
企 401
伊 1245
伏 1035
伐 1069
休 1038
会 814
伝 1036
充 823
兆 250
先 263
光 125
全 281
再 1934
刑 1956
列 734
劣 875
匠 926
印 1530
危 1520
各 311
合 269
吉 342
同 192
名 117
后 2005
吏 748
吐 162
向 195
吸 744
回 630
因 626
団 625
在 740
圭 167
地 554
壮 343
多 113
好 103
如 104

妃 566
妄 526
字 197
存 739
宅 2065
宇 1785
守 198
安 202
寺 170
尽 1152
州 135
当 1236
帆 434
年 1114
式 377
弐 379
忙 665
成 386
扱 745
旨 493
早 26
旬 71
旭 27
曲 1256
肌 70
有 83
朱 235
朴 220
机 223
朽 1331
次 510
死 878
毎 497
気 2030
汐 115
汗 1780
汚 1334
江 148
汎 147
池 555
灯 177

灰	180
百	38
竹	1007
米	987
糸	1431
缶	2116
羊	586
羽	615
老	1340
考	1341
耳	881
肉	1098
自	36
至	815
舌	41
臼	1531
舟	2012
色	1890
艹 芋	1784
芯	647
芝	1301
虫	556
血	1556
行	938
衣	423
西	1728
辶 巡	303
迅	298

7 画

串	649
乱	76
二 亜	1950
亻 伯	1041
伴	1287
伸	1199
伺	2008
似	1106
位	1028
低	1973
住	1027

佐	1024
体	1030
但	1026
何	1087
余	1786
作	1224
儿 克	109
児	62
兵	1429
冫 冷	1506
冶	808
初	431
判	1289
別	94
利	972
力 助	1921
努	929
励	931
労	924
医	1829
卩 即	1572
却	1497
卵	1526
口 君	1246
吟	1714
否	1303
含	1712
吹	506
吾	17
呂	24
呈	280
呉	2046
告	262
囗 困	621
囲	1948
図	1264
土 坂	780
均	172
坊	531
坑	328
士 声	2044

壱	496
売	345
妊	546
妙	130
妥	785
妖	458
妨	530
子 孝	1342
完	199
寸 対	1862
寿	1687
尾	2064
局	1147
尿	1132
山 岐	834
希	1602
序	1720
广 床	636
廷	547
弄	731
弓 弟	1328
形	1847
役	949
忌	644
忍	642
志	645
忘	640
応	653
快	1771
戈 我	690
戒	730
戻	1162
扌 扶	902
批	701
技	769
抄	699
把	1889
抑	1835
投	762
抗	700
折	1211

抜	761
択	1155
攵 改	567
攻	352
更	749
月 肖	119
肘	46
肝	1778
木 杉	1849
杏	215
材	738
村	221
束	1793
条	319
来	2029
求	1004
汽	2031
決	1770
沈	2033
沖	146
沙	151
没	763
汰	149
沃	459
沢	1153
火 災	179
状	254
狂	277
男	923
町	96
社	1173
禾 秀	980
私	968
究	1417
糸 系	1492
良	1578
艹 花	1084
芳	532
芸	450
臣	911
見	61

角	1953
言	357
谷	851
豆	1548
貝	56
赤	1880
走	410
足	1372
身	1337
車	304
辛	1612
辰	2164
辶 迎	1837
近	1210
返	782
邦	1991
酉	1534
里	185
麦	3
阪	1390
防	1399

8 画

並	1924
乳	786
事	1240
一 享	330
京	334
亻 佳	1044
併	1107
使	1065
例	1046
侍	1050
供	1935
依	1045
価	1729
侮	1064
八 具	78
典	1969
免	2126
函	2051

	到 817		孤 2024		抵 1974		果 1202		祉 1172
	制 447		学 346		抹 694		采 791		突 1416
	刷 1150	宀	宗 1181		押 1195		枝 770		空 1414
	券 1291		官 1363		抽 1187		枕 2034		糾 1627
	刺 446		宙 1190		担 721		枠 212		者 1345
	刹 1601		定 408		拍 704		枢 1832		舎 338
	刻 1639		宛 1521		拐 708	欠	欧 1834	廿	苑 1523
力	効 1369		宜 1922		拒 921		武 403		芽 2054
	劾 1642		宝 273		拓 703		歩 397		苗 249
十	卑 1629		実 1694		拘 706	殳	殴 1833		若 237
	卒 1102		尚 196		拙 831		毒 1651		苦 239
	卓 52	尸	居 1143		招 702		沫 232		苛 240
	阜 1360		屈 1140		拝 1686		河 157		英 1878
	協 937		届 1191		拠 722		沸 1325		茂 384
厶	参 1856	山	岡 2112		拡 801		油 1188		茎 772
	叔 775		岩 832		拉 696		治 807		虎 2145
又	取 882		岬 1196	攵	放 535		沼 145		表 1666
	受 794		岳 1428		斉 1866		沿 858	辶	迫 300
口	周 339		岸 1782	日	昆 483		況 156		迭 910
	味 233	干	幸 1622		昇 43		泊 158		述 1643
	呼 1597	广	底 1975		昌 25		泌 686		邸 1984
	呪 108		店 632		明 20		法 813		邪 2055
	命 1502		府 1077		旺 278		泡 572		那 1992
	和 963		延 419		易 1130		波 866		金 287
	固 622		弥 1322		昔 1268		泣 463		長 2070
	国 624		弦 1487	月	朋 19		泥 1135		門 1743
土	坪 1598		弧 2023		服 1501		注 285		阻 1919
	垂 1705	彳	彼 948		肢 771		泳 144		阿 1391
	夜 1115		往 945		肥 1893	火	炉 1161		附 1400
大	奇 133		征 946		股 764		炊 507		雨 451
	奈 1175		径 947		肩 1158		炎 174		青 1654
	奉 1695		忠 648		肪 533		版 1298		非 1760
	奔 1280		念 1715		肯 400	牛	牧 351		
女	妹 234		怖 670		育 821		物 1129		**9 画**
	妻 2035		性 1679	木	杯 1304		玩 276		乗 1709
	姉 442		怪 773		東 543	田	画 1254		亭 333
	始 809	戸	房 1159		松 848		的 73	亻	係 1493
	姓 1678		所 1208		板 781		盲 525		侯 1767
	妬 123		承 2050		析 1207		直 77		俊 1089
	委 979		披 868		林 208	目	知 1308		侵 1231
子	季 978		抱 697		枚 354		祈 1209		便 1066

	促	1373		帥	1362		胎	810		疫	1824		赴	412
	俗	1042		帝	466		胞	570		発	1840	車	軌	306
	保	1072	幺	幽	1480		栄	348	白	皆	484		軍	323
	侶	1025		度	1278	木	枯	219		皇	279	辶	迷	992
	信	1043		建	417		査	1920		盆	1557		追	1359
門	冒	18		彦	1852		架	934	目	看	688		退	1575
	冠	326	彳	待	944		柄	1097		県	552		送	2172
	則	92		律	939		柏	211		盾	1997		逃	301
	削	124		後	1479		柿	441		省	131		逆	2109
	前	309		怒	759		某	1896		相	222		郊	1987
力	勅	1796		思	651		染	548		眉	2045		郎	1995
	勃	930		怠	806		柔	1312	石	砂	122		限	1576
	勇	1509		急	1229		柱	286		研	729	里	重	1805
	南	1740		怨	1524		柳	1525		砕	121		面	2039
	卸	1499		恒	667		栃	553		祖	1918	革	革	2041
厂	厘	190		恨	1570		柵	1968		祝	1170		音	518
	厚	132		悔	672		段	2003		神	1200		頁	64
	叙	1789		括	714		泉	140	禾	秋	966		風	563
口	咲	2174		拷	1344		洋	588		科	1263		飛	2032
	咽	628		拾	720		洗	264		秒	965		食	1582
	哀	428		持	712		洞	193	穴	窃	1419		首	74
	品	23		指	711		津	350	糸	紀	1454		香	977
土	型	735		拭	695		洪	1939		約	1462			
	垣	165		挑	710		活	154		紅	1455	**10 画**		
	城	387		挟	1357		派	1999		級	1453	イ	修	1858
	変	1882	攵	政	407		浄	1239	美	美	587		俳	1761
大	契	1669		故	355		浅	395		耐	1248		俵	1667
	奏	1693		施	1124		海	500		臭	128		俸	1696
女	姻	627	日	星	1676	火	炭	833	艹	茨	511		倉	1758
	姿	513		映	1879		為	2067		茶	267		個	1047
	威	389		春	1690		点	181		草	238		倍	1067
宀	客	315		昧	231		牲	1680		荒	527		倒	1055
	室	816		昨	1222		狙	1917		荘	344		候	1769
	宣	200		昭	91		狭	1356	虍	虐	2153		借	1270
	専	47		是	414		狩	258		虹	559		倣	1053
ツ	単	2078		昼	1156		独	561		要	1730		値	1052
	屋	1138	月	肺	443		珍	1859	言	訂	362		倫	1962
	封	168		胃	29	甘	甚	1905		計	359		倹	1804
山	峠	835		胆	31	田	界	266		訃	363		俺	1091
	峡	1355		背	481		畑	178		貞	58		党	860
	巻	1292					畏	2069		負	67	八	兼	1723

氵	准	602		帯	444		朕	2183	
	凍	545		帰	1316		胴	194	
	凄	2036	广	座	1100		能	2160	
	剖	517		庫	633		脈	2000	
	剛	2115		庭	634		朗	1579	
	剣	1801	弓	弱	1323		脊	268	
	剤	1867	彳	徐	1788	木	案	227	
	剥	1227		徒	943		桜	2082	
	冥	322		従	942		核	1639	
力	勉	2129		恋	1885		格	312	
	匿	1827		悦	666		桂	210	
	原	142		恐	660		校	1371	
口	員	59		恥	886		根	1571	
	唆	828		恩	652		栽	382	
	唄	57		恭	1943		桟	393	
	哺	1979		息	657		株	236	
	哲	1212		恵	659		栓	282	
	唇	2169		恣	641		桑	754	
	唐	1241		悟	669		桃	251	
	埋	191		悩	2085		桐	216	
夂	夏	317		扇	1160		梅	499	
女	姫	912		挙	2088		栗	1735	
	娘	1581		振	2167		桁	956	
	娠	2168		挿	1197	歹	残	871	
	娯	2047		捕	1978		殊	873	
	孫	1494		捜	1201		殉	872	
宀	宮	1110		捉	1374		殺	1607	
	宰	1615		挨	1310		泰	1692	
	害	1671		挫	1101		消	155	
	宴	203		拳	1290		浸	1232	
	宵	201	攵	敏	498		浜	1430	
	家	580		旅	1127		浮	787	
	容	853		既	1593		浦	1980	
寸	射	1338	斗	料	1262		浴	852	
	将	789	日	時	171		流	826	
	尉	1537		書	349		涙	1163	
	展	2075	月	胸	1604		浪	1580	
山	峰	1683		望	528		烏	2094	
	島	2098		脅	936		烈	877	
	差	593		脇	935		特	261	
巾	席	1277		脂	494		珠	274	

	班	1315		蚊	1864
	畜	1485		衰	2037
田	畔	1288		衷	2038
	畝	1093		袖	1189
	留	1529		被	870
	疾	1819	自	師	1361
	症	1816	言	記	568
	疲	1823		訓	365
	病	1813		託	2066
	益	2026		討	364
	真	79	貝	貢	85
	眠	1977		財	737
石	破	869		軒	1781
	砲	571		起	565
	祥	1169	辰	辱	2165
禾	称	971	辶	逝	1213
	租	1916		造	299
	秘	970		速	1799
	秩	969		逐	578
	竜	575		通	1511
	笑	1008		逓	2002
米	粋	993		途	1790
	粉	988		透	981
糸	索	1465		連	305
	紙	1971		郡	1986
	純	1609	酉	酌	1536
	素	1652		酒	1535
	納	1456		配	1544
	紋	1863		針	292
	紡	1457		院	1401
	紛	1458		陥	1412
	翁	849		降	1405
耒	耕	1949		除	1787
	耗	2063		陣	1402
至	致	818		陛	1407
	航	2014		釜	1367
	般	2016	隹	隻	755
艹	華	1704		飢	1585
	荷	1088		馬	2132
	荻	257		骨	1383
虫	蚕	562		高	329

鬼 2175

11画

乙 乾 502
亻 偏 1964
停 1051
健 1048
側 1049
偵 1056
偶 2105
偽 2068
副 93
剰 1710
力 動 1806
勘 1906
務 1313
口 唯 595
唱 21
商 471
問 1744
啓 1166
喝 491
唾 1706
土 域 380
執 1623
培 516
基 1904
埼 164
堀 1142
堂 861
堆 596
女 婆 867
婚 1972
婦 1234
宀 宿 1070
寂 777
寄 204
寅 2162
密 837
尉 1176
巣 2077

崇 1182
山 崎 840
崩 836
崖 841
巾 帳 2072
常 862
康 1243
庶 1275
庸 1266
弓 張 2071
強 1321
彡 彩 1850
彫 1846
得 941
悠 1031
患 650
悪 1951
悼 668
情 1657
惜 1271
惨 1857
惧 680
捨 707
据 1144
掃 1235
授 795
排 1762
掘 1141
掛 727
採 792
探 1425
接 725
措 1272
控 1415
推 716
描 723
掲 726
捗 728
捻 1716
攵 救 1006
教 1343

敗 353
斎 1869
斜 1791
断 1218
方 旋 1125
族 1307
日 曹 1257
曽 540
月 脱 537
脚 1498
脳 2084
豚 577
木 梓 1614
梢 213
梨 973
械 732
梗 751
戚 385
欲 855
殻 767
液 1116
涯 169
渇 488
渓 903
混 487
済 1868
渋 1875
淑 778
渚 1353
渉 398
深 1426
清 1659
淡 176
添 684
淫 788
涼 335
猪 1352
猫 259
猛 1566
猟 2090
玄 率 1874

爽 1608
王 球 1005
現 275
理 283
瓶 1109
産 1681
田 異 1936
略 314
皿 盛 1567
盗 1559
目 眼 1577
眺 252
祭 1183
票 1732
章 464
痕 1822
穴 窓 811
窒 1418
移 964
竹 第 1327
笛 1192
符 1076
笠 1009
笹 1010
米 粗 1915
粘 989
粒 990
糸 経 1460
紺 1895
細 1463
終 1452
紹 1459
紳 1461
組 1914
累 1464
羽 習 616
翌 617
聿 粛 1870
船 2019
舶 2013
舷 2015

艹 菓 1203
菊 996
菌 985
菜 793
著 1347
菱 1635
葛 492
萎 986
疒 虚 2148
虫 蛍 557
蛇 558
術 1644
袋 1081
羞 2198
見 規 904
視 1174
言 許 611
訟 850
設 765
訪 534
訳 1154
貝 貨 1085
貫 106
責 1661
販 783
貧 845
貪 1713
赤 赦 1881
車 軟 509
転 449
斬 1215
辶 逸 2127
進 603
週 340
逮 1244
郭 1985
郷 1993
都 1989
部 1988
郵 1990
酉 酔 1543

釆	釈	2057		嗅	129		掌	864	
	野	1722		喩	308		提	718	
	釣	291		喉	1768		揚	717	
	閉	1751	口	圏	1293		換	1122	
	陰	1718	土	堕	1411		握	1139	
	険	1802		堤	416		揮	715	
	陳	1398		堪	1907		援	2101	
	陶	2117		報	1625		揺	2118	
	陪	1396		場	584		搭	698	
	陸	1631		塀	1136	攵	敢	889	
	隆	1682		塁	1871		散	1273	
	陵	1636		塔	270		敬	356	
雨	雪	1225		塚	1117		斑	1865	
	頂	98		堅	917	日	普	1925	
	頃	479	大	奥	997		暁	1285	
	魚	183	女	婿	422		景	337	
	鳥	2091		媒	1898		晴	1658	
	鹿	2154		媛	2100		最	884	
	麻	637	宀	富	205		晶	22	
	黄	1887		寒	1645		替	905	
	黒	186	寸	尊	1547		智	1309	
	亀	573		尋	1228		晩	2128	
			尤	就	2121		暑	1350	
12画			尸	属	2103	月	腕	1522	
亻	傍	1090		嵐	839		朝	53	
	傘	1103	巾	帽	436		期	1902	
	備	1267		幅	435		脹	2073	
	偉	1772		幾	1481	木	棋	1900	
	僅	1699	广	廃	1841		棒	1697	
	割	1673		廊	1996		棚	214	
	創	1759	弓	弾	2081		棟	544	
力	勝	1294		衆	2001		森	209	
	募	925	彳	御	1500		検	1803	
	勤	1700		復	940		棺	1364	
	博	48		循	1998		植	217	
口	善	1112		悲	1763		極	2052	
	喚	1121		惑	661		椅	218	
	喜	1553		惰	676		椎	597	
	喪	2076		慌	671	欠	欺	1899	
	喫	1670		愉	675		款	1178	
	営	1111		扉	1766		殖	874	

	温	1560		筆	1014
	渦	1387		箋	1011
	減	391	米	粧	991
	湖	159	糸	絵	1446
	港	1940		給	1449
	滋	1489		結	1451
	湿	1927		絞	1448
	測	160		紫	1475
	渡	1279		絶	1891
	湯	585		統	1447
	満	1253		絡	1450
	湾	1886	艹	落	320
	湧	1510		葬	879
火	焼	1284		葉	243
	煮	1346		蛮	1884
	焦	599	行	街	955
	然	256		裁	424
	無	1913		装	425
	猶	1546		裂	876
	琴	1717		補	1983
田	畳	1923		裕	856
	番	2058	見	覚	347
	疎	1797	言	詠	369
	痛	1825		詐	1223
	痘	1815		証	406
	痢	1821		詔	366
癶	登	1838		詞	2009
	着	594		診	1860
	短	1550		訴	1221
石	硬	750		評	1599
	硝	120		象	2130
	硫	825	貝	賀	933
	痩	1818		貴	1908
禾	税	961		貸	1082
	程	960		貯	206
	童	468		買	894
竹	筋	1012		費	1326
	策	1019		貿	1529
	等	1016		貼	60
	筒	1015	走	越	413
	答	1018		超	411

	距	1375
車	軽	774
	軸	1193
辶	運	325
	過	1389
	遇	2106
	遂	579
	達	591
	遅	1148
	道	295
	遊	1126
	遍	1965
	酢	1542
里	量	189
金	鈍	1611
門	開	1750
	閑	1753
	間	1747
	階	1406
	隔	2108
	随	1395
	隊	1403
	陽	1397
	隙	1394
隹	集	601
	雇	1164
	雅	2056
	雄	804
雨	雲	452
	霧	2184
頁	項	86
	須	1854
	順	136
	飲	1584
	飯	1583
	歯	1255

13画

	催	1062
亻	傑	1074
	債	1664

	傷	1071
	傾	1086
	働	1809
	僧	1057
	傲	1054
力	勢	1633
	勧	928
口	嗣	2011
	嘆	1702
	園	629
土	塊	2180
	塑	2110
	塗	1792
	塩	1568
	墓	246
	填	166
夕	夢	327
	奨	790
女	嫁	581
	嫌	1724
	嫉	1820
宀	寛	241
	寝	1233
	塞	1646
巾	幌	438
	幕	437
干	幹	1783
	廉	1727
	彙	1237
	微	954
	愁	967
	想	656
	意	654
	愚	2107
	愛	796
	感	662
	慈	1490
	慎	677
	慨	1595
	慄	1736
戈	戦	2079

	損	719
	搬	2018
	携	742
	搾	1422
	摂	1876
支	鼓	1552
	数	998
	新	1619
日	暇	2027
	暖	2099
	暗	519
月	腸	583
	腹	503
	腰	1731
	腺	141
	膝	1002
	腎	916
	腫	1807
木	楽	1872
	棄	820
	業	1931
	椿	1691
	楠	1741
	楼	999
	楷	485
止	歳	551
	殿	1945
	毀	1532
	滑	1384
	漢	1701
	源	153
	溝	1960
	準	606
	滞	445
	漠	245
	滅	390
	蒲	1981
	溶	854
	滝	576
	溺	1324
火	煙	1739

	煩	175
	照	182
	煎	310
	献	1742
	猿	430
	痴	1814
	盟	1558
	睡	1707
	督	776
	睦	1632
石	碁	1903
	碑	1630
	禁	1179
	禍	1386
	禅	2080
	福	1171
	稚	962
竹	節	1574
糸	継	1470
	絹	1468
	続	1445
	罪	1764
	署	1349
	置	895
	群	1247
美	義	691
	羨	592
耳	聖	888
	艇	2021
艹	蒸	2049
	蓄	1486
	蓋	1561
虍	虞	2150
	虜	2146
	蜂	1684
	裏	426
	褐	490
	裸	1205
	裾	1145
角	解	1955
	触	1954

	該	1640
言	詰	367
	誇	1332
	試	378
	詩	370
	詳	589
	誠	388
	誉	2089
	話	368
	詮	360
	詣	495
辛	辞	1613
豆	豊	1551
貝	資	512
	賊	381
	賃	1079
	賄	84
	賂	313
⻊	跡	1883
	践	1380
	跳	1378
	路	1376
	踪	1382
車	較	1370
	載	383
辰	農	2170
辶	遠	429
	遣	1910
	違	1773
	遜	1496
	遡	2111
酉	酬	1540
	酪	1541
金	鉛	857
	鉱	802
	鉄	909
	鉢	289
	鈴	1508
雨	電	574
	雷	454
	零	1504

隔 1409	模 244	聞 1754	領 1507	撮 885
革 靴 2042	構 1959	肉 腐 1099	餌 1588	撤 822
頁 頑 65	様 1003	廿 蔦 2095	餅 1590	撲 1932
頌 846	止 歴 402	蔑 392	馬 駅 2138	攵 敵 475
預 1721	穀 984	裳 863	駆 2137	敷 2028
頓 1610	演 2163	製 448	駄 2140	暫 1216
飼 2010	漁 184	複 504	髪 2074	暴 1941
飾 1587	漬 1665	言 語 371	鬼 魂 2177	木 横 1888
飽 1592	漆 1001	誤 2048	鼻 733	槽 1260
鳥 鳩 2096	漸 1217	誌 646		権 613
	漕 1259	誓 1214	**15 画**	標 1734
14 画	滴 474	説 538	イ 儀 1059	欠 歓 612
イ 像 2131	漂 1733	読 372	億 1058	潔 1668
僕 1933	漫 893	認 643	劇 2152	潤 1755
僚 1842	漏 1149	誘 982	口 嘱 2104	潟 2195
口 鳴 2092	熊 2159	豕 豪 582	器 127	潜 907
土 塾 331	獄 361	貌 2125	噴 1281	潮 152
境 523	瑠 1528	足 踊 1512	嘲 54	澄 1839
増 541	疋 疑 1513	辣 1798	土 墜 1404	熟 332
墨 187	瘍 1817	辶 遮 1276	墳 1282	勲 1808
大 奪 608	磁 1491	遭 1258	嬌 461	熱 1634
嫡 472	察 1184	適 473	審 2059	璃 1606
寡 664	禾 種 1810	酉 酵 1538	寮 1844	畿 1483
寧 897	稲 976	酷 1539	寸 導 296	皿 監 1562
蜜 838	穴 窪 1421	酸 1545	履 1137	盤 2017
尸 層 1146	立 端 1251	金 銀 1569	幣 1118	確 609
彰 1851	罰 896	銃 824	弊 1119	禾 稼 959
彳 徳 950	竹 箇 2185	銭 394	影 1848	稿 958
徴 952	管 1365	銑 288	徹 951	穂 975
態 2161	算 1017	銅 290	潰 1911	稽 983
慕 683	箸 1348	銘 293	慰 1177	穴 窮 1424
慢 892	米 精 1655	門 閣 1752	慶 2157	窯 1423
憎 673	糸 維 1441	関 2173	憂 663	罷 2188
慣 674	綱 2114	閥 1746	慮 2151	罵 2143
摘 709	緒 1444	隠 1410	憤 1283	竹 箱 1013
歌 508	総 1466	際 1392	憬 682	範 1516
旗 1901	綿 1467	障 1393	憧 681	糸 縁 1472
日 暮 247	網 1473	隹 雑 604	戯 2149	緩 2102
暦 226	緑 1471	雌 605	撃 766	緊 1474
膜 248	練 1443	需 1249	摩 689	縄 1477
木 概 1594	綻 1439	青 静 1660	摯 1624	線 1438

締 1440
編 1966
舞 1912
舗 1982
艹 蔵 913
蔽 1120
膚 2147
蝶 560
行 衝 1811
褒 1073
言 謁 489
課 1204
諸 1351
請 1656
諾 375
誕 420
談 374
調 373
論 1961
諦 467
誰 598
貝 賛 906
賜 1131
賭 1354
質 1219
賞 859
賠 515
賓 550
賦 404
趣 883
⻊ 踏 1381
輝 324
車 輩 1765
輪 1963
辶 遺 1909
遵 2187
遷 1737
選 1944
金 鋭 539
鋳 1688
閲 1745
雨 震 2166
霊 1930
養 1591
餓 1586
頬 1358
馬 駒 2133
駐 2136
魅 2179
黒 黙 255

16 画

亻 儒 1250
冫 凝 1515
土 墾 2124
壁 1616
壌 1649
壇 631
壊 427
奮 607
女 嬢 1650
憩 658
憲 1674
憶 679
懐 891
憾 678
操 724
擁 1488
攵 整 1800
曇 453
木 機 1482
橋 460
激 536
濁 898
濃 2171
膨 1855
樹 1554
火 燃 549
獣 2083
獲 757
磨 638
禾 穏 1230
積 1663
竹 築 1021
篤 2142
篭 1022
糖 1242
糸 縦 1436
縛 1476
繁 1435
縫 1685
臼 興 1533
艹 薫 1812
薪 1620
薦 2156
薄 242
薬 1873
膳 1113
緻 1437
虫 融 1123
衡 957
衛 1775
親 1621
貝 賢 915
言 諮 514
謀 1897
諭 376
謡 2119
諧 486
輸 307
醒 1677
辶 還 900
避 1618
緯 1774
金 錦 439
鋼 2113
錯 1269
錠 409
錘 1708
錬 2186
録 1226
錮 623
隣 1408
隷 2192
頁 頭 1549
頼 1794
館 1589
骸 1641
麺 1654

17 画

亻 償 1060
優 1068
厳 2086
嚇 2182
懇 2123
戴 1938
擦 1185
擬 1514
濯 619
曖 797
臆 655
燥 228
爵 1573
犠 693
王 環 899
療 1845
瞳 469
瞭 1843
矯 1306
礁 600
翼 1937
糸 縮 1434
績 1662
繊 1929
聴 890
覧 919
言 謄 1296
謙 1726
講 1957
謝 1339
謹 1698
謎 994
購 1958
車 轄 1672
醜 2176
鍛 2004
鍵 418
鍋 1388
闇 1748
霜 455
頁 頻 399
鮮 590
齢 1505

18 画

懲 953
曜 618
濫 1563
藍 1565
璧 1617
癒 2193
癖 1826
瞬 880
礎 421
穫 974
竹 簡 1749
糧 995
織 1432
繕 1433
翻 2060
繭 2025
職 887
艹 藤 1295
藩 2061
襟 1180
覆 1738
臣 臨 918
観 614
贈 542
金 鎌 1725
鎖 2087
鎮 294
闘 1757
離 1605

難 1703
韓 1776
頁 題 415
額 316
顎 1333
顔 1853
顕 1928
類 1000
馬 騎 2135
騒 2139
験 2134
鯉 188

19 画
瀬 1795
璽 2194
爆 1942
竹 簿 1020
繰 1469
羅 1442
臓 914
艶 1892
艹 藻 2191
覇 2043
識 521
譜 1926
警 358

蹴 2122
金 鏡 522
霧 1314
韻 520
頁 願 143
髄 1385
鯨 337
鶏 2097
麓 2155
麗 2158

20 画
懸 1495
欄 1756

競 465
籍 1689
言 議 692
譲 1648
護 756
醸 1647
金 鐘 470
響 1994
騰 2144

21 画
艦 2020
躍 1379
露 1377

頁 顧 1165
鶴 2093
魔 2178

22 画
襲 2181
驚 2141

23 画
鑑 1564

29 画
鬱 2120

Key Words and Primitive Meanings

This final Index contains a cumulative list of all the key words and primitive meanings used in this book. Key words are listed with their respective kanji and frame number. Primitive meanings are listed in italics and are followed only by the number of the page (also in italics) on which they are first introduced.

I (one)	壱	496	add	加	932	amass	蓄	1486
II (two)	弐	379	address	宛	1521	ambition	望	528
			adhere	付	1075	ancestor	祖	1918
A			adjusted	斉	1866	*angel*		*165*
			admirable	偉	1772	angle	角	1953
abacus		*325*	admonish	警	358	angling	釣	291
abandon	棄	820	adore	崇	1182	angry	怒	759
abbreviation	略	314	adroit	巧	1329	animal	獣	2083
abdomen	腹	503	advance	進	603	*animal legs*		*35*
abet	援	2101	*aerosol can*		*134*	animal sacrifice	牲	1680
abide by	遵	2187	affair	件	1032	*animal tracks*		*406*
ability	能	2160	affinity	縁	1472	annexed	添	684
abolish	廃	1841	affixed	附	1400	anti-	反	779
about that time	頃	479	afflicted	患	650	*antique*		*167*
above	上	50	Africa	阿	1391	anxiety	煩	175
above-stated	該	1640	again	再	1956	apologize	謝	1339
abundant	裕	856	again, or	又	752	appear	顕	1928
abuse	弊	1119	age	齢	1505	appellation	称	971
accept	受	794	aggression	攻	352	*apple*		*379*
accept humbly	戴	1938	agreement	肯	400	apply	応	653
accidentally	偶	2105	agriculture	農	2170	apprehend	逮	1244
accompany	従	942	aid	扶	902	apprehensive	畏	2069
accomplished	達	591	aim at	狙	1917	approve	賛	906
accumulate	累	1464	alienate	疎	1797	apricot	杏	215
accusation	訴	1221	all	皆	484	*apron*		*161*
accustomed	慣	674	alliance	盟	1558	arc	弧	2023
achievement	功	927	allot	充	823	ardent	烈	877
acid	酸	1545	alms	施	1124	argument	論	1961
acknowledge	認	643	*altar*		*279*	*arm*		*442*
acorn		*344*	alternate	迭	910	arm	腕	1522
acquiesce	承	2050						
acupuncturist		*32*						

armor 甲 1194
armpit 脇 935
army 軍 323
aroused 憤 1283
arrest 拘 706
arrival 到 817
aroma 匂 478
arrogance 傲 1054
arrow 143
art 術 1644
artificial 46
artisan 匠 1828
artist, performing 伎 1040
ascend 登 1838
ashes 灰 180
Asia 亜 1950
aside, set 措 1272
assault 殴 1833
assembly line 268
assets 資 512
assistant 佐 1024
association 組 1914
assurance 確 609
astray 迷 992
astringent 渋 1875
atmosphere 雰 2184
attack 襲 2181
attend 仕 1033
attire 装 425
attitude 態 2161
attractive 嬌 461
audience 謁 489
augment 殖 874
auspicious 祥 1169
authority 権 613
autumn 秋 966
auxiliary 陪 1396
awakening 醒 1677
awe 敬 356
awl 368
ax 斤 1206
axis 軸 1193

B

babe, newborn 児 62
back 裏 426
bad 悪 1951

badge 章 464
bag 俵 1667
baggage 荷 1088
bake 焼 1284
ball 111
ball 球 1005
ballot 票 1732
bamboo 竹 1007
bamboo grass 笹 1010
bamboo hat 笠 1009
banner 272
banquet 宴 203
barbarian 蛮 1884
bargain 廉 1727
barley 麦 3
baron 爵 1573
barracks 屯 2189
bartending 酌 1536
baseball (team) 18
bases 塁 1871
basin 盆 1557
basket 篭 1022
bathe 浴 852
bay 浦 1980
beach 岸 1782
beans 豆 1548
bear 熊 2159
beat 撃 766
beautiful woman 媛 2100
beauty 美 587
beckon 招 702
bed 床 636
bee 蜂 1684
before 先 263
beforehand 予 1719
beg 乞 501
beginning 元 63
beguile 惑 661
behind 後 1479
bell 鐘 470
bell, small 鈴 1508
belong 属 2103
below 下 51
belt 161
bend 曲 1256
benefit 益 2026
benevolence 徳 950

bequeath 遺 1909
best regards 宜 1922
bestow 与 1335
bewitched 妖 458
Big Dipper 斗 1261
bill, post a 貼 60
bin 函 2051
bird 鳥 2091
bird, sign of the 酉 1534
bird, white 28
birdhouse 229
bitter 辣 1798
black 黒 186
black ink 墨 187
bladder, gall 胆 31
blade 刃 88
blame 責 1661
Bldg. 館 1589
blessing 福 1171
blind 盲 525
block letters 楷 485
block, printing 版 1298
blocks, building 299
block up 塞 1646
blood 血 1556
blossom 咲 2174
blow 吹 506
blue 青 1654
blue, marine 瑠 1528
blue, navy 紺 1895
bluffs 崖 841
boar 猪 1352
board 搭 698
boast 誇 1332
boat 舟 2012
body 体 1030
body, part of 19
boil 煮 1346
boisterous 騒 2139
bomb 爆 1942
bond 債 1664
bone 240
bonsai 352
book 本 224
boom 盛 1567
borrow 借 1270
bosom 胸 1604

both	両 1252	
bottle, genie in the	221	
bottle, whiskey	331	
bottom	底 1975	
bough	枝 770	
boulder	岩 832	
boulevard	249	
boulevard	街 955	
bound up	36	
boundary	境 523	
bountiful	豊 1551	
bow	弓 1317	
bowl	鉢 289	
bowstring	弦 1487	
box	371	
box	箱 1013	
box, measuring	升 42	
boy	坊 531	
bracing	爽 1608	
brain	脳 2084	
brains	19	
branch	支 768	
branch off	岐 834	
brandish	揮 715	
break	毀 1532	
breasts	54	
breath	息 657	
breed	牧 351	
brew	醸 1647	
briar	茨 511	
bribe	賄 84	
bridegroom	婿 422	
bridge	橋 460	
bright	明 20	
bring up	育 821	
broaden	拡 801	
brocade	錦 439	
broom	28(	
brother, elder	兄 107	
brother, younger	弟 1328	
brown	褐 490	
brush	134	
brush, writing	筆 1014	
brush-stroke	画 1254	
bubble	泡 572	
bubble up	湧 1510	
buckle	160	
bud	芽 2054	
Buddha	仏 1037	
Buddhist priest	僧 1057	
Buddhist temple	寺 170	
build	建 417	
building blocks	299	
bullet	弾 2081	
bullrush	蒲 1981	
bull's eye	的 73	
bullying	苛 240	
bundle	束 1793	
bungling	拙 831	
burdensome	駄 2140	
bureau	局 1147	
bureaucrat	官 1363	
burglar	賊 381	
burn	燃 549	
bury	埋 191	
bushel basket	380	
bushes	349	
bustle	奔 1280	
busy	忙 665	
but of course	況 156	
butcher	125	
butterfly	蝶 560	
buttocks	尻 1134	
buy	買 894	
by means of	以 1105	
by one's side	46	
bystander	傍 1090	

C

cabbage	351	
cadet	曹 1257	
calamity	禍 1386	
calculate	算 1017	
calendar	暦 226	
calf, golden	422	
call on	訪 534	
call	呼 1597	
calling card	391	
calm	穏 1230	
camellia	椿 1691	
camp	陣 1402	
camphor tree	楠 1741	
can	可 97	
can, aerosol	134	

can, tin	缶 2116	
candle	60	
candlestick	115	
cannon	砲 571	
canopy	幌 438	
canopy, glass	83	
cap	帽 436	
cape	埼 164	
capital	京 334	
capital suburbs	畿 1483	
capsize	覆 1738	
captive	虜 2146	
captured	囚 1094	
car	車 304	
carbuncle	瘍 1817	
carp	鯉 188	
carrier	般 2016	
carry	運 325	
cart	124	
carve	彫 1846	
cash	幣 1118	
casting	鋳 1688	
castle	城 387	
cat	猫 259	
catalpa	梓 1614	
catch	捕 1978	
cauldron	76	
cauldron	釜 1367	
cause	因 626	
cave	208	
cavern	窟 1420	
caverns	295	
cavity	孔 100	
cedar	杉 1849	
ceiling	15	
celebrate	祝 1170	
celery	345	
cell	350	
censure	劾 1642	
center	央 1877	
cereal	251	
cereals	穀 984	
ceremony	儀 1059	
chafe	摩 689	
chain	36	
chain	鎖 2087	
chair	椅 218	

challenge	挑	710	cleanse	汰	149	companion	朋	19
chamber, public	堂	861	clear the land	拓	703	company	社	1173
change	化	1083	clear up	晴	1658	compare	比	482
chant	唱	21	cleverness	敏	498	compass		181
chapel		247	cliff		59	compensation	賠	515
chapter	課	1204	climate	候	1769	compilation	編	1966
char	焦	599	climax	至	815	complete	了	101
character	字	197	clique	閥	1746	computer		80
charcoal	炭	833	cloak		156	comrade	輩	1765
chariot		129	clock		356	concave	凹	33
chase	追	1359	clod	塊	2180	conceal	隠	1410
chastise	討	364	closed	閉	1751	concentrated	濃	2171
checkup	診	1860	clothes hanger		397	concept	想	656
cheek	頰	1358	clothesline		365	concerning	就	2121
cheerful	快	1771	clothing	服	1501	concurrently	兼	1723
cherry tree	桜	2082	cloud	雲	452	condolences	弔	1319
chess piece	棋	1900	cloud of, rising		162	condor		415
chestnut	栗	1735	cloudy weather	曇	453	confectionary	菓	1203
chestnut, horse	栃	553	co-	協	937	confer	叙	1789
chic	粋	993	coach	督	776	conflagration		76
chicken	鶏	2097	coarse	粗	1915	confront	抗	700
chief	伯	1041	cocoon		322	Confucian	儒	1250
chihuahua		105	cocoon	繭	2025	confused	錯	1269
child	子	99	code	典	1969	congeal	凝	1515
child, with	娠	2168	coffin	棺	1364	congratulations	賀	933
chin	顎	1333	coin	銭	394	conjecture	推	716
chink	隙	1394	cold	寒	1645	connection	関	2173
chirp	鳴	2092	collapse	陥	1412	consent	諾	375
choose	択	1155	collar	襟	1180	consider	考	1341
chop	析	1207	colleague	僚	1842	consign	託	2066
chop off	斬	1215	collide	衝	1811	consolation	慰	1177
chop-seal		326	color	色	1890	consort	伴	1287
chopsticks	箸	1348	coloring	彩	1850	conspire	謀	1897
Christmas tree		352	column		248	constancy	恒	667
chronicle	紀	1454	column	欄	1756	constitution	憲	1674
chrysanthemum	菊	996	column, spinal	脊	268	consult with	諮	514
cinnabar	丹	2196	comb		290	consume	喫	1670
circle	円	1952	come	来	2029	consummate	遂	579
circumference	周	339	come apart			contact	触	1954
city walls		394	at the seams	綻	1439	contain	容	853
clam		37	come in		235	contend	争	1238
clan	藩	2061	comfortable	庸	1266	continue	続	1445
clap	拍	704	commander	帥	1362	contraption	械	732
clasp	摯	1624	commandment	戒	730	contrast	較	1370
class	級	1453	commence	始	809	control	轄	1672
claw	爪	784	committee	委	979	convenience	便	1066
clean	浄	1239	commoner	庶	1275	convex	凸	34

conveyor	搬	2018	crowded	込	843	deer	鹿	2154
cook	炊	507	*crown*		128	*deer, painting of*		421
cooking fire		76	crown	冠	326	defeat	負	67
cool	冷	1506	crude	朴	220	defense	衛	1775
copper	銅	290	cruel	酷	1539	defer	讓	1648
copy	写	1336	crumble	崩	836	defile	潰	1911
cord	索	1465	cry	泣	463	degenerate	堕	1411
core	奥	997	crystal	璃	1606	degrees	度	1278
corner	隅	2108	cultivate	培	516	deliberation	議	692
cornerstone	礎	421	*cup, measuring*		292	delicate	微	954
cornstalk		353	cupfuls	杯	1304	delicious	旨	493
cornucopia		343	current	流	826	delight	歓	612
correct	正	405	curriculum	歴	402	deliver	届	1191
corridor	廊	1996	curse	呪	108	deluge	洪	1939
cosmetics	粧	991	curtain	幕	437	delusion	妄	526
cottage	舎	338	cut	切	89	demand	需	1249
cotton	綿	1467	cylinder	筒	1015	demolition	壊	427
countenance	貌	2125				den	洞	193
country	国	624	**D**			departed	逝	1213
country, home	邦	1991	*dagger*		48	department	科	1263
county	郡	1986	dainty	細	1463	deposit	預	1721
courage	勇	1509	dairy products	酪	1541	depression	窪	1421
courts	廷	547	damage	損	719	derision	嘲	54
courtyard	庭	634	damp	湿	1927	descend	降	1405
cover over	蔽	1120	dance	舞	1912	descendants	昆	483
covet	貪	1713	dangerous	危	1520	design	柄	1097
cow	牛	260	daring	敢	889	desk	机	223
cow, sign of the	丑	2197	dark, pitch	闇	1748	destitution	乏	1300
cowardice	臆	655	darkness	暗	519	destroy	滅	390
cowl		83	darning	繕	1433	detach	離	1605
craft	工	80	dart	矢	1305	detailed	詳	589
cram school	塾	331	daughter	娘	1581	detain	留	1529
cramped	狭	1356	day	日	12	determine	定	408
crane	鶴	2093	daybreak	暁	1285	*devil*		183
crash	墜	1404	daytime	昼	1156	dew	露	1377
create	造	299	death	死	878	diagonal	斜	1791
creek	江	148	decameron	旬	71	diameter	径	947
crest, family	紋	1863	decay	朽	1331	diamond	菱	1635
cricket, game of		60	deceased	亡	524	diarrhea	痢	1821
Cricket, Talking		413	deceit	欺	1899	*dice*		406
crime	犯	1517	decide	決	1770	*diced*		17
crimson	紅	1455	decline	衰	2037	difference	違	1773
criticism	批	701	decorate	飾	1587	difficult	難	1703
crock, lidded		133	decrease	耗	2063	dig	掘	1141
crossing	辻	297	dedicate	奉	1695	dike	堤	416
crotch		223	deed, meritorious	勲	1808	dilate	脹	2073
crow	烏	2094	deep	深	1426	diligence	勤	1700

dilute 薄 242
dining tray 膳 1113
direction 方 529
director 司 2007
dirt 72
dirty 汚 1334
disaster 災 179
discard 捨 707
discharge 発 1840
discipline 修 1858
disclose 啓 1166
disconcerted 慌 671
discontinue 絶 1891
discreet 謹 1698
discriminating 識 521
discuss 談 374
dish 皿 1555
dislike 嫌 1724
dispatch 遣 1910
display 呈 280
dispose 処 318
disquieting 惧 680
dissolve 融 1123
distant 遠 429
distinction 差 593
distract 紛 1458
distress 愁 967
distribute 配 1544
disturb 妨 530
ditch 堀 1142
divide 剖 517
divining rod 32
do 為 2067
doctor 医 1829
document 誌 646
dog 犬 253
dog, large 57
dog, sign of the (戌) 427
dog, St. Bernard 57
dog tag 394
dollar sign 302
domesticate 飼 2010
don 着 594
donburi 丼 1947
door 戸 1157
door, front 扉 1766
dormitory 寮 1844

dose 剤 1867
doth 致 818
double 倍 1067
double back 175
doubt 疑 1513
dove 28
Dr. 博 48
draft 稿 958
drag 396
dragon 竜 575
dragon, sign
of the 辰 2164
drama 劇 2152
draw near 寄 204
dreadful 怖 670
dream 夢 327
drift 漂 1733
drink 飲 1584
drip 滴 474
drive 駆 2137
droop 垂 1705
drop of 27
drop, to 245
drought 乾 502
drown 没 763
drowning 溺 1324
drowsy 睡 1707
drum 333
drum 鼓 1552
drunk 酔 1543
dry 干 1777
ducks, migrating 412
dull 鈍 1611
duplicate 複 504
duty 役 949
dwell 住 1027
dwindle 減 391
dye 染 548

E

each 各 311
ear 耳 881
ear of a plant 穂 975
early 早 26
earnings 稼 959
earthworm 340
east 東 543

easy 易 1130
eat 食 1582
eaves 宇 1785
echo 響 1994
ecstasy 悦 666
edge 端 1251
edict, imperial 詔 366
eel 195
effulgent 旺 278
egg 卵 1526
ego 我 690
eight 八 8
elbow 229
elbow 肘 46
elder brother 兄 107
elder sister 姉 442
elect 選 1944
electricity 電 574
elementary 素 1652
elephant 象 2130
elucidate 詮 360
elude 逸 2127
embarrass 辱 2165
embrace 抱 697
eminent 卓 52
emotion 感 662
emperor 皇 279
employ 雇 1164
employee 員 59
empress 后 2005
empty 空 1414
emulate 倣 1053
enclosure 郭 1985
encounter 遭 1258
encourage 励 931
encroach 侵 1231
end 終 1452
endure 忍 642
enemy 敵 475
England 英 1878
engrave 刻 1639
enlightenment 悟 669
enroll 籍 1689
enter 入 842
entertain 興 1533
entice 誘 982
entrails 臓 914

entrust	嘱	2104
entwine	絡	1450
envious	羨	592
environs	辺	302
epidemic	疫	1824
envy	嫉	1820
equal	匹	1830
equestrian	騎	2135
equilibrium	衡	957
equip	備	1267
erect	架	934
erupt	噴	1281
escape	逃	301
Esq.	様	1003
establishment	設	765
esteem	尚	196
etc.	等	1016
eternity	永	139
ethics	倫	1962
Europe	欧	1834
evade	避	1618
evaluate	評	1599
even	平	1596
evening	夕	114
eventide	汐	115
every	毎	497
everywhere	遍	1965
evidence	証	406
exam	校	1371
examination	検	1803
example	例	1046
excel	秀	980
excellent	佳	1044
exchange	替	905
exclude	除	1787
excuse	免	2126
exertion	勉	2129
exhaust	尽	1152
exhort	奨	790
exist	在	740
exit	出	829
expand	伸	1199
expense	費	1326
expert	師	1361
explanation	説	538
exploits	績	1662
expose	披	868

exquisite	妙	130
extent	程	960
extinguish	消	155
extract	抄	699
extremity	末	230
eye	目	15
eyeball		20
eyeball	眼	1577
eyebrow	眉	2045
eyedropper		27

F

fabricate	築	1021
face	顔	1853
faceup	仰	1836
facsimile	謄	1296
faction	派	1999
failure	敗	353
faint	幽	1480
faith	信	1043
fall	落	320
falsehood	偽	2068
family crest	紋	1863
family name	氏	1970
fan	扇	1160
fare	賃	1079
farm	畑	178
fascination	魅	2179
fasten	括	714
fat	脂	494
fat man		30
fate	命	1502
father	父	1366
fathom	測	160
favor	恵	659
fear	恐	660
feathers	羽	615
feathers, tail		407
fee	料	1262
feed	餌	1588
feelings	情	1657
fell	伐	1069
female	雌	605
fence	塀	1136
fenceposts		377
fermentation	酵	1538
fertilizer	肥	1893

fervent	篤	2142
few	少	111
fiber	維	1441
field, rice	田	14
fierce	猛	1566
fiesta		144
fight	闘	1757
figure	姿	513
file	列	875
filial piety	孝	1342
fine	緻	1437
finger	指	711
fingerprint		328
fingers		216
finish	済	1868
fire	火	173
fire, cooking/oven		76
fireplace		76
firewood	薪	1620
first time	初	431
fish	魚	183
fish guts	乙	75
fishhook		44
fishing	漁	184
fist		221
fist	拳	1290
fit	合	269
five	五	5
flag		274
flag, national	旗	1901
flames		76
flats	軒	1781
flavor	味	233
fledgling		228
flesh		19
flip	翻	2060
float		148
floating	浮	787
flock	群	1247
flood		64
floor		15
flour	粉	988
flourish	栄	348
flower		97
flower	花	1084
flower pot	瓶	1109
fluid	液	1116

flute 笛 1192
fly 飛 2032
flying horse 203
focus 省 131
fog 霧 1314
fold 折 1211
follow 随 1395
following, the 翌 617
fond 好 103
food 336
foolish 愚 2107
foot of a mountain 麓 2155
footgear 履 1137
foothold 拠 722
footprint 149
forces 勢 1633
ford 渉 398
forehead 額 316
forest 森 209
forge 鍛 2004
forget 忘 640
formerly 曽 540
fortune-telling 占 49
foster 養 1591
four 四 4
fragrant 薫 1812
frame 枠 212
free, set 放 535
freight 貨 1085
fresh 鮮 590
friend 友 760
frolic 戯 2149
from 乃 741
front door 扉 1766
front, in 前 309
frost 霜 455
frozen 凍 545
frugal 倹 1804
fruit 果 1202
full 満 1253
fundamentals 基 1904
funnel 391
fur 毛 2062
furrow 畝 1093

G

gain 得 941

gall bladder 胆 31
gamble 賭 1354
game hunting 猟 2090
game of cricket 60
garden 苑 1523
garment 衣 423
gates 門 1743
gather 集 601
gauze 羅 1442
gem, holed 璧 1617
general 総 1466
generation 世 28
genesis 創 1759
genie (in the bottle) 221
genius 才 736
gentle 妥 785
gentleman 士 341
genuine 純 1609
germ 菌 985
ghost 鬼 2175
gigantic 巨 920
girder 桁 956
gist 趣 883
give 呉 2046
renunciation 諦 467
gland 腺 141
glass canopy 83
gloom 鬱 2120
glossary 彙 1237
glossy 艶 1892
glue/glued to 31
gnats 193
Go 碁 1903
go in 235
go upstream 遡 2111
goat, mountain 414
go-between 仲 1029
godown 倉 1758
gods 神 1200
going 行 938
gold 金 287
golden calf 424
gone 去 812
good 良 1578
good luck 吉 342
goods 品 23
goodwill 款 1178

gorge 峡 1355
government office 庁 635
grab 采 791
grace 恩 652
graceful 淑 778
gracious 雅 2056
grade 段 2003
gradually 徐 1788
graduate 卒 1102
graft 賂 313
grains 粒 990
grains of rice 255
grains of sand 沙 151
grandchild 孫 1494
grant 賜 1131
grasp 把 1889
grass 草 238
grass, bamboo 笹 1010
grass skirt 346
grate 擦 1185
grave 墓 246
graveyard 99
greatness 傑 1074
green 緑 1471
grind 磨 638
grip 握 1139
grope 探 1425
ground 72
ground 地 554
*ground, sitting
on the* 169
groundbreaking 墾 2124
group 団 625
grove 林 208
grow late 更 749
grow up 347
grudge 怨 1524
guard 守 198
guess 察 1184
guest 客 315
guidance 導 296
guillotine 363
guilt 罪 1764
gulf 湾 1886
gully 237
gun 銃 824
gunwale 舷 2015

gutter	溝	1960	hear	聞	1754	horse		203
guy	奴	758	hearing	審	2059	horse	馬	2132
			heart	心	639	horse chestnut	栃	553
H			*hearth*		76	*horse, flying*		203
Hades	冥	322	hearth	炉	1161	horse, sign of the	(午)	427
haiku	俳	1761	heat	熱	1634	*horses, team of*		418
hair		408	heavens	天	457	hot water	湯	585
hair of the head	髪	2074	heavy	重	1805	hours, wee	宵	201
hair, lock of		407	hedge	垣	165	*house*		85
hairpin		408	hegemony	覇	2043	house	家	580
halberd	矛	1311	Heights	阪	1390	how many	幾	1481
half	半	1286	heir	嗣	2011	however	但	1026
hall	堂	861	*helmet*		83	hug	擁	1488
halo		336	help	助	1921	*human legs*		35
halt	停	1051	hem	裾	1145	humanity	仁	1063
hand	手	687	hemp	麻	637	humiliate	羞	2198
handle	扱	745	hermit	仙	1061	humility	慎	677
hands, outstretched		222	hide	匿	1827	hump	隆	1682
hands, two		219	high, piled	堆	596	hundred	百	38
hang	掛	727	highness	陛	1407	hundred million	億	1058
hanging scroll	幅	435	hill	丘	1427	hungry	飢	1585
hanker	憬	682	hillock	塚	1117	hunt	狩	258
happenstance	故	355	hinder	障	1393	hunting, game	猟	2090
happiness	幸	1622	hinge	枢	1832	hurry	急	1229
harbor	港	1940	history	史	747	husband	夫	901
hard up	窮	1424	hit	当	1236	husk	殻	767
harden	固	622	hoarse	喝	491			
hare, sign of the	卯	2199	hog, sign of the	亥	1637	**I**		
harm	害	1671	hoist	揚	717	I	吾	17
harmony	和	963	hold	持	712	*I beam*		46
harp	琴	1717	hole	穴	1413	*ice*		164
harvest	穫	974	holed gem	璧	1617	icicle	氷	138
hat, bamboo	笠	1009	holy	聖	888	idea	意	654
hat, top		130	home	宅	2065	ill	病	1813
hate	憎	673	home country	邦	1991	illuminate	照	182
haven	津	350	homecoming	帰	1316	imitation	模	244
hawser	綱	2114	hometown	郷	1993	immature	稚	962
haystack		295	honey	蜜	838	immediate	頓	1610
he	彼	948	honorable	御	1500	immersed	浸	1232
head		39	hooch	酎	1537	imminent	拶	713
head	頭	1549	*hood*		83	impart	授	795
head, place on the	頂	98	hooked	勾	800	imperial edict	詔	366
headland	岬	1196	hop	跳	1378	imperial order	勅	1796
headway, make	捗	728	hope	希	1602	in	中	39
heal	療	1845	horizon	涯	169	*in a row,*		
healing	癒	2193	horizontal	緯	1774	*upside down*		386
healthy	健	1048	*horns*		36	in front	前	309

incense 香 977
include 含 1712
income 収 1628
increase *184*
increase 増 541
incur 被 870
indications 徴 952
indigo 藍 1565
individual 個 1047
infancy 幼 1478
infant *232*
inferiority 劣 926
inflammation 炎 174
inflation 騰 2144
inherit 継 1470
ink, black 墨 187
inlay 填 166
inmost 衷 2038
inn 宿 1070
inquire 尋 1228
inscription 銘 293
insect 虫 556
insert 挿 1197
inside 内 1095
inspection 視 1174
Inst. 院 1401
instant 即 1572
instead 却 1497
instruction 訓 365
insult 罵 2143
intelligent 賢 915
intention 志 645
inter- 相 222
intercept 遮 1276
interchange 換 1122
interment 葬 879
interpretation 釈 2057
interrogative 那 1992
interval 間 1747
interview 遇 2106
intestines 腸 583
intimate 睦 1632
intimidate 威 389
introduce 紹 1459
intuition 勘 1906
invariably 必 685
inverted 逆 2109

investigate 査 1920
iron 鉄 909
iron, pig 銑 288
irrigate 沃 459
island 島 2098
isolate 隔 1409
Italy 伊 1245
item 箇 2185
ivy *74*

J

jail cell *362*
jammed in 介 265
Japanese Judas-
  tree 桂 210
jawbone *311*
jealous 妬 123
jewel 玉 272
jewel, squared 圭 167
join 併 1107
journey 往 945
jubilation 慶 2157
Judas-tree,
  Japanese 桂 210
judgment 判 1289
jump 踊 1512
junior 徒 943
jurisdiction 領 1507
just so 是 414
juvenile 童 468

K

kazoo *179*
ketchup *341*
key *363*
key 鍵 418
kick 蹴 2122
kidnap 拐 708
kidney 腎 916
kill 殺 1607
kiln 窯 1423
king 王 271
knee 膝 1002
knot *273*
know 知 1308
Korea 韓 1776
kudzu 葛 492

L

labor 労 924
lack 欠 505
lacquer 漆 1001
lad 彦 1852
ladle 勺 72
lady 婦 1234
lagoon 潟 2195
laid waste 荒 527
lake 湖 159
lament 悼 668
lamp 灯 177
land *72*
land 陸 1631
lap *133*
large 大 112
large hill 阜 1360
lass 嬢 1650
late, grow 更 749
laugh 笑 1008
laundry 濯 619
lazy 惰 676
lead (metal) 鉛 857
leader 将 789
leaf 葉 243
leak 漏 1149
lean 傾 1086
leap 躍 1379
learn 習 616
leather 革 2041
lecture 講 1957
left 左 81
leg 足 1372
leg, wooden *309*
legitimate wife 嫡 472
legs, animal *35*
legs, human *35*
legs, walking *125*
leisure 閑 1753
lend 貸 1082
length 丈 746
lengthen 張 2071
letters, block 楷 485
level 均 172
levy 賦 404
lewd 淫 788
license 允 827

lid	蓋	1561	lower	低	1973	matter	事	1240
lidded crock		133	lowly	卑	1629	mausoleum	陵	1636
lie	詐	1223	loyalty	忠	648	me	僕	1933
lie down	寝	1233	lucidity	澄	1839	meadow	原	142
life	生	1675	luck, good	吉	342	meal	飯	1583
lightly	軽	774	lumber	材	738	measurement	寸	45
lightning bug	蛍	557	lunatic	狂	277	measuring box	升	42
likeness	如	104	lungs	肺	443	*measuring cup*		292
lily, water		339	luxuriant	繁	1435	meat	肉	1098
limb	肢	771	*lying (down)*		173	mechanism	機	1482
limit	限	1576				mediator	媒	1898
line		248	**M**			medicine	薬	1873
line	線	1438	made in…	製	448	mediocre	凡	66
line, assembly		268	*maestro*		308	*meeting*		110
line up	陳	1398	*magic wand*		32	meeting	会	814
lineage	系	1492	magnet	磁	1491	melancholy	憂	663
linen	布	433	mail	郵	1990	mellow	熟	332
liner	舶	2013	*mailbox*		328	melodious	朗	1579
lips	唇	2169	majestic plural	朕	2183	melon	瓜	2022
listen	聴	890	make	作	1224	melt	溶	854
little	小	110	make a deal	商	471	membrane	膜	248
livelihood	暮	247	make headway	捗	728	memorize	覚	347
lively	活	154	male	雄	804	*mending*		152
liver	肝	1778	mama	母	105	mention	述	1643
livestock	畜	1485	man	男	923	mercy	慈	1490
load	載	383	*mandala*		242	merit	効	1369
location	場	584	*mane*		408	meritorious deed	勲	1808
lock	錠	409	maneuver	操	724	*metal*		115
lock of hair		407	manipulate	掌	864	metallurgy	冶	808
locket		364	mannerism	癖	1826	metaphor	喩	308
logic	理	283	many	多	113	method	法	813
loins	腰	1731	many, how	幾	1481	metropolis	都	1989
loneliness	寂	777	map	図	1264	mid-air	宙	1190
long	長	2070	*march*		147	*migrating ducks*		412
long time	久	1092	marine blue	瑠	1528	military officer	尉	1176
long-distance	距	1375	market	市	440	milk	乳	786
longevity	寿	1687	marketing	販	783	mimic	擬	1514
longing	欲	855	marquis	侯	1767	*mind, state of*		209
look back	顧	1165	marriage	婚	1972	mineral	鉱	802
look to	臨	918	marrow	髄	1385	mingle	交	1368
loose	漫	893	marry into	嫁	581	*mirror*		180
lord	主	284	marsh	沼	145	mirror	鏡	522
lose	失	908	martyrdom	殉	872	miscellaneous	雑	604
lose weight	痩	1818	mask	面	2039	miss	喪	2076
lot	譲	1649	masses	衆	2001	*missile*		225
love	愛	796	mat, tatami	畳	1923	*mist*		34
lovely	麗	2158	matrimony	姻	627	mistake	誤	2048

mix 混 487
mochi 餅 1590
model 塑 2110
modest 遜 1496
moment 利 1601
monks 83
monkey 282
monkey 猿 430
monkey, sign
  of the (申) 427
monme 勹 1104
month 月 13
moon 19
mop 289
more and more 弥 1322
moreover 且 2190
morning 朝 53
mortar 臼 1531
mosaic 380
mosquito 蚊 1864
mould 型 735
Mount 岡 2112
mountain 山 830
mountain, foot of a 麓 2155
mountain goat 414
mountain pass 峠 835
mountain stream 渓 903
mourning 忌 644
mouth 口 11
move 動 1806
Mr. 殿 1945
mud 泥 1135
mulberry 桑 754
municipality 府 1077
muscle 247
muscle 筋 1012
music 楽 1872
music, play 奏 1693
musical score 譜 1926
mutually 互 819
muzzle 177
myself 俺 1091
mysterious 玄 1484

N

nab 捉 1374
nail 51

naked 裸 1205
name 名 117
name, family 氏 1970
Nara 奈 1175
national flag 旗 1901
nativity 誕 420
navigate 航 2014
navy blue 紺 1895
near 近 1210
neck 首 74
need 要 1730
needle 18
needle 針 292
negate 否 1303
negative 不 1302
neglect 怠 806
neighboring 隣 1408
nest 巣 2077
netting 網 1473
new 新 1619
newborn babe 児 62
next 次 510
nickname 号 1330
nifty 凄 2036
night 夜 1115
nightbreak 旦 30
nightfall 晩 2128
nine 九 9
nitrate 硝 120
No. 第 1327
node 節 1574
Noh chanting 謡 2119
noodles 麺 1654
noon 午 610
north 北 480
nose 28
nose 鼻 733
nostrils 28
not 勿 1128
not yet 未 229
notebook 帳 2072
nothingness 無 1913
notice, put up a 掲 726
nourishing 滋 1489
now 今 1711
nucleus 核 1639
numb 萎 986

number 数 998
nun 尼 1133

O

oak 柏 211
oak, sweet 椎 597
oaken tub 384
obese 肪 533
obey 順 136
obituary 訃 363
obscure 昧 231
obvious 瞭 1843
occasion 際 1392
occupation 営 1111
ocean 洋 588
of 之 1299
office,
  government 庁 635
offering 献 1742
officer 吏 748
officer, military 尉 1176
oil 油 1188
old boy 君 1246
old man 老 1340
old man,
  venerable 翁 849
Old West 358
old 古 16
old woman 婆 867
olden times 旧 35
once upon a time 昔 1268
one 一 1
oneself 自 36
one-sided 片 1297
only 只 55
ooze 泌 686
open 開 1750
open sea 沖 146
or again 又 752
order, imperial 勅 1796
orderliness 諧 486
orders 令 1503
organize 整 1800
orphan 孤 2024
other 他 1034
ought 須 1854
outburst 暴 1941

outhouse		239
outline	概	1594
outlook	観	614
outside	外	116
outskirts	郊	1987
outstretched hands		222
oven fire		76
overall	統	1447
overcome	克	109
overdo	過	1389
overflow	濫	1563
overgrown	茂	384
overnight	泊	158
overpowering	豪	582
oversee	監	1562
overthrow	倒	1055
owl		409
oyster		37

P

pack of wild dogs		105
packed	詰	367
paddy ridge	畔	1288
page	頁	64
pagoda	塔	270
pain	痛	1825
paint	塗	1792
painting of a deer		421
pair	双	753
palisade	柵	1968
pan-	汎	147
paper	紙	1971
paper punch		316
parade		145
paragraph	項	86
parcel post	逓	2002
parch	燥	228
pardon	赦	1881
parent	親	1621
park	園	629
parking	駐	2136
part	分	844
part of the body		19
partial	偏	1964
particularly	殊	873
partition	頒	846
partner	侶	1025

parts of speech	詞	2009
party	党	860
patent	彰	1851
path	路	1376
pathetic	哀	428
patrol	巡	303
pattern	範	1516
paulownia	桐	216
pavilion	亭	333
pay	払	798
pay respects	伺	2008
peaceful	泰	1692
peach tree	桃	251
peak, mountain	峠	835
pear tree	梨	973
pearl	珠	274
pedestal	台	805
peel off	剥	1227
Pegasus		203
pelt	皮	865
penal	懲	953
penalty	罰	896
penetrate	徹	951
pent in		206
people	民	1976
pepper, red		341
perfect	完	199
performance	演	2163
performing artist	伎	1040
perfumed	芳	532
period	期	1902
perish		180
permit	許	611
persimmon	柿	441
person	人	1023
person in charge	係	1493
persuade	勧	928
perusal	覧	919
petition	願	143
phantasm	幻	2006
philosophy	哲	1212
phrase	句	69
pick	採	792
pick up	拾	720
pickling	漬	1665
picture	絵	1446
pierce	貫	106

piety, filial	孝	1342
pig iron	銑	288
pigeon	鳩	2096
piggy bank		197
piglets		197
piled high	堆	596
pillar	柱	286
pillow	枕	2034
pinch	摘	709
pine tree	松	848
pining	慕	683
pinnacle		312
pipe	管	1365
pit	坑	328
pitch dark	闇	1748
pity	惜	1271
place	所	1208
place on the head	頂	98
placement	置	895
placenta	胞	570
plaid		377
plains	野	1722
plan	案	227
plane	削	124
plank	板	781
plant	植	217
plant, rice	稲	976
plantation	栽	382
play	遊	1126
play music	奏	1693
pleasure	愉	675
pledge	契	1669
plot	計	359
plow		269
pluck	抽	1187
plug	栓	282
plug up	窒	1418
plum	梅	499
plump	太	126
plural, majestic	朕	2183
pocket	懐	891
podium	壇	631
poem	詩	370
Point	岳	1428
pointed	鋭	539
poison	毒	1651
pole (wooden)		88

poles	極	2052
polish	研	729
politics	政	407
pond	池	555
pony	駒	2133
pop song	唄	57
pork	豚	577
portable	携	742
portent	兆	250
porter		185
possess	有	83
post	職	887
post a bill	貼	60
post, parcel	逓	2002
posture	構	1959
pot	鍋	1388
pot, flower	瓶	1109
potato		366
potato	芋	1784
pottery	陶	2117
pour	注	285
poverty	貧	845
power	力	922
pox	痘	1815
practice	練	1443
praise	褒	1073
pray	祈	1209
precious	貴	1908
precipitous	険	1802
preface	序	1720
prefecture	県	552
pregnancy	妊	546
present	現	275
presents	贈	542
pressure	圧	163
previously	既	1593
price	値	1052
priest, Buddhist	僧	1057
princess	姫	912
printing	刷	1150
printing block	版	1298
prison	獄	361
private	私	968
prize	賞	859
proceed	赴	412
proclaim	宣	200
products	産	1681

profession	業	1931
profit	利	972
prohibition	禁	1179
prolong	延	419
promise	約	1462
promontory	崎	840
-proof	耐	1248
property	財	737
proportion	割	1673
propose	提	718
prosperous	昌	25
prostrated	伏	1035
protect	保	1072
provisional	仮	1039
provisions	糧	995
prudence	慮	2151
public	公	847
publish	刊	1779
pull	引	1318
punish	刑	734
pup tent		374
pupil	瞳	469
puppet		306
pure	清	1659
purification	斎	1869
purple	紫	1475
purse		383
pursue	逐	578
push	押	1195
put in		235
put up a notice	掲	726
puzzle		269

Q

quake	震	2166
quandary	困	621
quantity	量	189
quarter		297
quasi-	准	602
queen	妃	566
question	問	1744
quick	速	1799
quiet	静	1660
quit	罷	2188
quiver		144

R

| *rabbit* | | 417 |

radiance	輝	324
rag		273
rain	雨	451
rainbow	虹	559
raise	挙	2088
rake		288
ram, sign of the	(未)	427
range	域	380
rank	位	1028
rapidly	疾	1819
rapids	瀬	1795
rare	珍	1859
rather	寧	897
rat, sign of the	(子)	427
ratio	率	1874
ray	光	125
re-	戻	1162
reach out	及	743
read	読	372
reality	実	1694
reap	刈	1600
rebuke	諭	376
receipt		329
receive	享	330
recess	憩	658
recitation	詠	369
reclining		173
recollection	憶	679
recommend	薦	2156
record	録	1226
recreation	娯	2047
recruit	募	925
rectify	矯	1306
red	赤	1880
red pepper		341
reed	荻	257
reef	礁	600
refined	精	1655
reflect	映	1879
reformation	改	567
refreshing	涼	335
regiment	隊	1403
register	簿	1020
regularity	秩	969
reign	治	807
reject	斥	1220
rejoice	喜	1553

relatives 戚 385
relax 安 202
reliant 依 1045
religion 宗 1181
remainder 残 871
remains 骸 1641
remorse 憾 678
remote 悠 1031
remove 撤 822
rend 破 869
renowned 著 1347
reparation 償 1060
repay 酬 1540
repeatedly 頻 399
repel 拒 921
repent 悔 672
report 報 1625
repress 抑 1835
repudiate 排 1762
reputation 誉 2089
request 求 1004
research 究 1417
resemblance 肖 119
resentment 恨 1570
reside 居 1143
residence 邸 1984
resign 辞 1613
resin 345
resist 抵 1974
respect 恭 1943
respects, pay 伺 2008
responsibility 任 1078
rest 休 1038
restore 復 940
retainer 臣 911
retreat 退 1575
return 返 782
revelation 告 262
revered 尊 1547
review 閲 1745
revile 蔑 392
revise 訂 362
revolve 転 449
rhyme 韻 520
rhythm 律 939
ri 里 185
rice 米 987

rice field 田 14
rice, grains of 255
rice plant 稲 976
rice seedling 343
riddle 謎 994
ride 乗 1709
ridge, paddy 畔 1288
ridgepole 棟 544
ridicule 慢 892
right 右 82
righteousness 義 691
rin 厘 190
ring 環 899
riot 乱 76
rise up 昇 43
rising cloud of 162
rising sun 旭 27
risk 冒 18
ritual 祭 1183
river 河 157
road 122
road-way 道 295
roast 煎 310
rob 奪 608
robust 壮 343
rock 59
rod 棒 1697
rod, divining 32
romance 恋 1885
roof 屋 1138
room 室 816
root 根 1571
roots 281
rope 36
rope, straw 縄 1477
rot 腐 1099
rotation 旋 1125
round 丸 44
rouse 起 565
route 途 1790
row 並 1924
rowboat 艇 2021
rowing 漕 1259
rub 抹 694
rue 慨 1595
rule 則 92
run 走 410

run alongside 沿 858
rut 軌 306

S

saber 48
saber 剣 1801
sack 袋 1081
sacrifice 犠 693
sacrifice, animal 牲 1680
sad 悲 1763
safeguard 護 756
sagacious 俊 1089
sail 帆 434
saké 酒 1535
salad 294
salary 給 1449
saliva 唾 1706
salt 塩 1568
salutation 礼 1168
salvation 救 1006
same 同 192
samurai 134
sand 砂 122
sand, grains of 沙 151
sandwiched 挟 1357
sane 康 1243
sash 帯 444
sated 飽 1592
savings 貯 206
saw 286
say 言 357
sayeth 曰 620
saying 139
scaffold 桟 393
scale 366
scar 痕 1822
scarecrow 354
scarf 156
scarf, top hat and 156
scatter 散 1273
scenery 景 337
scheme 策 1019
scepter 111
school, cram 塾 331
schoolhouse 135
scissors 307
scold 叱 477

score, musical	譜	1926	shade	陰	1718	sign of the bird	酉	1534
scorn	侮	1064	shadow	影	1848	sign of the cow	丑	2197
scorpion		*191*	shake	振	2167	sign of the dog	(戌)	427
scrapbook		*391*	*shaku*	尺	1151	sign of the dragon	辰	2164
screwdriver		*293*	*shakuhachi*		*276*	sign of the hare	卯	2199
scribe	記	568	shallow	浅	395	sign of the hog	亥	1637
scroll	巻	1292	shame	恥	886	sign of the horse	(午)	427
scroll, hanging	幅	435	*shape*		*375*	sign of the
sea	海	500	shape	形	1847	monkey	(申)	427
sea, open	沖	146	*sheaf*		*339*	sign of the ram	(未)	427
seacoast	浜	1430	sheep	羊	586	sign of the rat	(子)	427
seal	封	168	sheet of	枚	354	sign of the snake	巳	2200
seal, chop-		*326*	*shelf*		*384*	sign of the tiger	寅	2162
seams, come apart			shelf	棚	214	signature	署	1349
at the	綻	1439	shellfish	貝	56	signpost	標	1734
search	捜	1201	*shells*		*37*	*silage*		*354*
seasons	季	978	shield	盾	1997	silence	黙	255
seat	席	1277	shift	移	964	silk	絹	1468
seaweed	藻	2191	shining	昭	91	silkworm	蚕	562
second	秒	965	shins	脚	1498	*silver*		*334*
second		*176*	Shinto shrine	宮	1110	silver	銀	1569
secrecy	密	837	ship	船	2019	similar	似	1106
secret	秘	970	shish kebab	串	649	simple	単	2078
section	部	1988	shoes	靴	2042	simplicity	簡	1749
seduce	召	90	*shoot*		*280*	sincerity	誠	388
see	見	61	shoot	射	1338	single	独	561
seedling	苗	249	shop	舗	1982	sink	沈	2033
seethe	沸	1325	short	短	1550	Sino-	漢	1701
seize	獲	757	shoulder	肩	1158	sire	紳	1461
self	己	564	shouldering	担	721	sister, elder	姉	442
self-effacing	謙	1726	shout	叫	1626	sister, younger	妹	234
selfish	恣	641	shove	挨	1310	sit	座	1100
sell	売	345	*shovel*		*291*	*sitting on the*
semi-	準	606	show	示	1167	*ground*		*169*
send back	還	900	*shredder*		*271*	six	六	6
send off	送	2172	shrine, Shinto	宮	1110	skeleton	骨	1383
sentence	文	1861	shrine, visit a	詣	495	sketch	描	723
separate	別	94	shrink	縮	1434	skill	技	769
sequential	循	1998	shudder	慄	1736	skin	膚	2147
set	据	1144	sickle	鎌	1725	skirt	裳	863
set aside	措	1272	*sickness*		*370*	*skirt, grass*		*346*
set free	放	535	side	側	1049	*skunk*		*416*
settlement	納	1456	*side, by one's*		*46*	slacken	緩	2102
seven	七	7	sideways	横	1888	slap	撲	1932
severance	断	1218	*siesta*		*171*	*slave*		*245*
sew	縫	1685	*sieve*		*289*	slave	隷	2192
sex	性	1679	sigh	嘆	1702	sleep	眠	1977

sleeve	袖	1189	special	特	261	state	州	135
slender	繊	1929	specialty	専	47	*state of mind*		209
slingshot		*304*	species	種	1810	station	駅	2138
slip out	抜	761	specimen	鑑	1564	stationery	箋	1011
slippery	滑	1384	speckled	斑	1865	statue	像	2131
slope	坂	780	*speech*		*139*	stature	背	481
slow	遅	1148	speech, parts of	詞	2009	status	格	312
small bell	鈴	1508	sphere	圏	1293	status quo	状	254
smash	砕	121	spicy	辛	1612	steadily	漸	1217
smoke	煙	1739	*spike*		*51*	steal	盗	1559
snake		*193*	spinal column	脊	268	stealth	窃	1419
snake	蛇	558	spindle	錘	1708	steam	蒸	2049
snake, sign of the	巳	2200	spine	呂	24	steel	鋼	2113
snapshot	撮	885	spinning	紡	1457	step	踏	1381
snare		*303*	spiny	梗	751	stern	厳	2086
sniff	嗅	129	spirit	気	2030	*stick, walking*		*27*
snow	雪	1225	spirits	霊	1930	sticky	粘	989
so-and-so	某	1896	spit	吐	162	stiff	硬	750
sociable	懇	2123	splash	沫	232	stimulate	促	1373
soft	軟	509	splendor	華	1704	stinking	臭	128
soil	土	161	split	裂	876	stipend	俸	1696
soldier	兵	1429	sponsor	催	1062	stirred up	奮	607
solely	唯	595	*spool*		*226*	stocks	株	236
solemn	粛	1870	spoon	匕	476	stomach	胃	29
solicit	請	1656	spot	点	181	stone	石	118
solution	答	1018	sprain	挫	1101	stop	止	396
somebody	身	1337	spread	敷	2028	store	店	632
someone	者	1345	spring	泉	140	storehouse	蔵	913
son	郎	1995	springtime	春	1690	storm	嵐	839
song	歌	508	*sprout*		*280*	story	階	1406
song, pop	唄	57	spy	偵	1056	straightaway	直	77
sort	類	1000	squad	班	1315	strand	渚	1353
sort of thing	然	256	squared jewel	圭	167	strange	奇	133
soul	魂	2177	squeeze	搾	1422	strangle	絞	1448
sound	音	518	St. Bernard dog		*57*	stratum	層	1146
soup	汁	150	stab	突	1416	*straw man*		*296*
source	源	153	stagnate	滞	445	straw rope	縄	1477
south	南	1740	stalk	茎	772	stream	川	134
sovereign	帝	466	*stamp*		*325*	stream, mountain	渓	903
sow		*196*	stamp	印	1530	street	丁	95
span	亙	32	stand up	立	462	*stretch*		*154*
spare time	暇	2027	standard	規	904	strict	堅	917
spark		*60*	*staple gun*		*397*	strike	打	705
sparkle	晶	22	*staples*		*329*	strong	強	1321
sparkler		*378*	star	星	1676	*strung together*		*387*
speaketh	申	1198	stare	眺	252	stubborn	頑	65
spear		*301*	starve	餓	1586	study	学	346

stupid	痴	1814
sturdy	剛	2115
style	式	377
subjugate	征	946
submerge	潜	907
submit	供	1935
subscription	購	1958
substance	質	1219
substitute	代	1080
suburbs, capital	畿	1483
suck	吸	744
suckle	哺	1979
sue	訟	850
suffering	苦	239
sugar	糖	1242
suitable	適	473
sulfur	硫	825
sultry	暑	1350
summer	夏	317
summit	峰	1683
sun		19
sun, rising	旭	27
sunflower		24
sunglasses		241
sunglasses with		
one lens out		271
sunshine	陽	1397
superfluous	冗	321
superintend	宰	1615
supplement	補	1983
suppose	存	739
surface	表	1666
surname	姓	1678
surpass	越	413
surplus	剰	1710
surround	囲	1948
suspend	懸	1495
suspicious	怪	773
sūtra	経	1460
swamp	沢	1153
sweat	汗	1780
sweep	掃	1235
sweet	甘	1894
sweet oak	椎	597
swell	膨	1855
swift	迅	298
swim	泳	144

swing	揺	2118
sword	刀	87
symptoms	症	1816
system	制	447

T

table		332
tag	札	225
tail	尾	2064
tail feathers		407
tailor	裁	424
take	取	882
take along	連	305
tale	話	368
Talking Cricket		413
tall	高	329
T'ang	唐	1241
tariff	租	1916
task	務	1313
taskmaster		137
tassel	房	1159
tatami mat	畳	1923
tax	税	961
tea	茶	267
teach	教	1343
team of horses		418
tears	涙	1163
technique	芸	450
teenager		55
teepee		373
tempering	錬	2186
temple, Buddhist	寺	170
temporarily	暫	1216
tempt	唆	828
ten	十	10
ten thousand	万	68
tenacious	執	1623
tender	柔	1312
tenderness	優	1068
tense	緊	1474
test	試	378
texture	肌	70
Thanksgiving		145
thick	厚	132
thigh	股	764
thin	淡	176
thing	物	1129

think	思	651
third class	丙	1096
thirst	渇	488
thong	緒	1444
thorn	刺	446
thousand	千	40
thread	糸	1431
threaten	脅	936
three	三	3
throat	喉	1768
throw	投	762
thunder	雷	454
thwart	阻	1919
ticket	券	1291
tide	潮	152
tie	結	1451
tiger	虎	2145
tiger, sign of the	寅	2162
tighten	締	1440
tile	瓦	1108
till	耕	1949
timber-trees	樹	1554
time	時	171
time, spare	暇	2027
-times	回	630
tin can	缶	2116
tinker with	弄	731
tired	疲	1823
together	共	1934
toil	努	929
token	符	1076
tolerant	寛	241
tomb	墳	1282
tombstone	碑	1630
tome	冊	1967
tongue	舌	41
tongue wagging		
in mouth		19
too much	余	1786
tool		45
tool	具	78
tooth	歯	1255
top hat		130
top hat and scarf		156
topic	題	415
tortoise	亀	573
torture	拷	1344

touch 接 725	turn into 成 386	valve 弁 803
towel 巾 432	*turtle* 104	vapor 汽 2031
tower 閣 1752	tusk 牙 2053	various 諸 1351
town 村 221	twenty 廿 1274	*vase* 165
toy 玩 276	twig 条 319	vast 弘 1320
tracks 跡 1883	twist 糾 1627	vat 槽 1260
tracks, animal 406	two 二 2	vegetable 菜 793
trade 貿 1529	*two hands* 219	*vehicle* 124
traffic 通 1511	two-mat area 坪 1598	vein 脈 2000
trail 踪 1382	tyrannize 虐 2153	venerable old man 翁 849
training 稽 983		verification 験 2134
tranquilize 鎮 294	**U**	vermilion 朱 235
transcend 超 411	ugly 醜 2176	versify 吟 1714
transit 渡 1279	*umbrella* 109	vertical 縦 1436
transition 遷 1737	umbrella 傘 1103	vessels 隻 755
translate 訳 1154	un- 非 1760	vicarious 摂 1876
transmit 伝 1036	uncle 叔 775	vice- 副 93
transparent 透 981	unclear 曖 797	victory 勝 1294
transport 輸 307	uncommon 異 1936	vie 競 465
tray 盤 2017	undefiled 潔 1668	villa 荘 344
tread 践 1380	undertake 企 401	village 町 96
treasure 宝 273	undress 脱 537	villain 凶 1603
tree 木 207	uneasiness 虞 2150	vine 蔦 2095
tree trunk 幹 1783	unfold 展 2075	vinegar 酢 1542
treetops 梢 213	*United States* 255	violent 激 536
tremendously 甚 1905	universal 普 1925	V.I.P. 賓 550
tribe 族 1307	unlucky 厄 1519	virtuous 善 1112
tribute 貢 85	unravel 解 1955	vis-à-vis 対 1862
triceps 248	unusual 変 1882	visit 参 1856
trifle 僅 1699	upbraid 嚇 2182	visit a shrine 詣 495
trip 旅 1127	upright 貞 58	voice 声 2044
trouble 悩 2085	uprising 勃 930	voiced 濁 898
truckers' convoy 125	*upside down*	void 虚 2148
true 真 79	*in a row* 386	volume 積 1663
trunk 胴 194	upstream, go 遡 2111	vow 誓 1214
trunk, tree 幹 1783	urge 迫 300	vulgar 俗 1042
truss 縛 1476	urine 尿 1132	*vulture* 227
trust 頼 1794	use 使 1065	
tub, oaken 384	usual 常 862	**W**
tucked under	utensil 器 127	*wagging tongue*
the arm 222	utilize 用 1265	*in a mouth* 19
tumor 腫 1807	utmost 最 884	*wagon* 124
tune 調 373		wait 待 944
turf 芝 1301	**V**	waiter 侍 1050
turkey 200	vague 漠 245	*waitress* 337
turkey house/coop 202	*valentine* 209	walk 歩 397
turn 番 2058	valley 谷 851	*walking legs* 125
	value 価 1729	

walking stick		27
wall		231
wall	壁	1616
wand, magic		32
wandering	浪	1580
war	戦	2079
ward	区	1831
ward off	防	1399
warehouse	庫	633
warm	温	1560
warmth	暖	2099
warrior	武	403
warship	艦	2020
wash	洗	264
waste, laid	荒	527
watch over	看	688
watchtower	楼	999
water	水	137
water, hot	湯	585
water lily		339
waterfall	滝	576
waver	猶	1546
waves	波	866
weak	弱	1323
wealth		50
wealth	富	205
weather		163
weather vane		36
weave	織	1432
wee hours	宵	201
week	週	340
weekday	曜	618
weight, lose	痩	1818
welcome	迎	1837
weld	鋼	623
welfare	祉	1172
well	井	1946
west	西	1728
West, Old		358
wet	潤	1755
whale	鯨	337
what	何	1087
wheat		251
wheel	輪	1963
wherefore	由	1186
whirlpool	渦	1387
whirlwind		130
whiskey bottle		331
white	白	37
white bird		28
who	誰	598
whole	全	281
wholesale	卸	1499
wick	芯	647
wicked	邪	2055
wicker basket		381
wide	広	799
widespread	氾	1518
widow	寡	664
wife	妻	2035
wife, legitimate	嫡	472
wild dogs, pack of		105
willow	柳	1525
wind		36
wind	風	563
winding	繰	1469
window	窓	811
windpipe	咽	628
wing	翼	1937
wings		204
wink	瞬	880
winter	冬	456
wipe	拭	695
wisdom	智	1309
wish	念	1715
wisteria	藤	1295
witch	魔	2178
witch		164
with child	娠	2168
withdraw	控	1415
wither	枯	219
withstand	堪	1907
woman	女	102
woman, beautiful	媛	2100
womb	胎	810
wonder	驚	2141
wood		88
wooden leg		309
wooden pole		88
wool		199
word	語	371
words		137
work	働	1809
world	界	266
worship	拝	1686
wound	傷	1071
wrap	包	569
wrench	捻	1716
wretched	惨	1857
write	書	349
writing brush	筆	1014

Y

yank	拉	696
yarn		324
yawn		175
year	年	1114
year-end	歳	551
yearn	憧	681
yell	喚	1121
yellow	黄	1887
yesterday	昨	1222
yield	屈	1140
yonder	向	195
young	若	237
younger brother	弟	1328
younger sister	妹	234

Z

Zen	禅	2080
zero	零	1504
zoo		155